AT EDEN'S DOOR

THE LITTMAN LIBRARY OF
JEWISH CIVILIZATION

Dedicated to the memory of
LOUIS THOMAS SIDNEY LITTMAN
*who founded the Littman Library for the love of God
and as an act of charity in memory of his father*
JOSEPH AARON LITTMAN
and to the memory of
ROBERT JOSEPH LITTMAN
who continued what his father Louis had begun

יהא זכרם ברוך

*'Get wisdom, get understanding:
Forsake her not and she shall preserve thee'*

PROV. 4:5

*The Littman Library of Jewish Civilization is a registered UK charity
Registered charity no. 1000784*

AT EDEN'S DOOR

❋

The Habsburg Jewish Life of Leon Kellner
1859–1928

❋

DAVID RECHTER

London
The Littman Library of Jewish Civilization
in association with Liverpool University Press
2023

The Littman Library of Jewish Civilization
Registered office: 4th floor, 7–10 Chandos Street, London W1G 9DQ

in association with Liverpool University Press
4 Cambridge Street, Liverpool L69 7ZU, UK
www.liverpooluniversitypress.co.uk/littman

Managing Editor: Connie Webber

Distributed in North America by
Oxford University Press Inc., 198 Madison Avenue
New York, NY 10016, USA

© David Rechter 2023

All rights reserved.
No part of this publication may be reproduced,
stored in a retrieval system, or transmitted, in any form or by
any means, without the prior permission in writing of
the Littman Library of Jewish Civilization

Catalogue records for this book are available from the
British Library and the Library of Congress

ISBN 978–1–789621–03–7

Publishing co-ordinator: Janet Moth
Copy-editing: Claire Taylor-Jay
Proof-reading: Andrew Kirk
Index: Sarah Ereira
Production, design, and typesetting by
Pete Russell, Faringdon, Oxon.

Printed and bound in Great Britain by
TJ Books Limited, Padstow, Cornwall

In memory of my teachers
EZRA MENDELSOHN *and* JONATHAN FRANKEL

ACKNOWLEDGEMENTS

❈

I COULD NOT HAVE WRITTEN THIS BOOK without the generous help of friends, colleagues, and acquaintances and it is a pleasure to record my gratitude to all of them.

A number of people took the time to read and comment on all or part of the work. I am grateful to Peter Bergamin, Abigail Green, Mitch Hart, and Derek Penslar, all of whom offered good advice that improved the final product. My sister Sue was kind enough to do the same.

Astrid Freuler deciphered some particularly difficult handwriting, as did Marco Brandl. I owe a huge debt to Rebekka Grossmann and Andreas Pfützner for their crucial work in trawling through enormous amounts of archival material in Jerusalem and Vienna. Jordan Finkin sent me an important collection of correspondence from the archives of Hebrew Union College in Cincinnati. I was fortunate to receive valuable material from Renate Evers at the Leo Baeck Institute archives at the Center for Jewish History in New York; Marcus Patka of the Jewish Museum of Vienna; Ramon Pils in Vienna; Camelia Crăciun and Lucian Herşcovici in Bucharest; Edina Meyer-Maril in Tel Aviv; and Philip Steele in Warsaw. I particularly want to thank Andrei Hoisie of the University of Iaşi for his support and help. The University of Vienna library and the Austrian National Library were gracious in providing otherwise unavailable source material. Closer to home, the Bodleian Library, and especially its Inter-Library Loan service and the Leopold Muller Memorial Library, were indispensable.

As ever, the team at Littman have been exemplary and a pleasure to work with. I am extremely grateful to Connie Webber and Janet Moth for many years of support. Copy-editor Claire Taylor-Jay's exacting eye for detail and sensitivity to language ironed out infelicities and corrected numerous mistakes.

I wish to thank the following for permitting me to use material from previously published articles, in revised form: Indiana University Press for 'Improving the Volk: Leon Kellner and the Jewish Toynbee Hall Movement (1900–39)', *Jewish Social Studies*, 24 (2019), 51–79; and Hartung-Gorre

Verlag Konstanz for 'The Education of Leon Kellner: A Galician Jew Between East and West', in Francisca Solomon and Ion Lihaciu (eds.), *Terra Iudiaca* (Konstanz, 2020), 101–22.

I could have done none of this without my wife Lynne and our children Ella, Noah, and Laura. They will be pleased to have heard the last of Kellner.

CONTENTS

List of Abbreviations x
Note on Transliteration xi

Introduction 1

1. The Education of Young Leon 5
2. The Making of an Intellectual 25
3. Herzl and Zionism 45
4. The Jewish Toynbee Hall 76
5. The Czernowitz Years 94
6. Post-Habsburg Twilight 128

Conclusion 161

Bibliography 167
Index 191

ABBREVIATIONS

Archives

AJA			American Jewish Archives
	GDP		Gotthard Deutsch Papers
ANL			Austrian National Library, Vienna
ATUW			Archiv der Technischen Universität Wien
AUW			Archiv der Universität Wien
	PUW		Personalakt Universität Wien
CAHJP			Central Archives for the History of the Jewish People, Jerusalem
CZA			Central Zionist Archives, Jerusalem
NLI			National Library of Israel
OS			Österreichisches Staatsarchiv, Vienna
	AdR		Archiv der Republik
	AV		Allgemeines Verwaltungsarchiv
		5C/Cz	5C/Czernowitz
		PCK	Professorenakt-Czernowitz, Kellner
		PUW	Professorenakt-Uni Wien, Kellner (PUW)
WSL			Wiener Stadt- und Landesarchiv

Periodicals

AZ	*Allgemeine Zeitung*
CAZ	*Czernowitzer Allgemeine Zeitung*
CAZ/CT	*Czernowitzer Allgemeine Zeitung/Tagblatt*
CT	*Czernowitzer Tagblatt*
JC	*Jewish Chronicle*
JV	*Der Jüdische Volksrat*
JZ	*Jüdische Zeitung*
NFP	*Neue Freie Presse*
NWT	*Neues Wiener Tagblatt*
OW	*Dr. Bloch's Österreichische Wochenschrift*
VW	*Die Volkswehr*
WZ	*Wiener Zeitung*

NOTE ON TRANSLITERATION
AND PLACE NAMES

❧

THE TRANSLITERATION of Hebrew in books published by the Littman Library reflects consideration of the type of books they are, in terms of their content, purpose, and readership. The system adopted therefore reflects a broad, non-specialist approach to transcription rather than the narrower approaches found in the *Encyclopaedia Judaica* or other systems developed for text-based or linguistic studies. The aim has been to reflect the pronunciation prescribed for modern Hebrew rather than the spelling or Hebrew word structure, and to do so using conventions that are generally familiar to the English-speaking reader.

In accordance with this approach, no attempt is made to indicate the distinctions between *alef* and *ayin*, *tet* and *taf*, *kaf* and *kuf*, *sin* and *samekh*, since these are not universally relevant to pronunciation; likewise, the *dagesh* is not indicated except where it affects pronunciation. Following the principle of using conventions familiar to the majority of readers, however, transcriptions that are well established have been retained even when they are not fully consistent with the transliteration system adopted. On similar grounds, the *tsadi*, although generally *ts*, is rendered by 'tz' in such familiar anglicized words as 'barmitzvah'. Likewise, the distinction between *het* and *khaf* has been retained, using *h* for the former and *kh* for the latter; the associated forms are generally familiar to readers, even if the distinction is not always borne out in pronunciation, and for the same reason the final *heh* is indicated too. As in Hebrew, no capital letters are used except that an initial capital has been retained in transliterating titles of published works (for example, *Shulhan arukh*).

Since no distinction is made in this transliteration system between *alef* and *ayin*, they are both indicated by an apostrophe, but only in intervocalic positions where a failure to do so could lead an English-speaking reader to pronounce the vowel-cluster as a diphthong—as, for example, in *ha'ir*—or otherwise mispronounce the word. An apostrophe is also used, for the same reason, to disambiguate the pronunciation of other English vowel clusters, as for example in *mizbe'ah*.

The *sheva na* is indicated by an *e*—*perikat ol*, *reshut*—except, again, when established convention dictates otherwise.

The *yod* is represented by *i* when it occurs as a vowel (*bereshit*), by *y* when it occurs as a consonant (*yesodot*), and by *yi* when it occurs as both (*yisra'el*).

Personal names have generally been left in their familiar forms, even when this is inconsistent with the overall system.

Place Names

Where a place has a widely used name in English, such as Vienna or Prague, I have used it. Where no such English version exists, I have generally used the name current in the period under discussion, giving the present-day name in parentheses: Czernowitz (Chernivtsi); Bielitz (Bielsko).

INTRODUCTION

❧

'THERE is properly no history; only biography', wrote Ralph Waldo Emerson in 1841, an exaggeration masking the truth that, as he also noted, 'there is a relation between the hours of our life and the centuries of time'.[1] This book is more history than biography, a distinction which is sometimes unhelpful in an account such as this; in reality, the two cannot be separated. Nonetheless, the balance in the following pages is tilted towards the historical.[2] In the case of Leon Kellner, once an eminent public intellectual, scholar, and politician, historians have done little to connect the life with the times. By writing Kellner back into the historical record and telling the story of the man, his ideas, and his work, I hope to bring to light a Jewish life that, although exceptional in the breadth and quality of its individual achievement, reveals much about Jewish life more generally in east-central Europe in the second half of the nineteenth and the early twentieth century.

There is a vast ocean of biographies of greater and lesser figures. Why add another? In other words, why write a historical biography about a relatively obscure figure who makes only the occasional appearance in Jewish and Habsburg historiography and collective memory? Historiography and collective memory, however, are fickle and malleable, and need not determine historians' choices. Reputations rise and fall, sometimes more than once. Kellner was one of the great and good of Habsburg Austria. A close friend and confidant of Theodor Herzl, he was a central actor in the very earliest days of the Zionist movement in Vienna. He was an English language and literature scholar of international repute and a celebrated Shakespeare specialist, at home among the literary elites of Vienna and of Victorian and Edwardian London; he was instrumental, for example, in bringing George Bernard Shaw's work to German-speaking Europe. He was a public intellectual who lectured and taught widely, and for more than

---

[1] Emerson, *Self-Reliance and Other Essays*, 4, 1.

[2] On the relationship between history and biography, see e.g. Caine, *Biography and History*; Renders et al., *The Biographical Turn*; Lee, *Biography*.

four decades wrote essays of style and substance for the quality press in Austria and Germany. He created the Jewish Toynbee Hall in Vienna, a cultural and educational institution that became a movement across central and eastern Europe. He was a regional political leader and parliamentarian, and the press recorded his presence at events, noted his daughters' marriages—he was the father-in-law of Walter Benjamin—and reviewed his publications. In the post-Habsburg Austrian republic, he was a friend and adviser on Anglo-American affairs to the president. All this has long slipped out of sight. His writings are neglected, his scholarship is dated, his political engagement was overtaken by revolution and wars. I have set out neither to praise nor to bury Kellner. As will become evident, he received the former in abundance during his lifetime, and the weight of historical change and the passage of time have seen to the latter. I do, however, wish to rescue him from the historiographical shadows.

We can sketch the intersection of the hours of his life with the centuries of time. Born in 1859, as neo-absolutist rule in Austria gave way to liberalism, he came of age as liberalism itself gave way to nationalism. Liberalism and nationalism brought with them, respectively, emancipation and antisemitism, forming the political and cultural matrix that shaped his life and work. He became and remained a liberal nationalist; emancipation made his success possible, but antisemitism imposed limits upon it. He was a man of imperial Austria, although he survived a decade beyond the empire, and we can connect the trajectory of his life and career with fundamental themes of the post-Enlightenment history of Habsburg Austrian Jewry, a population of 1.4 million just prior to the First World War. The most obvious of these themes is the east–west axis, a long-standing discourse that cast Jewish eastern Europe as the west's insufficiently modern cousin: east European Jews were numerous, poor, Orthodox, Yiddish-speaking, and unacculturated, whereas Jews in western Europe were fewer, more homogeneous, religiously moderate, middle-class, and better integrated. Siegmund Kaznelson, a Prague Zionist intellectual and activist, wrote in 1921 that Austrian Jewry had been 'a union of an entirely western with an entirely eastern Jewry', and Kellner's biography is a case in point.[3] The divide between east and west, however, is only a partial truth which is

---

[3] Hellmann [Kaznelson], 'Die Geschichte der österreichisch-jüdischen Kongressbewegung', 394.

qualified by the powerful imprint of regional diversity, itself reflected in Kellner's experience of living in four different crownlands. Through the prism of his belief in liberalism and nationalism we can detect traces of the relationship of Jews as a collective to Habsburg state and society. We can observe in the arc of his career the 'half-open door' for Jews, the uneasy co-existence of opportunity and constraint, demonstrating what Jews could achieve in Austria but showing the profound resistance they faced too.[4] Studying an individual life allows us to glimpse the ways in which the individual is embedded in society—in other words, how and where the particular meets the universal. Kellner was embedded in two societies, Jewish and Habsburg Austrian, and saw no contradiction in fully inhabiting both, although he was acutely aware of the boundaries of each. In this, he provides a case study of the challenge so often posed to Jews in modern Europe: how to balance the pressures of tradition and acculturation.

Beyond the Jewish dimension, an account of Kellner's life has a part to play in the historiographical repositioning of the Habsburg monarchy that has taken place in recent decades. No longer regarded as a weak state and a prison of nations, the monarchy is now seen instead as an imperfect democracy with a vibrant, relatively pluralist, civil society. The exploration of a less commonly observed type of Jewish life adds to this revised picture by bringing a novel perspective to familiar narratives about one of the empire's minorities. Kellner's story, the rise to worldly success of a Galician Jew from a strictly Orthodox milieu, says a great deal about the dynamics of acculturation and nationalism as Jewish variants of the experiences of other Habsburg peoples. It also speaks to another key concern in the Habsburg territories, the balancing act between capital and province. The Galician Jewish writer Joseph Roth commented that 'the essence of Austria is not the centre, but the periphery';[5] Kellner was at home in both. He moved from the Galician periphery to Vienna but spent the peak of his professional career in Czernowitz (Chernivtsi), Austria's easternmost regional capital. A man of east and west, of periphery and centre, he gave unusually literate and articulate expression to what were for him two points on a continuum rather than polar opposites. Kellner's life makes visible the complex circulation of ideas, movements, and people between these two sides of the same imperial coin and, in doing so, enables us to trace

[4] Pulzer, 'Legal Equality and Public Life', 154.   [5] Roth, *Die Kapuzinergruft*, 18.

the development of interlocking themes—minorities, east and west, centre and periphery, regions—that are indispensable to understanding Habsburg Austria and its Jews.

A biography is at most the sketch of a life distilled from the available material, and it should be kept in mind that the unavailable material outweighs the accessible by an order of magnitude. I have been mindful of a paraphrase of Yeats (with whom Kellner had a passing acquaintance) reminding biographers, on behalf of their subjects, 'to tread softly for you tread on my life'.[6] My account of Kellner's life and work is therefore of necessity selective and incomplete. I have let him speak in his own words as far as possible in order to convey a flavour of his sensibility. He was above all a man of words, whether written or spoken, and his eloquent writing offers access to his temperament, character, and preoccupations.

The narrative is chronological. Chapter 1 recounts Kellner's childhood and education, taking us from western Galicia to Vienna. In Chapter 2 he establishes himself professionally as a scholar and writer in Vienna and London. Chapter 3 turns to politics, telling the story of his friendship with Herzl and his Zionist work, a corollary of which was the Jewish Toynbee Hall, discussed in Chapter 4. Chapter 5 takes us to Czernowitz and to the zenith of his scholarly and political success as a professor of English language and literature, a regional parliamentarian, and the leader of a popular nationalist movement. The final chapter finds Kellner in the transformed and much-reduced world of post-war and post-imperial Vienna, brutally excluded from academia, no longer a politician, and in dramatically straitened circumstances.

[6] King, *Tread Softly*. The reference is to the final line of Yeats's poem 'He Wishes for the Cloths of Heaven', 'Tread softly because you tread on my dreams'.

ONE

❊

THE EDUCATION OF
YOUNG LEON

Galicia and Its Jews

Some 2 million Jews lived in Europe near the end of the eighteenth century, constituting approximately 90 per cent of the world's Jewish population and 1.5 per cent of Europe's. Half of them lived in territory seized by the Austrians, Russians, and Prussians when they dismantled the Polish–Lithuanian Commonwealth between 1772 and 1795; some 200,000 could be found in a part of southern Poland that the Austrians renamed Galicia.[1] Austrian observers noted with distaste the area's extreme and pervasive poverty, along with the 'backwardness' of many of its people, not least the Jews, a view that persisted until the collapse of the Habsburg empire in 1918.[2] Empress Maria Theresa responded with 'horror and disgust' at the prospect of ruling over so many Jews.[3] Her son Joseph II, equally dismayed but better informed due to his travels in the province, launched a far-reaching programme of reform, aiming to transform Galicia into a model of enlightened governance, and its Jews—whom he regarded as insular, poor, and unproductive—into useful subjects.

These imperial attitudes were merely the tip of the iceberg. In the early nineteenth century, government officials described Galician Jews as 'particularly depraved' and advocated their 'de-judaization'. Joseph Rohrer, professor of statistics at the university in Lemberg (now Lviv) and an avid ethnographer who travelled widely in Galicia, thought the province was 'flooded' with Jews, their filthy, 'teeming' residential streets spreading illness to their 'blameless' Christian neighbours. He recorded with disdain

---

[1] Bihl, 'Die Juden', 881–2; Wolff, *The Idea of Galicia*, 13–19.

[2] Good examples of this attitude in the nineteenth and early twentieth centuries are Rohrer, *Versuch*; Szczepanowski, *Nędza Galicyi*; Tenenbaum, *Żydowskie problemy gospodarcze*.

[3] Beales, *Joseph II: In the Shadow of Maria Theresa*, 363.

the 'busy idleness of the dirty Jews', their 'immoral propensity for lies and deception', and the 'foul breath' of Jewish women. Forced-labour camps or penal colonies abroad, such as those the English had established in Australia, were Rohrer's solution.[4] Such sentiments were widespread, reflecting the legacy of Counter-Reformation Austria, which was inhospitable to Jews and other non-Catholics. Towards the end of the eighteenth century, long-standing anti-Jewish hostility of this sort was supplemented by a current of Enlightenment opinion that saw Jews as debased but ultimately redeemable, all of which was embedded in the perception of Galicia as part of 'primitive' eastern Europe. Jews, as the Austrians now saw at first hand, were an inescapable part of the east European landscape, a large and unacculturated population representing an obstacle to a state looking to modernize. (In parts of northern and western Europe, by contrast, Jews were numerically inconsequential and their elites had already set their sights on modernization and acculturation.)

Joseph's Jewish policies, at least in part shaped by his face-to-face encounter with Galician Jews, offered opportunity, but only at a price. What Joseph gave with one hand, he took away with the other. The state conceded that Jews could join society; in return, the Jews were expected to reform themselves. The government relaxed strictures on Jewish occupation, residence, movement, and property ownership, opened up previously closed trades and crafts, allowed Jews to attend state schools and universities, and encouraged them to establish factories. Influenced by physiocratic ideas, the authorities pressed them to move from trade and commerce to agriculture in order to improve both their character and productivity. Measures were taken that might begin to loosen entrenched social divides. Jews were free to leave home before midday on Sundays and Christian festivals, to enjoy places of public entertainment, and were no longer to be marked out in public by the infamous yellow badge on clothing or by the obligation imposed on Jewish men to sport a beard. These new freedoms, though, were hedged about with exceptions and qualifications. The toleration tax, along with other burdensome levies imposed exclusively on Jews, remained in force, as did certain restricted rights of residence and property ownership. With the aim of attenuating Jewish autonomy and reducing

---

[4] Quotes in Robertson, 'Joseph Rohrer', 36; Rohrer, *Versuch*, 21, 26–7, 29, 182. On penal colonies, see ibid. 200–2. On government views, see Pribram, *Urkunden und Akten*, ii. 164–5.

Jewish difference, the state extended its reach deep into individual and collective life. It began to take control of Jewish education, diluted the judicial and fiscal prerogatives of the Jewish community (the *kehilah/Gemeinde*), mandated that all communal records be kept in German, rather than Hebrew or Yiddish, and demanded that Jews take German family names.[5]

Joseph's push to modernize and assimilate the Jews was sweeping and hasty, and, like almost all other aspects of the reform crusade in his decade of sole rule (1780–90), was bitterly contested on all sides and unevenly implemented. Refashioning the Jews in this way, though stopping short of emancipating them, was a radical *ancien régime* experiment, long acknowledged by historians as a 'new era', a 'decisive turning point', and even a kind of 'Archimedean point' in Habsburg Jewish history.[6] It marked the beginnings of the evolution of a collective sense of 'Habsburg Jewry' and remained a touchstone for Jewish fidelity to the Habsburg state.[7] Part of what so indelibly imprinted this period on Jewish collective memory was that it was often seen, as a historian from the 1930s remarked, as 'the one bright spot in the history of the Austrian Jews from the time of the Babenberg Frederick II to the later years of Francis Joseph I'.[8]

A long period of 'stagnation and regression' for Jewish rights followed the helter-skelter Josephinian decade.[9] Joseph's brother, Leopold II (1790–2), a reforming leader as Grand Duke of Tuscany, had more pressing issues to deal with, having inherited a number of regime-threatening crises from Joseph. The absolutist 'byzantine administration' of Leopold's son Franz (1792–1835) struggled to formulate a systematic policy towards Jews, save a consistent concern to limit their numbers, extract the maximum possible revenue from them, and further reduce what was left of their communal autonomy.[10] Josef Wertheimer, a contemporary businessman,

---

[5] On Joseph II and the Jews, see Silber, 'The Making of Habsburg Jewry', 789–92; Karniel, *Die Toleranzpolitik Kaiser Josephs II.*, ch. 5; Beales, *Joseph II: Against the World*, 196–213.

[6] Grunwald, *Vienna*, 147, 154; Lewin, 'Geschichte der Juden in Galizien unter Kaiser Joseph II.', 15, 28. On the 'Archimedean point', see Wolf, *Die Juden*, 43. For similar encomiums, see Wolf, *Joseph Wertheimer*, 12–13; Sznajdman, 'Die Zeit der Aufklärung und die Juden in Österreich', 159–60.

[7] A similar point is made in Tietze, *Die Juden Wiens*, 123; Stein, *Der Mensch im Bilde Gottes*, 12.

[8] Grunwald, *Vienna*, 164.

[9] Wertheimer, *Die Juden in Oesterreich*, iii. 215. For details on Galicia, see Mahler, *History of the Jewish People* (Heb.), i. 38–40; Friedler, 'Die galizischen Juden'.

[10] Quote from Laven, *Venice and Venetia*, 22.

communal leader, and author, observed that Franz lacked the 'fatherly love' for Jews that he demonstrated towards his other subjects, and commented that Jews 'played the undeserved role of Cinderella' among Austria's peoples.[11] The government had neither sufficient will nor incentive to improve this Cinderella status. The occasional breach in the mass of restrictive legislation that shackled Jewish daily life was offset by persistent social and political exclusion. Recognition of Jewish equality, said one of Franz's advisers in 1834, would at a stroke 'unsettle' the civic and religious status quo, offend public opinion, and lead to an 'alarming increase of Jewish influence on the income, property, and morality of the Christian population'.[12] While rejected by the government, emancipation of the Jews was on the agenda of the 1848 revolutionaries; it in fact came as a gift of the counter-revolution, when the new emperor, Franz Joseph, imposed a constitution in March 1849 that guaranteed equal rights to all, irrespective of religion. (Hungary's revolutionary government granted emancipation at the end of July 1849, shortly before its defeat by the Habsburg and Russian armies.[13])

Long awaited and much anticipated, emancipation proved not to be straightforward. Jews had been declared equal but were still subject to a multitude of special regulations; even the government was unsure about the Jews' status.[14] Jews were quick to test the limits of what was now possible, living in areas formerly closed to them, buying property, and taking up new educational and career opportunities. Displeased, many provincial and local authorities took refuge in the lack of clarity regarding Jewish rights: the Krakau (Kraków) municipality, for example, was not inclined to accept the principle of confessional equality, and a number of towns in Galicia barred Jews from settling. Local officials in Moravian Nikolsburg (now Mikulov) thought the Jews had become 'impudent' and asked the provincial administration to 'curtail' their rights. The government in Vienna by and large stood firm in response to such objections, reiterating that it expected all branches of the state to respect the principle of equality

[11] Wertheimer, *Die Juden in Oesterreich*, iii. 214–16.

[12] Pribram, *Urkunden und Akten*, ii. 350–1. On Franz's Jewish policies, see also Bato, *Die Juden im alten Wien*, 119–38, 148–64.

[13] On the new constitution, see Deak, *Forging a Multinational State*, 83–94.

[14] Leitner, 'Die Judenpolitik der österreichischen Regierung', 42–7; Wolf, *Josef Wertheimer*, 74, 78–9.

THE EDUCATION OF YOUNG LEON

enshrined in the new constitution.[15] The efforts of all parties to adjust to the new dispensation were cut short at the end of December 1851 when Franz Joseph abolished the constitution, the implementation of which was in any case patchy, initiating what came to be known as the period of neo-absolutism.[16] Brief as it was, this first emancipation nonetheless lodged firmly in Jewish memory. In a sixtieth anniversary commemoration, Austria's leading Zionist newspaper acclaimed the 1848 revolution as the catalyst for the delivery of Habsburg Jews from the 'most intolerable bondage' and the 'most brutal mistreatment'.[17]

The implications for Jewish rights in a neo-absolutist state, with its centralization of power and antipathy to liberalism, were revealed only incrementally during the 1850s, as the new government's Jewish policies demonstrated a similar repressive intent and lack of system to those of its Vormärz predecessor. Once more, Jews found themselves hemmed in by a labyrinth of stifling legislation, despite Minister-President Felix zu Schwarzenberg's alleged admonition that 'every government that has persecuted the Jews since the time of the pharaohs has fared badly'.[18] Heinrich Jaques, a Viennese lawyer and liberal parliamentary deputy, remarked unhappily in 1859—exaggerating for effect—that everything not expressly sanctioned was forbidden, and likened Jews to people 'living at the summit of a high, entirely inaccessible mountain . . . vegetating in total seclusion and isolation'.[19] By the middle of the nineteenth century, some 1 million Jews lived in the monarchy, perhaps 3 per cent of the total population: in the Austrian lands an estimated 620,000 in 1857, rising to 820,000 by 1869; in Hungary 450,000 in 1857 and 540,000 in 1869.[20] This was a diverse set

---

[15] Wolf, *Josef Wertheimer*, 73–9, 147; Miller, *Rabbis and Revolutions*, 269–74 (Nikolsburg quotation on p. 274); Friedmann, *Die galizischen Juden im Kampfe*, 73–6; Jaques, *Denkschrift über die Stellung der Juden*, pp. xviii–xxii, xxxix–xliv; Leitner, 'Die Judenpolitik der österreichischen Regierung', 51–73.

[16] On the so-called Sylvester Patent of 31 December 1851, see Deak, *Forging a Multinational State*, 101–5. [17] *JZ*, 13 Mar. 1908, 1. See also *OW*, 11 Mar. 1898, 181–4.

[18] Leitner, 'Die Judenpolitik der österreichischen Regierung', 105–8. See also Friedmann, *Die galizischen Juden im Kampfe*, chs. 4 to 8. For Schwarzenberg's comment, see Friedjung, *Österreich von 1848 bis 1860*, ii. 285.

[19] Jaques, *Denkschrift über die Stellung der Juden*, pp. ix–x, lxxxix. On this pamphlet, see Kwan, 'Liberalism, Antisemitism and Everyday Life in Vienna', 136–8.

[20] All sources insist that such figures are estimates at best. See Thon, *Die Juden in Oesterreich*, 7–8; Silber, 'Hungary before 1918', 770–82 (table 1); Bihl, 'Die Juden', 881–3.

of communities, ranging from a select group of ennobled bankers and industrialists in Vienna, the nucleus of a few hundred 'tolerated' families in the capital, to the hundreds of thousands of pedlars, traders, artisans, innkeepers, labourers, and agricultural workers who lived at subsistence level in Galicia, Bukovina, north-eastern Hungary, and Subcarpathian Rus. Between these extremes, an urban commercial and professional middle class developed rapidly when liberal constitutionalist ideas loosened the absolutist grip in the 1860s and, in particular, once emancipation had been secured in 1867.

Numbers and poverty were greatest in Galicia, home in the second half of the nineteenth century to nearly 70 per cent of Austrian Jewry, some 575,000 people in 1869 and just over 800,000 by 1900, making up some 10 per cent of the total population (with a far higher proportion in urban areas and in eastern Galicia).[21] As was the case elsewhere in eastern Europe, Jews in Galicia had long occupied an important niche in the feudal economy as intermediaries between peasantry and nobility, and between town and countryside. Many were agents and leaseholders on noble estates, but most worked in petty trade and commerce, in which they had a dominant role, as well as in a range of crafts—as tailors, furriers, cap-makers, goldsmiths, cobblers, glaziers, bakers—and in all branches of the alcohol industry (distilling, brewing, running taverns), despite sporadic government efforts to dislodge them. The upper reaches of the Jewish economy comprised a thin stratum of successful merchants and industrialists, a similarly small professional class, a slightly more substantial agricultural sector and, from the 1870s, a surprisingly sizeable contingent of estate owners, principally in eastern Galicia.[22] These modest pockets of growth and success were overshadowed by endemic poverty; a German travel writer remarked in 1840 that an ox in Switzerland lived better than a Jew in Galicia, and some half of Galician Jewry at the beginning of the twentieth century constituted what has been aptly called an 'underclass.'[23] Such acute poverty triggered mass

[21] Thon, *Die Juden in Oesterreich*, 10–13; Wróbel, 'The Jews of Galicia under Austrian-Polish Rule', 105–8.

[22] On the Galician Jewish economy, see Friedmann, *Die galizischen Juden im Kampfe*, 7–29; Mahler, *History of the Jewish People* (Heb.), i. 11–22. See also Gąsowski, 'From Austeria to the Manor', 120–36.

[23] Lichtblau and John, 'Jewries in Galicia and Bukovina', 35; for the comment by Johann Georg Kohl in 1840, see Häusler, *Das galizische Judentum*, 75.

migration. Over the course of the years of Austrian rule, Galician Jews moved away in their hundreds of thousands, primarily to the United States but also to other areas of the monarchy, in particular to Hungary and Vienna.[24]

The advent of a form of home rule for Galicia in the wake of the establishment of the Dual Monarchy of Austria-Hungary in 1867 signalled a major political and cultural reorientation for the province, reversing nearly a century of centralization and Germanization: the Sejm (the Galician parliament) became a significant legislative chamber, the regional government carved out considerable freedom of manoeuvre from Vienna, and Polish became the language of education and administration at all levels.[25] This 'de facto autonomy' posed a challenge to Jews, who since the Josephinian era had been pushed by the state to adopt German.[26] As already noted, German had replaced Hebrew and Yiddish in communal record-keeping and for family names, and German-language Jewish schools, funded by the Jews but supervised by the state, had provided a basic secular education.

Competence in German, the language of imperial administration and of most educational institutions as well as of Habsburg supra-national 'high' culture, was a necessity for daily life and a prerequisite for social mobility in the first half of the nineteenth century. By contrast, fluency in Polish, familiarity with Polish culture, or identification with the increasingly influential Polish national cause were rare among Galician Jews before the 1870s.[27] Moreover, as Jews tended to look to the central authorities in Vienna for protection from Polish antisemitism, they were often viewed as more loyal to the imperial government than to its provincial counterpart in Lemberg. For the Polish liberal nationalist statesman Franciszek Smolka, debating Jewish emancipation in the Galician Sejm in 1868, the 'Jewish Question' was the most pressing 'national and social' issue of the day, and a secure future was 'dependent' on its satisfactory resolution.[28]

From the 1870s, as more Jews received a Polish-language education in towns and cities, a political and cultural realignment from German/

---

[24] On migration, see Wróbel, 'The Jews of Galicia under Austrian-Polish Rule', 108–12.

[25] Wandycz, *The Lands of Partitioned Poland*, 214–21; Maner, *Galizien*, 139–46.

[26] For 'de facto autonomy', see Wandycz, *The Lands of Partitioned Poland*, 220.

[27] For background, see Polonsky, *The Jews in Poland and Russia*, vol. i, ch. 8. A useful summary of government policy regarding Galician Jewry is Friedmann, *Die galizischen Juden im Kampfe*, 189–97.   [28] Cited in Friedmann, 'Die Judenfrage im galizischen Landtag', 386.

Austrian to Polish took hold, in particular among the educated middle classes. The Deutsch-Israelitisches Bethaus (German-Israelite House of Prayer), for example, a Reform synagogue opened in 1846 in Lemberg to cater for the city's small but expanding liberal Jewish bourgeoisie, appointed as its first preacher a Prague-educated, German-speaking rabbi who established a German-language Jewish school.[29] Towards the end of the nineteenth century, though, the synagogue changed its name to the Gminna Synagoga Postępowa, and sermons in Polish were introduced very soon after.[30] Emerging out of the same milieu in 1868, just as Galicia was granted home rule, was Shomer Yisra'el (Guardian of Israel), a cultural and political association made up of self-declared 'Austrian patriots' who at that time were devoted to German culture and ambivalent at best about Polish nationalism. Their somewhat anachronistic stance did not last: in 1879, when Shomer Yisra'el members were elected to the central Austrian parliament, they joined the 'Polish Club' parliamentary faction, and by 1885 the association called for Galician Jews to define themselves first and foremost as 'Poles of the Mosaic persuasion'.[31] For most Orthodox Jews, and in particular for hasidic Jews, a formidable force in Galicia, Polish culture remained a largely closed world, and German, tainted by its association with the Haskalah (Jewish Enlightenment), was a sure route to assimilation.[32] Even with the ever-rising tide of Polonization and the continuing powerful grip of Orthodoxy, German culture, and the imperial capital Vienna, remained attractive to many Galician Jews until the end of the empire, and even beyond. Kellner was a case in point.[33]

---

[29] Manekin, 'Gaming the System', 359–67; Mendelsohn, 'Jewish Assimilation in Lvov', 578.

[30] Bussgang, 'The Progressive Synagogue in Lwów', 135; Bałaban, *Historia Lwowskiej synagogi postępowej*, 170–1.

[31] Mendelsohn, 'Jewish Assimilation in Lvov', 578–81; Manekin, *The Jews of Galicia and the Austrian Constitution* (Heb.), chs. 2 and 3.

[32] Galicia was a stronghold of hasidism, a form of religious revivalism that emerged in the first half of the eighteenth century. See Biale et al., *Hasidism: A New History*, 141–8 and ch. 13; Wodziński, *Historical Atlas of Hasidism*, 38–40.

[33] For the post-imperial decades, see e.g. Aleksiun, 'The Galician Paradigm?', 159–78. On the processes of Germanization and Polonization, see also Lichtblau and John, 'Jewries in Galicia and Bukovina', 31–9.

From Tarnów to Bielitz

Leon Kellner was born in 1859 in Tarnów into a religious family of modest means. Jews had a long history in Tarnów, as was the case in many Galician towns and cities, settling there soon after its foundation in the fourteenth century. Always a considerable proportion of the population, they comprised some 40 per cent of its residents for most of the second half of the nineteenth century, reaching perhaps 12,000 by the 1880s. In western Galicia, only Krakau, 45 miles to the west, was larger and was home to more Jews.[34] Leon's parents, Rafael and Leah, lived on the semi-rural outskirts of town, at a considerable distance from the more central residential districts favoured by most of Tarnów's Jews.[35] Tall, voluble, and tempestuous, Rafael was an overbearing father who regularly administered corporal punishment. Leon's mother, Leah Goldstein, was enterprising, competent, and more even-tempered than her husband, often mediating between her strictly hasidic family—she was one of eight or nine children—and Rafael, a bitter opponent of hasidism.[36]

Rafael worked in the grain trade, a mainstay of the Galician economy in which Jews played a disproportionately prominent role. A small-scale dealer, he was a link in the supply chain between producer and consumer, delivering his goods by horse and cart until the advent of the railway in the mid-1850s began to transform the economic landscape.[37] Self-employed traders made up a significant proportion of the Galician Jewish economy in the second half of the nineteenth century, although many, if not most, were pedlars who barely made a living.[38] In Tarnów, as in most other Galician towns and cities, Jews were instrumental in the development of commerce

[34] For estimates of Tarnów's population, see Thon, *Die Juden in Oesterreich*, 17, 20; Herzig, 'Tarnów od r. 1567 do r. 1907', 187, 250; *Encyclopedia of Jewish Communities. Poland* (Heb.), iii. 178.

[35] Leon's early years are recounted in A. Kellner, *Leon Kellner*, 7–13; Arnold, *Memoirs* (Heb.), 35–8; Spann, 'Dr. Leon Kellner' (Yid.), 270–4.

[36] A number of hasidic dynasties enjoyed support in the city, principal among them Sandz, but also Belz, Rimanov, and, later, Bobov, Ruzhin, and Boyan. See Chomet (ed.), *The Life and Destruction of a Jewish City* (Yid. and Heb.), 189–231. On Rafael, an avowed *mitnaged* ('opponent' of hasidism), see also Leon's thinly disguised autobiographical sketch, 'Der erste Schultag'.

[37] On the railway and its effect on the grain trade in Galicia, see Tokarski, *Ethnic Conflict and Economic Development*, 203–18; Lipp, *Verkehrs- und Handels-Verhältnisse Galiziens*, 3–5, 8–9.

[38] Rosenfeld, *Die polnische Judenfrage*, 113–19; Friedmann, *Die galizischen Juden im Kampfe*, 8–14.

and industry, notwithstanding the overwhelming poverty of the great majority. They owned and operated mills, brickworks, glassworks, tanneries, factories, and banks, and were a commanding presence in wholesale manufacture and trade as well as in the textile and clothing industries (hats were a local speciality).[39]

By the late 1860s Rafael's business was melting away, a casualty of the quickening pace and expanding volume of grain commerce in the wake of the railway's arrival. The consequent decline in the family's fortunes was reversed by Leah, who converted the front room of their home into a household goods store. That Leah had learned Polish and German at school stood her in good stead in her new role, as the bulk of her clientele were Polish-speaking peasants and workers living in the immediate vicinity. A degree of fluency in non-Jewish languages was not unheard of among Orthodox Jewish women in eastern Europe. Unlike men, they were neither required nor indeed expected to devote themselves to intensive study of religious texts (Torah and Talmud), and in fact were generally not permitted to do so. Excluded from the higher-status public religious sphere and not expected to be learned, Jewish women were often required to contribute economically to the family, and in this respect the benefits of acquaintance with non-Jewish society were obvious. The utility of attending government schools to acquire practical skills such as languages, literacy, and numeracy outweighed any risk that came with exposure to secular knowledge.[40] Leah's store proved a reasonably successful venture, thanks in large measure to her commercial acumen and language skills. Before long, Rafael had liquidated his business and joined his wife in running the store, taking care of the accounts and procuring supplies. Theirs was a frugal, lower-middle-class household of five: Leon had two younger sisters (three other children had died young). Their home was small and sparingly furnished, comprising four rooms and a kitchen; when business was good, they could afford a live-in maid, who occupied the attic. A sizeable garden, with a pear tree and a vegetable allotment, surrounded the house, provid-

---

[39] Chomet, 'On the History of the Jews in Tarnów' (Yid.), 50–1, 63–5.

[40] Parush, *Reading Jewish Women*, 38–46; Stampfer, *Families, Rabbis, and Education*, 183–6; Dynner, 'Those Who Stayed', 307–11. In Leon's later extended family in Austrian Silesia, for example, his wife's aunt ran the Troppau (Opava) branch of a Viennese clothing business established by his uncle, while his mother-in-law was in charge of a tailor's shop in Bielitz. See Arnold, *Memoirs* (Heb.), 16, 31.

ing a space sufficiently large for Rafael, an animal lover, to keep the horses he had used when travelling on business.

As was customary in Orthodox families, Leon was sent from the age of 3 to a traditional Jewish school, a *heder* (lit. 'room'), where the curriculum was limited exclusively to Judaism, Hebrew, and religious texts. Throughout the nineteenth century, elementary education in a *heder*—typically located in a room in the teacher's house—was the most popular form of Jewish education in much of eastern Europe. With little state regulation or supervision, the *heder* was deeply traditional in its pedagogy and curriculum. For reformers, the *heder* was an abomination, serving only to perpetuate cultural and social isolation; its teachers, notoriously cruel and untrained, were 'despots', 'imbeciles', and 'ignoramuses'.[41] Until the 1860s, and even later in Galicia, most Jewish children in Austria attended *heder* rather than a state primary school.[42] Both the standard of educational provision and the rate of school attendance improved in Austria from the 1870s, once school had become obligatory and free for children aged 6 to 14, as stipulated by the Imperial Elementary School Law of 1869.[43] But despite the best efforts of the state and of Jewish reformers to encourage families to send their children either to state schools or to reformed Jewish schools that taught both secular and religious studies, the *heder* remained a popular choice well into the twentieth century for Jewish parents wary of the assimilatory potential of state education.[44]

Leon attended *heder* for ten years, between the ages of 3 and 13. It was a gruelling schedule and a brutal regime: a typical day began at 6 in the morning (or 7 in winter) and finished in the late afternoon, punctuated by a one-hour break for lunch, with discipline enforced by regular caning. He proved to be a gifted student. Already by the age of 7 or 8 he had been enlisted by the teacher to help instruct other children, employing a version of the pedagogical method developed in the early nineteenth century by the English Quaker Joseph Lancaster.[45] At the same time, he began to write

[41] Zalkin, *Modernizing Jewish Education*, ch. 1 (pp. 28, 31).

[42] Cohen, 'Education and the Politics of Jewish Integration', 480.

[43] Cohen, *Education and Middle-Class Society*, 38, 55.

[44] Thon, *Die Juden in Oesterreich*, 90–1 (table LVI). In 1880, the Galician Sejm estimated that there were some 1,200 *heders* in Galicia, with nearly 24,000 students, more than half of Jewish children of compulsory school age (6 to 14). See Manekin, *The Jews of Galicia and the Austrian Constitution* (Heb.), 233–4 n. 85.   [45] Dickson, *Teacher Extraordinary: Joseph Lancaster*.

THE EDUCATION OF YOUNG LEON

his own commentaries on biblical passages. Such was his promise as a religious scholar that Moritz Güdemann, later the chief rabbi of Vienna, reportedly referred to him as the 'Ilui [talmudic prodigy] of Tarnów'.[46] Students of exceptional calibre were commonly expected to continue full-time religious study after 'graduation' from *ḥeder* at the age of 12 or 13 in the hope of carving out a career as a rabbi or scholar, both of which enjoyed great prestige in Orthodox circles. In nineteenth-century Galicia, the most common route to this goal was individual or small-group study with an established teacher.[47] This was precisely the path that Leon's parents wished him to follow. To this end, they sent him to study with Rabbi Yeshayahu Mann, one of a good number of noted local teachers. Leon was the youngest of Mann's students, and here too he excelled.[48]

Hedging their bets, Leon's parents also hired a tutor to acquaint him with the rudiments of reading and writing in German. Hiring a tutor was not unusual among Orthodox Jewish parents, relatively few of whom had attended state secondary schools. Jewish attendance at state schools increased in Austria from the 1870s, at which point Jews made up around 8 per cent of secondary-school students in Galicia, proportionate to their percentage of the general population although lower than their percentage of the urban population, where most schools were located.[49] German was not a self-evident choice of language for an Orthodox Yiddish-speaking family in a predominantly Polish-speaking city such as Tarnów, given the increasing importance of Polish in Galicia in the early 1870s. As noted above, Leon's mother had learned Polish at school, and the majority of her shop's clientele were Polish-speaking; his father had needed Polish to do business as a travelling grain dealer, and Leon's German, his daughter

[46] A. Kellner, *Leon Kellner*, 7–8; Arnold, *Memoirs* (Heb.), 38; Spann, 'Dr. Leon Kellner' (Yid.), 270–1.

[47] This generally took place in a 'study house' such as a *beit midrash* (Yid. *bes medresh*) or *kloyz*. See Gertner, 'Battei Midrash in Galicia' (Heb.).

[48] Spann, 'Dr. Leon Kellner' (Yid.), 272; Kahane, 'Tarnów, A Center of Torah' (Yid.), 190. On study houses in Tarnów, including mention of Kellner and Salo Baron as students who went on to become 'eminent', see Blazer, 'A Survey of Religious Jewry in Tarnów' (Yid.), 219–20. See also Margoshes, *A World Apart*, 52–7.

[49] Adamczyk, *Edukacja a przeobrażenia społeczności żydowskich*, 60–4. In 1869, Jews were 12.4% of the population in eastern Galicia and 7.5% in western Galicia: see Friedmann, *Die galizischen Juden im Kampfe*, 3–4. In 1880, Jews made up more than 20% of the population of some thirty Galician cities; see Thon, *Die Juden in Oesterreich*, 20.

THE EDUCATION OF YOUNG LEON   17

recalled, had a slight Polish, rather than Yiddish, lilt to it.[50] Choice of language, and the supposed political and cultural preferences it expressed, was for Jews often fraught with difficulty. The Josephinian reforms had obliged them to become familiar with German, and in many areas of the monarchy Jews continued to speak German alongside another (non-Jewish) language even as the rise of nationalist movements exerted pressure on them to identify as speakers of Czech, Hungarian, or Polish. Increasing adoption of Czech by Jews in Bohemia and Moravia in the latter decades of the nineteenth century, for example, did not entirely eclipse their use of German, particularly in larger cities. In Hungary in 1910, three-quarters of Hungarian Jews declared Hungarian as their mother tongue, but nearly two-thirds also spoke German.[51]

As for many Habsburg Jews, the choice of a German tutor was for Leon's parents a practical matter, more a kind of insurance policy than a statement of ideological intent. It was in their eyes a lesser risk than allowing their intellectually capable and inquisitive son to attend a state school. Even so, his hasidic maternal grandparents strenuously objected to this departure from tradition. Their suspicions turned out to be well founded: Leon's tutor went far beyond the basics, not only teaching him to read and write in German but also introducing him to grammar, history, geography, and literature, all of which he tackled with enthusiasm. Leon read contemporary 'middlebrow' historical fiction by Jewish authors such as the brothers Ludwig and Phöbus Philippson; this was a genre 'European in form and Jewish in content' that combined 'high cultural forms with sensationalist melodrama'.[52] Alongside this, he took in such German writers as Schiller and Lessing. The study of geography, a particular favourite, led him to *Robinson Crusoe*, a staple of nineteenth-century east European Haskalah literature in Yiddish and Hebrew translation.[53] The exposure to unfamiliar worlds and new modes of storytelling was revelatory for Leon, who until that point had been fed solely on a diet of Talmud and Torah.

His appetite whetted, he struck out on his own. Saving the pittance of

---

[50] Arnold, *Memoirs* (Heb.), 71. On language use in Tarnów, see *Die Ergebnisse der Volkszählung*, 107.

[51] Silber, 'Hungary before 1918', i. 778–9 (table 3); Kieval, 'Bohemia and Moravia', i. 210; id., *Languages of Community*, 161–2.

[52] Hess, *Middlebrow Literature*, 68–9.   [53] Moseley, *Being for Myself Alone*, 446–7.

daily lunch money he received from his parents, he purchased a second-hand Latin textbook instead of food. The need for secrecy was paramount, as this was a grave infraction: not only was he misleading his parents, but he was pursuing illicit knowledge. One afternoon, he reportedly fell asleep in a meadow clutching the textbook. Who should chance upon him but, conveniently, the teacher of classical languages at the city's Gymnasium?[54] Intrigued—why was this sleeping Jewish youth learning Latin alone in a field?—the teacher tested him, pronounced himself impressed, and subsequently recounted the story to his own students. Leon's parents were less impressed and meted out a severe punishment to the boy for his brazen defiance of family and community. This was not the only such episode. At around the same time, when he was 13 or 14, Leon applied his new-found expertise in geography to the perennial riddle of the precise location of the biblical Garden of Eden (Gen. 2: 8–14). Answer in hand, he proudly informed Rafael of his discovery, only to be told that his solution contradicted the great eleventh-century biblical commentator Rashi (Rabbi Shelomoh Yitshaki). Rashi, announced Leon, must be mistaken. For this effrontery, Rafael beat his son, burned his secular books, and dismissed his tutor. A crisis point was soon reached. Leon had all the while been diligently attending Rabbi Mann's study house in tandem with his secular studies, yet the temptations of the latter intruded into the former. When it was discovered that Leon had smuggled a secular book into this religious space, hiding it inside a sacred text, he was summarily expelled, bringing shame and disgrace to his family. At 14, this talented, highly intelligent boy was in educational limbo, no longer attending any sort of school nor receiving private tuition.[55]

For all its intensity, this impasse was unremarkable: a familiar confrontation between generations and a routine stand-off between the demands of tradition and the lure of acculturation. This description of Leon's intellectual development is a version based in family lore, presented in the first instance by his wife Anna (1862–1941) and subsequently embellished by his daughter Paula and by a younger Tarnów acquaintance, the lawyer

---

[54] See Herzig, 'Tarnów od r. 1567 do r. 1907', 204–5, on the Tarnów Gymnasium in the late 1860s.

[55] Arnold, *Memoirs* (Heb.), 38–9; A. Kellner, *Leon Kellner*, 11–12; Spann, 'Dr. Leon Kellner' (Yid.), 273–4; Arnold, 'Leon Kellner', 173.

and Zionist leader Samuel Spann. It recalls nineteenth-century Haskalah narratives that recount the 'awakening' of Orthodox youths as they seek new knowledge in heroic defiance of familial and communal pressure. Not only is the arc of Leon's story similar to these narratives but so too are its individual components, such as the figure of the tutor as catalyst, the self-directed reading, the conflict with authority within the family and beyond, and the learning of non-Jewish languages. The bucolic setting of the Latin textbook episode, its invocation of solitary reading, and the element of a surprise encounter are all frequent motifs in Haskalah literature.[56] That the template is recognizable should not, though, be cause to dispute the account's basic authenticity. His wife and daughter, both accomplished authors, present an intimate but not uncritical portrait in which the advantages and drawbacks of first-hand recollections are evident. If they, like Spann, are undeniably laudatory in intent, the details that they all provide nonetheless mostly ring true.

Parents and son, stubborn in equal measure, remained at cross-purposes for many months. Leon was keen to continue his education, but refused to return to exclusively religious study. His parents were understandably wary of further secular study and anxious about his prospects, given that he had burned his bridges in Tarnów. Shortly after he reached 15, his parents turned for advice to the teacher of Judaism at the Tarnów Gymnasium, who suggested that Leon seek admission to the Jüdisch-Theologisches Seminar (Jewish Theological Seminary) in Breslau (now Wrocław), a modern, scholarly rabbinical training school. The first of its kind in Germany, the seminary had opened in 1854 as an alternative to the traditional yeshiva, hoping to shape a new generation of rabbis in the spirit of the 'Positive-Historical Judaism' movement. Led by Zecharias Frankel, a rabbi and scholar educated at yeshiva in Prague and university in Budapest, the seminary, like its parent movement, steered a middle course between Reform Judaism and Orthodoxy, although closer to the latter than the former. An institutional embodiment of the increasing embourgeoisement of German Jewry, it aimed to produce scholarly rabbis, academically rigorous and professionally competent, imbued with the gravitas needed to function as the public face of Judaism. In addition to advanced rabbinical tuition,

---

[56] Moseley, *Being for Myself Alone*, 303–6, 448; Parush, *Reading Jewish Women*, 98–106. See also Werses, *'Awake, My People'* (Heb.), 67–114.

until the late 1880s the seminary also offered regular Gymnasium-level studies—Greek, Latin, German, ancient history, geometry, maths, physics —for students who had not completed Gymnasium elsewhere.[57] For Leon the prospect was enticing, but for his parents it represented a worrying leap into the unknown. He would receive a more thorough modern education than they had envisaged, without the traditional separation of religious and secular studies, and the religious studies would differ in style and substance from his experience in *ḥeder* and study house. They worried, too, about sending him alone to a new and much larger city in a different country. These risks notwithstanding, it was at least a Jewish institution rather than a state school, and Leon could train there to become a rabbi, even if a kind of rabbi unfamiliar to his parents. It represented a limited rather than complete parting of the ways, and was a compromise they were willing to make.

To prepare him for the entrance examination they hired another tutor, a local Gymnasium student just a year older than Leon, to coach him in Latin, Greek, French, mathematics, and natural sciences.[58] Ever the diligent student, he was admitted to the seminary and set off for Breslau in the autumn of 1876, his first foray beyond Tarnów and its immediate surrounds. A fellow newcomer, Gotthard Deutsch, a graduate of the Gymnasium in Nikolsburg and later a professor of Jewish history and philosophy at Hebrew Union College in Cincinnati, Ohio, described Breslau as a 'different world' for provincial Austrian Jews.[59] As if to emphasize the break with his life to date, Leon effected a radical change of style, readying himself for life in a Prussian city by transforming himself from a strictly Orthodox Polish Jew into a German-style modern Orthodox Jew, trimming his *peyes* (sidelocks) and casting off his long black coat in favour of a shorter jacket.[60]

The seminary, however, fell short of Leon's expectations, and it took little more than a year in Breslau for disappointment to set in. He found

[57] Brämer, 'Die Anfangsjahre des jüdisch-theologischen Seminars', 99–112; Brann, *Geschichte des jüdisch-theologischen Seminars*, 65–6.

[58] The tutor was David Spitzer, later a court official in Krakau; see Fragebogen zur Erfassung der jüdischen Bevölkerung der Stadt Krakau (Dec. 1940), Starosta Miasta Krakowa, 1939–1945. Wykazy dowódow osobistych (Kennkartenlisten) wydanych Żydom. Sygn. 450/ID 25039, United States Holocaust Memorial Museum; A. Kellner, *Leon Kellner*, 13.

[59] Deutsch, *Scrolls: Essays on Jewish History and Literature*, i. 43. Leon was one of eight new students in a class of thirty-four; *Jahresbericht des Jüdisch-Theologischen Seminars*, pp. i, iv–v; Deutsch, *Scrolls: Essays on Jewish History and Literature*, i. 45.

[60] A. Kellner, *Leon Kellner*, 10–11; Arnold, *Memoirs* (Heb.), 39.

the intellectual horizons narrow and the teaching methods surprisingly reminiscent of his *ḥeder* days. The great historian Heinrich Graetz, for example, whose work he had read and much admired, was less inspiring as a teacher; Leon agreed with Deutsch that Graetz's teaching lacked 'imaginative intuition'.[61] An exit route was provided by a seminary teacher, David Rosin. Like Leon, Rosin had moved from *ḥeder* and advanced Talmud study (in his case in Prussian Silesia and Prague) to Gymnasium in Breslau, and then onto a doctorate on Homer's Agamemnon at the University of Halle. Prior to his appointment at the seminary, where he not only taught homiletics and exegetical literature but was also in charge of the Gymnasium-level teaching (and was therefore well acquainted with Leon), he had been director of a Jewish school in Berlin. With this wealth of experience, some of which perhaps predisposed him to sympathy with Leon's frustration, Rosin suggested that a period away from formal Jewish study might be beneficial, and advised Leon to try his luck instead at the Gymnasium in Bielitz (now Bielsko), some 150 miles south-east of Breslau, on the Silesian–Galician border in Austria. Following graduation he would be welcome, should he wish, to return to the seminary and resume his rabbinical studies.[62]

Increasingly drawn to secular study, Leon readily agreed. His parents, though not without hesitation, acquiesced, since the plan offered grounds for cautious optimism that he was not permanently alienated from their traditions and values. In May 1878, at the age of 19, he left Breslau, hoping to begin study at the Gymnasium in Bielitz in September. There were only a handful of Gymnasien in Silesia and just over twenty in Galicia;[63] they were the pinnacle of the Austrian school system, reserved for an academic elite. Admission required an entrance examination, and graduation from a Gymnasium was the prerequisite for a university place. In 1880 only twenty in every thousand of the school-age population in Austria attended secondary school, and just over five per thousand of those aged 19 to 22 made it to uni-

---

[61] Kellner, 'Gotthard Deutsch', 12–13. See also Deutsch, *Scrolls: Essays on Jewish History and Literature*, i. 49; A. Kellner, *Leon Kellner*, 14.

[62] On Rosin, see Brann, *Geschichte des jüdisch-theologischen Seminars*, 98–9; A. Kellner, *Leon Kellner*, 14–15.

[63] *Statistik der Unterrichts-Anstalten*, 14. Government statistics merged Gymnasien with Realgymnasien; the latter were a hybrid of the Gymnasium and the slightly less academically rigorous Realschule. See Cohen, *Education and Middle-Class Society*, 41–2.

versity. Jews made up nearly 15 per cent of secondary-school pupils, more than three times their proportion of the population, and were between 15 and 20 per cent of university students.[64] Despite his patchy and idiosyncratic education, Leon passed the entrance exam—with tests in German, mathematics, and religion—with ease.[65] The Bielitz Gymnasium had admitted its first students in 1871, and in the summer of 1878 had graduated its first finishing class of five students. Leon was one of 333 students in September 1878, 134 of whom were Jews, alongside 113 Catholics and 70 Protestants. Some 30 per cent of the students were from Bielitz; a little over 20 per cent came from Biała, the other part of the city just across the River Biała, and nearly 25 per cent were from elsewhere in Galicia. Two-thirds claimed German as their mother tongue and just over a quarter registered as native Polish speakers; many of the Jews, of course, were Yiddish speakers, but were not permitted to register as such. At some 40 per cent, the disproportionate Jewish representation was striking, given that in 1880 Jews comprised only 1.5 per cent of the Silesian population (although nearly 12 per cent of neighbouring Galicia's).[66]

The two years in Bielitz were crucial for Leon's personal and intellectual development. His wife Anna (née Weiss), whom he met almost immediately upon arrival in the city, recalled that he began at the Gymnasium as a 'restless, sceptical, querulous hothead' and emerged two years later 'happy, more content, and full of confidence in the future'.[67] Anna's family, part of the city's German-speaking Jewish bourgeoisie, gave him entrée into a social and cultural milieu far removed from that of his own family and upbringing in Tarnów. In Breslau he had sat in on classes in English language and literature at the university (all seminary students were expected to attend some university classes), but living in the seminary building and surrounded by other rabbinical students as he was, this was little more than a glimpse of the wider world.[68] In Bielitz he was part of this world for the

---

[64] Cohen, *Education and Middle-Class Society*, 56 (table 2/1), 145, 277 (table 4); id., *The Politics of Access to Advanced Education*, tables 1, 2, 4. See also id., 'Education and the Politics of Jewish Integration', 485.

[65] Cohen, *Education and Middle-Class Society*, 42; Spann, 'Dr. Leon Kellner' (Yid.), 274.

[66] *Jahresbericht des k. k. Staatsgymnasiums zu Bielitz*, 9–11; Thon, *Die Juden in Oesterreich*, 8 (table 1).   [67] A. Kellner, *Leon Kellner*, 17.

[68] Nachtrag zum Curriculum Vitae, 10 May 1890, k. k. Ministerium für Cultus und Unterricht, OS, AV/PUW, Zl. 18771/1890.

first time, although still anchored in a comfortable, if different, Jewish environment thanks to the Weiss family, whom he met through one of his few contacts in Bielitz, a former business acquaintance of Rafael. In 1880 Bielitz was an overwhelmingly German-speaking city of some 13,000 people, of whom 1,660—just over 12.5 per cent—were Jews.[69] Present in small numbers since the mid-eighteenth century, by the second half of the nineteenth century Jews were prominent in all branches of one of the town's signature industries, textile manufacture and trade. Bielitz's economic growth attracted Jews from Galicia, Moravia, Hungary, Slovakia, Germany, and the Polish lands, leading to a threefold increase in the Jewish population between 1870 and 1910. By reputation, Bielitz Jewry was prosperous and burgeoning. Jews were well represented among factory owners (for instance, with factories making brushes, drinks, nails, and rope) and in the growing middle class of commercial and white-collar workers and professionals; many of the town's teachers were Jews, as were half of its doctors and most of its lawyers.[70] The Weiss family, balancing tradition with acculturation and aspiration, was not untypical of Bielitz's ascendant Germanized Jewish middle class.

When she first met Leon, Anna was just shy of 16 years old, one of a dozen children.[71] Her mother, Klara, was from a well-to-do family in Berdychiv, where Klara's father ran a flourishing import business that required considerable travel, on occasion as far as India. Soon after his wife's death, he sent the 15-year-old Klara to marry a merchant in Bielitz; a second daughter was sent to Leipzig where, unusually, she married a non-Jewish man. Klara never saw her father again. Anna's father, a wool trader with interests in literature, music, and politics—he professed a great admiration for Napoleon—travelled regularly on business to Poland, Hungary, and Russia. As he grew older his sight failed, and his business slowed significantly. With a large family to support, Klara stepped into the breach, as had

---

[69] Spyra, *Żydowskie gminy wyznaniowe na Śląsku*, 230; *Die Ergebnisse der Volkszählung*, 84–6. Biała and the adjoining district of Kunzendorf (Lipnik), on the Galician side of the river, were home to nearly 1,200 Jews in 1880, just over 10% of the population. See 'Bielsko-Biała', *Encyclopedia of Jewish Communities. Poland* (Heb.), iii. 78, 81–2.

[70] 'Bielsko-Biała', *Encyclopedia of Jewish Communities. Poland* (Heb.), iii. 78–81. See also Maser and Weiser, *Juden in Oberschlesien*, 87–95.

[71] Thirteen according to her daughter, at least one of whom died young: Arnold, *Memoirs* (Heb.), 30. See also *NFP*, 8 Feb. 1911, 25, where eleven children are noted.

Leon's mother in Tarnów. She was installed as the manager of a newly opened tailor's shop owned by a relative of Leon, a position she held until her death in 1911. A confirmed traditionalist, Klara had received almost no education bar a smattering of French and embroidery, and claimed to see little utility in education for girls.[72] Nonetheless, Anna attended a private German-language girls' school; girls were not permitted to attend state secondary schools and her parents chose not to send her to the town's Jewish school.[73]

Anna, like Leon, was partial to language and literature, her sights set on a teaching career. She studied piano and singing, took private English lessons, taught herself Italian, and learned French at school. Leon introduced Anna and her sisters to contemporary German authors such as Gustav Freytag, Theodor Storm, and Theodor Fontane, along with the German Jewish writer Berthold Auerbach, the Romantic novelist Jean Paul, and the Norwegian novelist and poet Bjørnstjerne Bjørnson. This was a meeting of hearts and minds that laid the foundation for a lifelong partnership.[74] After two years working his way through the Gymnasium curriculum of Greek, Latin, natural sciences, mathematics, and religion, Leon graduated with distinction.[75] Despite his parents' entreaties, a return to Breslau and to the prospect of becoming a rabbi was out of the question for him, as he was no longer observant. As he wrote to Anna in October 1880, he had made 'a transition from purely Jewish life and thought to freethinking'.[76] Armed with his Gymnasium diploma, he set out for Vienna and the university.

[72] On Anna's family, see A.K. [Anna Kellner], 'Unsere Mutter'; Arnold, *Memoirs* (Heb.), 28–34.

[73] Cohen, *Education and Middle-Class Society*, 73–5. On the local Israelitische Volksschule (the Jewish primary school), see Aronsohn, 'Zur Geschichte der schlesischen Juden', 17–18.

[74] A. Kellner, *Leon Kellner*, 16–17, 25.

[75] AUW, PUW/2172, Zl. 709; *Jahresbericht des k. k. Staatsgymnasiums zu Bielitz*, 13. For the curriculum, see also Sirka, *The Nationality Question in Austrian Education*, 111.

[76] A. Kellner, *Leon Kellner*, 117.

TWO

❀

THE MAKING OF
AN INTELLECTUAL

A S A GALICIAN JEW in Vienna, Kellner was not alone. The imperial capital had been a magnet for Jewish immigration from all corners of the Habsburg lands since the revolution of 1848 had eased residence restrictions on Jews in the city. As the empire's largest, most glittering metropolis and as the seat of government, its appeal was obvious: it represented economic opportunity and the prospect of broader cultural and social horizons. Of the roughly 72,500 Jews in Vienna in 1880, some 10 per cent of the city's population, nearly 20 per cent were Galician-born, and most of these had arrived in the previous two to three decades, along with Jews from the Czech lands and the western regions of Hungary. Kellner was part of an even larger wave of Galician migration that began in the 1880s, made up for the most part of poor, uneducated, and Orthodox Jews looking to escape the province's notorious poverty. By 1910 nearly a quarter of Vienna's Jews had been born in Galicia.[1] Kellner, like many others, had family and acquaintances in Vienna, in his case an uncle, a second cousin, and two of Anna's elder brothers, both of whom were university students. In 1880 around a third of students at the University of Vienna were Jewish; some 60 per cent of these were in the medicine and law faculties, with nearly 16 per cent choosing the philosophy faculty, where Kellner enrolled.[2] In 1910 Galician Jews still constituted well over 20 per cent of the Jewish student body.[3]

Kellner's area of interest was comparative linguistics, within which he gravitated in particular to English philology, requiring the study of, inter alia, phonetics and Indo-European and Semitic languages (the last of these taught by David Heinrich Müller, who, like Kellner, was born in Galicia to

[1] On Galician Jews in Vienna, see Wistrich, *The Jews of Vienna*, 49–51; Rozenblit, *The Jews of Vienna*, 40–5; Oxaal and Weitzmann, 'The Jews of Pre-1914 Vienna', 398–400.
[2] Beller, *The Jews of Vienna*, 34; Cohen, 'Die Studenten der Wiener Universität von 1860 bis 1900', 296–7.   [3] Rozenblit, 'The Assertion of Jewish Identity', 184.

26 THE MAKING OF AN INTELLECTUAL

an Orthodox family and studied for a period at the seminary in Breslau).[4] His initial focus was classical languages, but he quickly found that he was 'in his element' in the study of the historical development of modern languages; this, he told Anna, was the 'holy ground' on which he felt 'at home'. Pragmatic considerations also played a role. He thought the field of classical philology 'overcrowded', whereas opportunities for modernists, primarily in schoolteaching, were more plentiful.[5] The field of English philology was of very recent vintage in German-speaking academia, and in Vienna the first chair in the subject was only established in 1876.[6] Even at this stage of his life, though, Kellner was concerned that employment prospects for Jews in a largely state-controlled sector such as teaching were 'very, very bleak', given the eruption in the 1870s in Austria of 'racial conflict' and 'religious hatred'.[7]

Kellner experienced this at first hand, as his arrival in Vienna coincided with a surge of antisemitism at the university, catalysed in part by a polemic written in 1875 by the eminent surgeon Theodor Billroth aimed squarely at Galician and Hungarian Jewish medical students. Jews made up nearly half of all medical students at the university in the 1880s (a proportion that subsequently declined), and Galicians in particular were a visible presence among them.[8] 'I am not a pessimist by nature', Kellner wrote, 'but I must confess that the situation is very grave.' His response combined liberal optimism with ethnic pride. 'When the ghetto walls were torn down last century, Jews were still a despised people of junk dealers and profiteers. And now? . . . By and large, the wall separating the confessions has collapsed and in practical terms there is no difference.' The current wave of 'anti-Jewish hostility', at the university and in the city more generally, was surely a temporary phenomenon; what was therefore required from Jews, ever the 'scapegoats', was perseverance. Jews must 'brace themselves' and rely on 'skill and knowledge to compensate for the advantages that Christians have'

---

[4] AUW, PUW/2172, Zl. 709; A. Kellner, *Leon Kellner*, 18–19. On Müller, see Landesmann, *Rabbiner aus Wien*, 252–5; *Ost und West* (Feb. 1913), 161–6.

[5] A. Kellner, *Leon Kellner*, 108–9, 119.

[6] Reiffenstein, 'Zu den Anfängen des Englischunterrichts', 171–4; Schipper, 'Über die Stellung und Aufgabe der englischen Philologie'. [7] A. Kellner, *Leon Kellner*, 113.

[8] Rathkolb, 'Gewalt und Antisemitismus an der Universität Wien', 71–4; Wistrich, *The Jews of Vienna*, 215–18. See also Billroth, *Über das Lehren und Lernen*, 148–52. For enrolment figures, see Cohen, 'Education and the Politics of Jewish Integration', 486.

THE MAKING OF AN INTELLECTUAL 27

over them.[9] This mixture of steadfastness and self-esteem in the face of antisemitism, shored up by a faith in liberal values, was not unlike the defiant posture adopted at this time by Joseph Samuel Bloch, the Galician-born activist and rabbi who in 1883 was elected to the Reichsrat (the Austrian parliament) and who in 1884 launched, as editor and publisher, the *Österreichische Wochenschrift*, one of Austrian Jewry's most important and long-lived newspapers.[10] An overtly nationalist option did not yet appeal to Kellner (nor at any time to Bloch). He did not, for example, join the Kadimah, the pioneering Jewish nationalist student association formed by his contemporaries at the university in 1882. Kellner would not have been out of place there, as most of the Kadimah's first members were students from Galicia, Romania, and Russia.[11]

In addition to his university classes in French and English language and literature, Kellner took private lessons in these languages during his first year in Vienna from a secondary-school teacher, paid for by his work as a tutor for the family of a local pipe manufacturer. Fortunate enough to find steady employment as a tutor for the duration of his studies, Kellner so impressed one employer that he was offered a permanent position, once he had graduated, overseeing business correspondence in English and French.[12] A secure income would have made marriage with Anna feasible, a notion uppermost in Leon's mind since leaving Bielitz in the summer of 1880. Immediately following his departure, they had begun a covert correspondence, initiated by Leon; by October of that year, they had agreed upon marriage. Her parents were neither thrilled nor surprised; her father had already cautioned her against taking this adolescent infatuation seriously.[13] She revealed her intentions to her mother in writing rather than in person, using an extended passage from a Gustav Freytag novel, *Die verlorene Handschrift* (*The Lost Manuscript*), to express her sentiments. Klara

---

[9] A. Kellner, *Leon Kellner*, 113–14.

[10] On Bloch, see Ian Reifowitz, *Imagining an Austrian Nation*, ch. 3; Wistrich, *The Jews of Vienna*, ch. 9.

[11] Olson, *Nathan Birnbaum and Jewish Modernity*, 24–6; Wistrich, *The Jews of Vienna*, 348–9.

[12] The French and English teacher was Professor Emil Seeliger of the Ober-Realschule am Schottenfeld; see *Hof- und Staats-Handbuch*, 133. In his second year, Kellner's employer was Ludwig Sobotka, owner of an import–export trading business; see *Annalen des k. k. naturhistorischen Hofmuseums*, 46, 54. See also A. Kellner, *Leon Kellner*, 18–19.

[13] A. Kellner, *Leon Kellner*, 20–1.

was ambivalent but made no attempt to dissuade her. This was far from what she had hoped for, she wrote. She acknowledged that Leon was 'congenial, very talented, industrious, [and] mature beyond his years', but was alarmed by his 'precarious situation'. Although she grudgingly approved of his ambition, she told Anna that his 'lofty plans for an academic career seem impracticable to my modest bourgeois sensibility', and she worried that 'terrible disappointments' were in store for the young couple.[14] Undeterred, they maintained their informal engagement during Leon's three years at university. Leon visited Bielitz as often as his schedule allowed and was welcomed into the Weiss family's routines at home and on holiday, although he and Anna were invariably closely chaperoned. Leon's parents similarly travelled from Tarnów to meet Anna's family. Eager to marry, in the summer of 1882 Leon conceived of a plan to seek a teaching post at an elementary school in Bielitz.[15] Anna, however, took a longer view. She felt sure that neither teaching in Bielitz nor the offer of managing business correspondence was likely to prove satisfying for him. Even as an 18-year-old in Breslau, Leon had written to her that he wished above all 'to serve knowledge', and his true goal now, which Anna fully supported, was an academic career, as her mother had noted.[16] He had been encouraged in this by his teacher Jakob Schipper, professor of English philology in Vienna, who recommended that he spend time in Britain and France upon completion of his doctorate.[17] Marriage, counselled Anna, could wait.

In October 1883 Kellner completed his dissertation, a study of verb classes in Shakespeare. He continued with occasional work as a private tutor (teaching English, for example) but was in need of a more adequate and secure income, fearing that without this his marriage might be indefinitely postponed. By February 1884 he had found his first teaching post – not in language or literature, as he had hoped, but as a substitute religious studies (Judaism) teacher at the prestigious Franz-Joseph Gymnasium in Vienna, where more than 40 per cent of students were Jewish. For the next three years, he drew on his thorough training in Tarnów and Breslau to teach biblical texts, liturgy, ethics, history, and literature.[18] At about the

[14] A. Kellner, *Leon Kellner*, 24.   [15] Ibid. 19.   [16] Ibid. 80.
[17] Kellner retained a lifelong affection for Schipper; see Kellner, 'Jakob Schipper'.
[18] *Zehnter Jahresbericht über das k. k. Franz-Josephs Gymnasium in Wien 1883/84*, 47, 64; *Vierzehnter Jahresbericht über das k. k. Franz-Josephs Gymnasium in Wien 1887/88*, 2, 21. See also Rozenblit, *The Jews of Vienna*, 101–5.

THE MAKING OF AN INTELLECTUAL

time he took up this position, he was also hired by Ignaz Kuranda, the distinguished liberal parliamentarian, veteran journalist and author, and president since 1872 of the Vienna Kultusgemeinde (the city's formal Jewish representative institution), to catalogue the Gemeinde's library of some 8,000 volumes. Kuranda took a particular interest in the library, overseeing its rapid expansion from 2,000 volumes in the early 1870s to more than 10,000 by the 1890s, as well as purchasing Hebrew books and donating the bulk of his own collection.[19] There is a certain irony in the fact that these initial employment opportunities, welcome as they were, relied more upon Kellner's store of Jewish knowledge than on his more recently acquired academic skills. A modicum of security now assured, the couple married in Bielitz in February 1884, and Anna moved to Vienna.[20]

Kellner soon added a third string to his career bow, alongside scholarship and teaching. A voracious reader with eclectic taste and broad cultural horizons, he was a gifted writer with a flair for engaging prose. He did not lack ambition. In his very first published essay, in Heinrich Friedjung's new *Deutsche Wochenschrift*, he took aim at the views of the 'curmudgeonly' philosopher Arthur Schopenhauer on the origins of language, taking him to task for wilful ignorance of developments in linguistic theory.[21] Friedjung, an Austrian Jewish historian and journalist with pan-German sympathies and strong assimilationist inclinations, wanted his weekly (other contributors included Arthur Schnitzler and Hermann Bahr) to 'constitute a journalistic bridge between Austria and Germany', appealing beyond a 'superficial readership interested only in gossip and novelty'.[22] At the same time, Kellner looked further afield and began to publish regularly in the renowned Munich-based *Allgemeine Zeitung*. For the next four decades, he produced a steady flow of material—essays, feuilletons, stories, reviews—for the quality press. His first forays into this territory were an indication of what was to come, moving deftly between contemporary and historical perspectives on German, French, and English culture and society. A piece

[19] Kristianpoller, 'Die Bibliothek der Wiener Kultusgemeinde', 198–9; *OW*, 12 Oct. 1906, 705. On Kuranda, see Wistrich, *The Jews of Vienna*, 140–2.

[20] A. Kellner, *Leon Kellner*, 27–8; A.K. [Anna Kellner], 'Unsere Mutter' (1926), 124–5.

[21] *Deutsche Wochenschrift*, 24 Feb. 1884 (no. 8), 6–7. See also ibid., 18 Jan. 1885 (no. 3), 9; 22 Mar. 1885 (no. 12), 2–3; 25 Oct. 1885 (no. 43), 7–8.

[22] *Mährisches Tagblatt*, 13 Oct. 1883, Suppl. 235, 1. On Friedjung, see Wistrich, *Laboratory for World Destruction*, 74–6.

marking the 200th anniversary of the death of the seventeenth-century French dramatist Pierre Corneille demonstrated his familiarity with different genres and periods of French literature, as did an article celebrating the work of Victor Hugo on the occasion of the writer's death in May 1885. He used a review of a book on the psychology of French literature by Eduard Engel (a German Jewish literary scholar and writer who later developed extreme German nationalist views) to discuss German perceptions of French literature and the scholarly perils of using the popular new 'science' of *Völkerpsychologie* (ethnopsychology) as a prism through which to read the literature of a nation, an approach, Kellner wrote, that 'brushed alarmingly against the boundary separating the daring from the false and preposterous'.[23]

Closer to home intellectually was his review of Friedrich Müller's *Grundriss der Sprachwissenschaft* (Outline of Linguistics), a multi-volume investigation of the world's language families. Kellner called Müller, with whom he had taken classes at university, the last representative of the 'heroic age' of comparative linguistics, part of the discipline's founding generation which built comprehensive systems and typologies. Müller's work was a 'bequest from the old school to the new'; now, said Kellner, the field was characterized by 'division of labour and detail'. This was an angle that allowed him gently to critique Müller's purportedly empirical classification of language families along racial lines according to hair type—woolly, straight, curly, or tufted. Contrary to the claims of ethnopsychologists, said Kellner, 'soil and climate' are not reflected in the 'detail' of language, and their efforts to find traces of the desert's 'uniformity' in the structure of Semitic languages, for example, were 'not very clever'.[24] He voiced a similar critique of the appropriation of scholarship for political purposes in his sketch of the International Congress of Orientalists held in Vienna in late September 1886: the government ought not to expect from scholars, 'fanatics for peace', any 'assistance and support for a future politics of conquest in the east'. Poorly understood research about Asia and Africa should not be used to justify the 'colonization fever of our age' and the related 'ugly excesses of national egoism, which in better days will be identified as the stigma of our time'. He was particularly exercised by the 'baseless formulas

---

[23] *Die Presse*, 5 Mar. 1885, 1. For Corneille, see ibid., 1 Oct. 1884, 1–3. For Victor Hugo, see ibid., 23 Mar. 1885, 1–2.   [24] *Die Presse*, 17 Sept. 1886, 1–2.

THE MAKING OF AN INTELLECTUAL   31

of Semitic and Aryan' adopted with 'juvenile overzealousness' by a 'semi-educated crowd'. A true appreciation of orientalist research—embracing Indian hymns, Hebrew psalms, Zoroastrian Avesta, cuneiform script, arch-aeology, biblical and quranic studies, and the centuries-long Arab presence in Europe—belied the false and simplistic dichotomy of Semitic and Aryan that was fuelling the new antisemitism. Scholarship of this sort had an alto-gether higher mission: helping east and west to live peacefully side by side and to understand that together they constituted the 'family of humanity'. As in nature, so too in scholarship: 'Ex oriente lux'.[25]

His oblique reference to antisemitism was in keeping with his future practice in this kind of forum, where he only fleetingly addressed the issues of explicitly Jewish concern that continued to preoccupy him. He was not averse, though, to showing occasional glimpses of his intimate familiarity with Jewish matters. In one of his early pieces in the *Allgemeine Zeitung*, he approvingly remarked in passing on the use of *Midrash rabah*, a com-pilation of Hebrew biblical commentary, in a work tracing the sources of Boccaccio's *Decameron*.[26] A few months later, he commented on the sud-den appearance in Elizabethan literature of 'exotic' Jews such as Shylock and the Jew of Malta; far from displaying the expected 'angst and humility', these Jews had 'seized the offensive to engage in open battle' with Chris-tians, who responded with 'mortal hatred'.[27] These infrequent instances declined over time and he mostly pursued Jewish themes in the more par-ticularist confines of the Jewish press. Writing in the empire's premier Jew-ish newspaper, the liberal weekly *Die Neuzeit*, a few weeks after his portrait of Victor Hugo had appeared in *Die Presse* (a liberal daily established in 1848), he touched once more upon the theme of antisemitism.[28] It was an 'old historical truth', he noted ruefully in a review of a history of the Jews in Bohemia, that 'Jews were better appreciated as one of the state's invigorat-ing elements in the Middle Ages than today'. One would have hoped that,

[25] *Die Presse*, 3 Oct. 1886, 1–2.
[26] *AZ*, 13 Dec. 1884, Suppl. 346, 5113–14. The work in question was by Markus Landau, like Kellner a Galician Jew who had settled in Vienna.
[27] *AZ*, 14 Feb. 1885, Suppl. 45, 659–60. See also *AZ*, 21 Aug. 1885, Suppl. 231, 3401–3; 13 Dec. 1887, Suppl. 345, 5089–91; *NFP*, 25 Oct. 1888, 1.
[28] On *Die Neuzeit*, see Toury, *Die jüdische Presse*, 39–42, 69–72. On *Die Presse*, a rival to the more exalted *Neue Freie Presse* for which Kellner also wrote, see Walter, *Österreichische Tages-zeitungen der Jahrhundertwende*, 45–51.

given the 'always lively interplay between contemporary political and social questions and [the study of] history', the 'medieval Jew-baiting of recent years' might at least have led to greater scholarly attention to Jewish history. Unfortunately, this was not the case, despite the wealth of relevant holdings in the Habsburg archives.[29]

Kellner's passing mention of the 'interplay' between scholarship and society reflected his assumption that the former grew out of, and should be relevant to, the latter. 'As sharp as the distinction between scholarship and life might appear, the daily hubbub penetrates the tranquil, research-consecrated rooms of scholars, setting the orientation and objectives of their thinking.'[30] Rejecting the 'narrow-minded aesthetic' that artificially separated a work from its creator, he believed that scholarship had 'its genesis in life, and in fact often in its most ordinary, everyday needs'.[31] Even the Bible was not immune to this approach. In a breezy historical survey of English Bible translations, written to mark the completion and publication of the English Revised Version, he observed that every rendering of the Bible was as much a reflection of its time as of any eternal truths.[32] He held fast to this conviction throughout his career, whether writing for the public or for the academy. A corollary of this was his view that scholarship ought not to remain solely in scholars' rooms or books. He chided the orientalists' congress, for example, for neglecting to hold 'popular lectures . . . to engage the interest of the educated public', and his conception of this educated public went well beyond the readership of quality newspapers.[33] That knowledge should be accessible to as broad an audience as possible was for him a fixed principle, grounded in his unshakeable belief in the power of education to improve individual lives and, by extension, to benefit society at large. He put this belief into practice above all in his teaching, although he also published a number of successful popular and semi-popular books for a non-specialist readership on English and North American literature and literary history.[34]

[29] *Die Neuzeit*, 1 May 1885, 175. [30] Ibid.
[31] *AZ*, 21 Aug. 1885, Suppl. 231, 3401 for 'narrow-minded aesthetic'; for the second quotation, see *Die Presse*, 3 Oct. 1886, 1.
[32] *Die Neuzeit*, 18 Sept. 1885, 352–3; 25 Sept. 1885, 362–3. [33] *Die Presse*, 3 Oct. 1886, 2.
[34] For example, *Englische Märchen; Englische Epigonenpoesie; Ein Jahr in England; Geschichte der nordamerikanischen Literatur; Nursery Rhymes; Die englische Literatur im Zeitalter der Königin Viktoria*.

Kellner's early newspaper pieces display an exceptional breadth of learning and stylistic assurance for a writer still in his mid-twenties, and served to announce his presence as a distinctive voice in the public sphere, a remarkable achievement given that he had only been speaking German for just over a decade. As a Berlin observer noted in 1899, he wielded 'the pen of a refined feuilletonist'.[35] Following the requirements of the genre, he joined an elegance of expression and a critical—in his case, liberal—perspective with dry humour and sharp observation.[36] For Kellner, none of this was an end in itself but rather a vehicle for thoughtful commentary on contemporary culture and politics. These qualities remained the hallmark of his writings. From the outset, his intellectual curiosity led him to range freely across cultural, political, and social topics, undeterred by constraints of geography and chronology. Most often, though, literature occupied pride of place, providing a springboard for wide-ranging discussion, and without relinquishing variety of subject matter he soon carved out a niche of his own which built on his academic expertise in English literature and language: the culture, society, and politics of Victorian Britain. In so doing, he tapped into a well-established current of Anglophile sentiment in Austria, manifested, as Sigmund Freud wrote in 1882, in an admiration for Britain's 'sober industriousness [and] its generous devotion to the public weal'.[37] Among the imperial bourgeoisie in particular, many looked to Britain as a model of stable and moderate liberalism, and of proven parliamentary government.[38] In time, Kellner became an important mediator between the two cultures.

With the birth of Leon and Anna's first daughter, Paula, in February 1885 and their move to a larger apartment, the family needed more, and more predictable, income than was provided by their piecemeal work—Leon's journalism, part-time schoolteaching, cataloguing at the Kultusgemeinde library, and occasional private tutoring, and Anna's earnings as an English and French translator. To this end, Leon soon took the obvious step, which he had already considered upon arrival in Vienna in 1880, of

[35] *Die Nation*, 14 Jan. 1899, 234.

[36] Kernmayer, 'Zur Frage: Was ist ein Feuilleton?' See also id., *Judentum im Wiener Feuilleton*.

[37] Schorske, *Thinking with History*, 194.

[38] Wadl, *Liberalismus und soziale Frage in Österreich*, 153–7; Ng, *Nationalism and Political Liberty*, 19–24.

qualifying as a secondary-school teacher of English, French, and German. He harboured no illusions regarding his chances of quickly landing a permanent teaching post—these were in the gift of the government and opportunities for Jews were 'limited'—but the formal qualification led to more regular teaching stints at a number of schools in Vienna in the following years.[39]

If Anna was of the view that writing for the public sphere was his 'greatest talent', Leon insisted that he was not a 'journalist', nor did he wish to be; as he wrote in 1888, he was, and wished to remain, a 'teacher and scholar'. Although not dissatisfied with the balance he had struck between what he called his 'careers', he wished to make his mark above all in scholarship, which he saw as his 'only future' and to which he devoted more and more of his time, looking to establish a reputation as a specialist in English language, literature, and culture.[40] In 1885 he published a version of his dissertation, now focusing on verb syntax in Shakespeare. That it was reviewed in the leading German scholarly Anglicist journal *Englische Studien*, where its 'linguistic excursions through centuries and millennia' were praised as a 'superb scholarly achievement' that would 'afford all its readers great intellectual pleasure', was to be expected.[41] More surprising, and a feather in Kellner's cap, was that the *Neue Freie Presse*, the empire's premier newspaper, saw fit to publish a review, calling the book an 'admirable contribution to the lexicography and elucidation of Shakespeare' and admiring the 'rigorous scholarly fashion' in which Kellner had led comparative linguistic research in Germany and Austria along an 'untrodden path' by applying to syntax a methodology more commonly associated with the study of morphology and phonetics.[42] He followed this study up before too long with two essays on Shakespeare's contemporary, Christopher Marlowe. The first, published in *Englische Studien*, investigated the mystery of Marlowe's historical sources for his play *The Jew of Malta*, and in particular for its cen-

[39] He qualified for French and English in 1886 and for German in 1888; AUW, PUW/2172, Zl. 709; Nachtrag zum Curriculum Vitae, 10 May 1890, OS, AV/PUW, Zl. 18771/1890. See also *Jahresbericht des k. k. Staatsgymnasiums im IX. Bezirke*, 27; A. Kellner, *Leon Kellner*, 30. For his views, see ibid. 114, 120. On 'limited' opportunities, see Cohen, *Education and Middle-Class Society*, 62.
[40] A. Kellner, *Leon Kellner*, 29, 133–5.
[41] *Englische Studien*, 9 (1886), 84, 91.
[42] *NFP*, 5 June 1885 (Abendblatt), 4.

tral character, Barabas.[43] The second, framed as a 'contribution to the study of Elizabethan English grammar', drew on the entire corpus of Marlowe's poetry and plays to illustrate his use of adjectives, adverbs, articles, verbs, conjunctions, prepositions, pronouns, and concordances.[44]

From the summer of 1885 Leon and Anna made almost annual trips to London. Most of his time there, and much of hers, was spent in the library of the British Museum (his annual pilgrimage, as he called it) but, eager to acquire greater fluency in spoken English, they also assiduously attended the theatre, lectures, and even church services.[45] Besides his works on Marlowe, his time at the library resulted in a lengthy essay examining the question of the authorship and provenance of the unremarkable but popular sixteenth-century romance *Sir Clyomon and Sir Clamydes*. Just as when he wrote on the riddle of Marlowe's sources, here too he employed close textual analysis alongside literary-historical argument, combing through the play's language (orthography, vocabulary, syntax), metre, and use of alliteration, and examining its dramatic techniques and characters.[46] These visits, and in particular an Austrian government-funded stay for the better part of a year, from July 1888 to April 1889, enabled Leon and Anna to develop a substantial network of contacts, both professional and personal. A key figure for Kellner was Frederick James Furnivall, whom he had befriended on his first trip. Furnivall, a prominent scholar with an interest in Chaucer and Shakespeare, founder of the (still extant) Early English Text Society, and an instrumental figure in the creation of the *Oxford English Dictionary*, introduced him to colleagues and friends among the literati of late-Victorian London. It was through Furnivall, for example, that Kellner met the publisher Alexander Macmillan, along with Henry Bradley, one of the editors of the *Oxford English Dictionary* (later the senior editor), and Richard Morris, a pioneering philologist with an interest in early English and

[43] Kellner, 'Die Quelle von Marlowes Jew of Malta'. He had already touched on this theme in *AZ*, 14 Feb. 1885, Suppl. 45, 659–60 and 21 Aug. 1885, Suppl. 231, 3401–3.

[44] Kellner, 'Zur Sprache Christopher Marlowe's', 3.

[45] For 'pilgrimage', see *NFP*, 3 Oct. 1891, 1. See also A. Kellner, *Leon Kellner*, 31–2.

[46] Kellner, 'Sir Clyomon and Sir Clamydes'. He completed this in January 1889. The play's full title is *Sir Clyomon and Sir Clamydes: The History of the Two Valiant Knights, Sir Clyomon Knight of the Golden Shield, Son to the King of Denmark, and Clamydes the White Knight, Son to the King of Swabia*. For a critical response, see Fischer, 'Zur Frage nach der Autorschaft von Sir Clyomon and Sir Clamides'.

Pali, the language used in early Buddhist texts.[47] At Morris's suggestion, Kellner, with Bradley's assistance, revised Morris's popular and successful grammar and teaching text, *Historical Outlines of English Accidence: Comprising Chapters on the History and Development of the Language, and Word-Formation*, publishing it with Macmillan in 1895. It did not go unnoticed in Germany that a 'foreigner' had been entrusted with this task, evidence of the 'high regard' in which Kellner was held 'on the other side of the Channel'.[48] With Furnivall's 'help and untiring kindness', Kellner had also published *Historical Outlines of English Syntax* with Macmillan in 1892, a volume of detailed and technical exposition of syntactical principles intended to accompany Morris's book.[49]

During these repeated visits to London, Kellner's scholarly interest in the intricacies of the history and grammar of the English language bloomed into a complementary broader fascination for, and love of, English society and culture. What began as abstract philology became cultural immersion, and for the next forty years he pursued both in parallel. In tandem with his scholarly work, he began in these years to write regularly about English cultural life for the press in Germany and Austria, wanting 'to sketch a picture of art and literature in London'.[50] He wondered, for example, at the success of Samuel Smiles (author of the books *Self-Help, Character, Thrift,* and *Duty*), a 'moralist' for whom the 'gospel of work and duty was life's beginning and end, content and purpose', and whose enormous popularity demonstrated that while it was perhaps unfair to call the English a nation of shopkeepers, they were 'categorically a nation of business'.[51] He mined past and present in his dispatches: on the 200th anniversary of the death of John Bunyan, author of *The Pilgrim's Progress*, he endeavoured to explain to a German-speaking public the book's phenomenal success in England. But the non-English reader, he thought, would be hard-pressed to get much beyond the Slough of Despond in this 'quintessentially English book . . . Only in England could such a book emerge; only in England can such

---

[47] For 1888 and 1889 in London, see AUW, PUW/2172, Zl. 709; A. Kellner, *Leon Kellner*, 31–3. For Kellner on Furnivall, see *NWT*, 27 Sept. 1889, 1–2.

[48] *AZ*, 18 June 1890, Suppl. 139, 4. For 'foreigner', see *JC*, 12 Apr. 1889, 19.

[49] For Morris's suggestion to revise his book, see Morris, *Historical Outlines of English Accidence*, p. v. For 'help and untiring kindness', see Kellner, *Historical Outlines of English Syntax*, p. ix.

[50] *NFP*, 25 Oct. 1888, 3.   [51] *AZ*, 14 Sept. 1886, Suppl. 225, 3747–8 (p. 3747).

a book be understood.'[52] Disconcerted as he watched London turn into a 'ghostly city' in October 1888, its population gripped by near-hysteria about the marauding Jack the Ripper, he diagnosed a 'curious affliction in the inner life of our English contemporaries', the 'apogee and triumph of sensation' in literature and theatre.[53] A prime culprit was Robert Louis Stevenson, whose *Strange Case of Dr Jekyll and Mr Hyde* (and its successful stage adaptation of that summer) Kellner mocked as straddling 'the frontier between the sublime and the ridiculous'. Stevenson, as well as Rider Haggard, the 'idol of the lending-library public on both sides of the Atlantic', strove to be fashionably 'enigmatic and unfathomable' but instead produced 'unwitting comedy and satire'.[54] In April 1889, having been in London since the previous summer, he penned an entertaining and provocative overview of the London theatre scene, outlining its recent history and offering opinions on the quality and quantity of genres, venues, repertoires, producers, directors, and actors.[55]

This extended stay in 1888 and 1889 proved particularly fruitful. When not poring over sixteenth-century texts or writing about theatre and literature, Kellner found time to blend his scholarly and more general cultural interests in an exploration of the state of contemporary English poetry, which he thought 'verbose' and 'journalistic'.[56] Given that the most prominent poets of the generation—Tennyson, Browning, Swinburne—had, he believed, 'passed their zenith', he set out to find other 'bards of the first rank'.[57] In a series of portraits, published initially in the *Allgemeine Zeitung* in February 1889 and subsequently in book form, he somewhat uncharitably characterized the poets he had chosen as epigones, discerning in their work 'an artificial, antique-like language and a certain blasé fatigue'.[58] His assessments, intended to inform a German readership, couched exacting exposition of the poetry in succinct accounts of the poets and their respective milieus, mixing empathetic praise with astringent critique. William Morris, 'one of England's most multi-talented and remarkable men', was

---

[52] *NFP*, 29 Aug. 1888, 1–3 (p. 1). [53] *NFP*, 25 Oct. 1888, 1–3 (p. 1).

[54] *AZ*, 18 Nov. 1888, Suppl. 321, 4730–1 (p. 4731). See also *AZ*, 26 Sept. 1888, Suppl. 268, 3937–8.

[55] *AZ*, 13 Apr. 1889, Suppl. 103, 1–2; *AZ*, 14 Apr. 1889, Suppl. 104, 2–3.

[56] *AZ*, 2 Oct. 1891, Suppl. 230, 5–6.

[57] For the first quotation, see Kellner, *Englische Epigonenpoesie*, 34; for the second, see *AZ*, 6 Nov. 1891, Suppl. 260, 3. [58] Kellner, *Englische Epigonenpoesie*, 5.

'a poet drunk with beauty who has landed in the camp of socialist material-ists', while Robert Buchanan was 'a preacher in the wasteland of a secular age, a proselytizing apostle in the midst of a ... self-absorbed generation'.[59] George Meredith's work, marked by his 'penchant for symbolic meditation on nature', was shrouded in 'enigmatic gloom', an 'irredeemable knot of ideas'.[60] By contrast, the 'secret of success' for Coventry Patmore lay in his 'idylls of love and marriage' and, even if he was not an original thinker, he had to his credit 'created a space for the English woman in poetry'.[61] Kellner judged Edwin Arnold, although an editor for the *Daily Telegraph* in his day job, to be 'one of the authentic poets of the age', but was less impressed by Andrew Lang and Austin Dobson, men of 'genial nonchalance who act as though they have examined the peaks and troughs of human wisdom but have through their own experience arrived at Ecclesiastes' truth: *Vanitas vanitatum vanitas!*'[62] This collection of 'brilliant and interesting essays', all appearing in February 1889, was part of a sustained burst of essay writing in this period, testimony not only to Kellner's talent and confidence but also to a relentless work ethic. Anna recalled that her husband worked eighteen-hour days, like 'a man possessed'.[63] His work habits remained obsessive to the end of his life, sometimes at the expense of his emotional well-being; he was, as Anna wrote, 'always at work', even on holiday.[64]

Shortly after returning to Vienna, he completed an article apprais-ing three manuscript versions of Chaucer's translation into English of *De Consolatione Philosophiae* (*The Consolation of Philosophy*) by the sixth-century Roman writer, philosopher, and statesman Boethius.[65] In the course of preparing an edition of William Caxton's *Blanchardyn and Eglantine*, an English translation of a medieval French romance, he had chanced upon Chaucer's translation of Boethius. Comparing the manuscript used by Caxton, a translator, publisher, and pioneer of printing in fifteenth-century England, with two manuscripts used by Richard Morris in a publication for the Early English Text Society in 1868 of Chaucer's translation of Boethius, he became aware of significant discrepancies between them, not just in

[59] For the quotations on Morris, see Kellner, *Englische Epigonenpoesie*, 6, 10; for Buchanan, see ibid. 13.   [60] Ibid. 17–18.   [61] Ibid. 28.

[62] For Arnold, see ibid. 23. For Lang and Dobson, see ibid. 32.

[63] A. Kellner, *Leon Kellner*, 29–30. For 'brilliant and interesting', see Körting, *Grundriss der Geschichte der englischen Literatur*, 403.

[64] A. Kellner, *Leon Kellner*, 52.   [65] Kellner, 'Zur Textkritik von Chaucer's Boethius'.

THE MAKING OF AN INTELLECTUAL   39

phonetics, syntax, and lexicography but also in elements of translation and interpretation. Kellner was moved to compile an exhaustive list of variations—running into the thousands—between the three manuscripts in the hope that this might prove useful for future editions. The philologist and Cambridge professor of Anglo-Saxon Walter Skeat confirmed in 1899 that Kellner's readings of the manuscripts showed 'all possible care and minuteness', adding that 'this excellent piece of work has saved me much trouble'.[66]

The same kind of punctilious manuscript study underpinned his work on Caxton. In this instance, Kellner used the original French version of *Blanchardyn and Eglantine* along with English translations—eleven versions in all, mostly in manuscript—to produce a scholarly edition of Caxton's translation.[67] Dedicated to Furnivall, 'the disinterested furtherer of true scholarship', this book was published in 1890 for the Early English Text Society. A lengthy introduction was published as a separate volume—*Caxton's Syntax and Style*—in the same year. The project was a labour of love, but Kellner pulled no punches in describing the 'main feature' of Caxton's style as 'tiresome tautology'.[68] His orthography was 'very trying', his printing 'seethed with typographical errors', and he wished to make his work 'as showy as possible', reflecting his period's 'intolerable verbosity ... There are very few passages in which Caxton is less verbose than the original.'[69] Meticulous textual parsing of this sort, not unlike that at which he had excelled in Tarnów or at the Breslau seminary, remained a core dimension of his scholarship. He was aware, though, even at the beginning of his career, that philology was with some justification sometimes disparaged as mere 'syllable-counting' and 'decrepit text criticism'. As part of a younger generation he wished to convey a different image of the discipline by broadening its scope and, in the 'century of the natural sciences', portraying it as an 'inductive, exact science'.[70] He treated it as a discipline with flexible boundaries, routinely leavening his work on philology, comparative linguistics, and phonetics with his knowledge of, and passion for, literature

---

[66] Skeat (ed.), *The Complete Works of Geoffrey Chaucer*, vol. ii, p. xliv.

[67] Kellner, *Caxton's Blanchardyn and Eglantine*, p. cxvi.   [68] Ibid., p. cxii.

[69] Ibid., p. cxiv. For the comments on orthography and printing, see Kellner's review of Thomas Malory's 'Le Morte Darthur', *Englische Studien*, 15 (1891), 425.

[70] *AZ*, 13 Dec. 1884, Suppl. 346, 5113.

and its history. For the latter, he laid out a credo of sorts in 1888: 'Authors and literary historians who take their calling seriously do not burden their minds with an interminable list of good and bad books but listen carefully to the divine language of literature, which tells stories about people before us who have striven and suffered, worried and struggled.'[71] He certainly took his calling as scholar and essayist seriously. Fuelled by the need to engage and inform, he wanted on the one hand to 'serve knowledge' (as he had earlier expressed it) and on the other 'to tell stories' about past and present. For him, these were two sides of the same coin.

Confirmation of his growing reputation as a scholar came in the summer of 1890 with his appointment as Privatdozent (external lecturer) in English philology at the University of Vienna, an essential rung on the academic career ladder.[72] As Jakob Schipper (the senior English philologist at the university) proclaimed, English was well on its way to becoming the 'global language', primarily as a consequence of the British empire's vast reach. Along with the Germans and the French, the English, Schipper believed, were now the 'mainstays of modern education and cultural development', and the English language was 'of epochal importance in almost all areas of science and humanities scholarship.'[73] With this position Kellner acquired a foothold, albeit neither secure nor remunerated, in the milieu to which he had for some years aspired. Securing a Privatdozent post was more readily possible for Jews in Vienna than elsewhere in Austria, but offered no guarantee of further advancement due to the not inconsiderable anti-Jewish sentiment at universities throughout the empire.[74] It was nonetheless a significant milestone, representing formal recognition of the quality of his work from the heart of the academic world and permitting him to lecture at the university. His lectures mixed literature and linguistics, introducing students, inter alia, to Middle English, Shakespeare and Elizabethan drama, nineteenth-century English literature, the history of English syntax, the development of English prose, and phonetics and morphology.[75]

※

[71] *AZ*, 22 Jan. 1888, Suppl. 22, 321.
[72] AUW, PUW/2172, Zl. 228, 605, 697, 709; *Die Neuzeit*, 17 Oct. 1890, 409.
[73] Schipper, 'Über die Stellung und Aufgabe der englischen Philologie', 140–1.
[74] Surman, *Universities in Imperial Austria*, 240–1.
[75] The lectures are listed in OS, AV/PUW, Zl. 18771/90. See also A. Kellner, *Leon Kellner*, 53.

THE MAKING OF AN INTELLECTUAL   41

Kellner's three part-time careers—teaching, journalism, and scholarship —brought in a barely adequate income for a family with one child, and the arrival of a second daughter, Dora, in early 1890 made financial stability an ever more pressing concern. At this stage, it was only teaching that could offer security. In the summer of 1891 Leon took up his first full-time teaching post ('finally!', as Anna wrote), at a school in Troppau (now Opava), the capital of Austrian Silesia.[76] The move from imperial capital to provincial city was not without its challenges. Troppau, with a population of some 23,000, predominantly German-speaking and including just over 1,000 Jews, was terra incognita for Leon and Anna.[77] As in Vienna, family proved helpful: Anna's recently widowed sister Rosa, along with her two children, had not long before moved from Dortmund to Troppau to manage a clothing store that was part of Leon's uncle's Vienna-based business. For Anna, Rosa's presence was a 'stroke of good fortune'.[78] If Troppau was entirely unfamiliar, Silesia was a known quantity, with Anna's family home being in Silesian Bielitz, some 50 miles east of Troppau, and Leon having spent his final two years of school there. Even so, this was a new start in a new city, far removed from their social and professional lives in Vienna, and for Leon it was a matter of particular regret that he was forced to relinquish his newly acquired university appointment.[79]

Kellner taught English, German, and French at the Oberrealschule, a type of secondary school with a curriculum oriented more towards natural sciences than humanities. In a school of some 350 students, of whom nearly 20 per cent were Jewish, the overwhelming majority of students were German-speaking and Catholic, mostly born in Troppau or elsewhere in Silesia.[80] A 'born teacher', as the writer Richard Beer-Hofmann described him, Kellner's dedication to teaching, for him both vocation and avocation, never wavered.[81] He was, he wrote, a teacher in 'heart and soul . . . When

---

[76] A. Kellner, *Leon Kellner*, 54. On the appointment to Troppau, see OS, AV/PUW, Zl. 27124/1891; *WZ*, 14 July 1891, 3.

[77] For Troppau's population, see *Special-Orts-Repertorium*, 1; Spyra, *Żydowskie gminy wyznaniowe na Śląsku*, 92.   [78] A. Kellner, *Leon Kellner*, 54.

[79] On his university post, see Kellner to Professoren-Collegium, 18 Nov. 1891, AUW, PUW/ 2172, Zl. 241; Ministerium für Cultus und Unterricht, 29 Dec. 1891, AUW, PUW/2172, Zl. 27124.

[80] *Jahres-Bericht der Staats-Oberrealschule . . . 1891/92*, 61–2; *Jahres-Bericht der Staats-Oberrealschule . . . 1892/93*, 47–8.

[81] From Richard Beer-Hofmann's introduction to Kellner, *Meine Schüler*, 13.

42 THE MAKING OF AN INTELLECTUAL

I stand before my class, the chaotic hustle and bustle, vanities, discord, and disagreements of the world outside subside: I create for my students and myself a more beautiful world of peace and harmony.'[82] School, he believed, should be a site 'not merely of instruction but of nurture', more than just 'an interminable series of monotonous, dreary days, a protracted struggle with one's own nature ... and with implacable teachers'. At its best, a school should provide a 'sense of home' for its students.[83] He was well aware, of course, that reality often fell far short of this, reserving his harshest criticism for the 'torture' of the final graduation examinations. Crucial rites of passage that opened the way to higher education, they often constituted little more than a test of memory ('the countless details of history') that 'demanded the impossible' from students.[84] Pedantry, rote learning, and poor pedagogy were the result. His idealism about the mission of teaching was balanced by a healthy pragmatism. Advising a young relative considering a teaching career, he noted sardonically that teachers were rarely rewarded with 'accolades or medals for their distinguished service'. Theirs was 'a quiet, monastical profession that demands sacrifice', its work 'silent, slow, almost invisible'. If the pupil fails, the teacher is to blame; should the child succeed, 'credit belongs to the home or the student's talent'.[85]

His commitment to teaching went beyond the confines of formal schooling. Otto Koenig, a veteran adult education activist and editor in the 1920s of the socialist newspaper the *Arbeiter Zeitung*, called Kellner, who became a sought-after adult education lecturer, an 'exemplary' teacher whose 'insight and humanity' distinguished him from his contemporaries.[86] Soon after leaving university he took to the public lecture circuit, speaking to learned societies and cultural associations, both general and Jew-

---

[82] Kellner, *Meine Schüler*, 182.   [83] Ibid. 137.   [84] Ibid. 179–80.

[85] Ibid. 187–8. Credit was sometimes given where it was due: the painter Oskar Kokoschka attributed his 'fondness' for England to Kellner's influence and recalled his teaching of Shakespeare as one of the rare highlights of his school years. See Kokoschka, *Mein Leben*, 43–4.

[86] *Arbeiter Zeitung*, 9 Sept. 1930, 5. See also Kellner, *Meine Schüler*, 13. In a review of the latter, a posthumously published book of his essays about students, he was described as 'a true educator of youth, a born teacher, an authority on boys' souls'; see *WZ*, 9 Sept. 1930, 3; see also *Chwila*, 1 Mar. 1931, 10. Roman Dyboski, professor of English literature at the University of Kraków, praised his 'innate pedagogic talent'; 'Leon Kellner: Ein Gedenkblatt zum fünften Jahrestag seines Todes', ANL, Nachlass Luick, 274/113 (Leon Kellner).

ish.[87] So committed was he to extramural education that in 1900 he created the Jewish Toynbee Hall movement, a network of innovative adult education institutions that spread quickly from Vienna across central and eastern Europe.[88] The Jewish Toynbee Halls merged education, culture, and welfare work; they presented lectures, musical performances, and literary readings, dispensed food, drink, and advice, and provided a forum for social activity, all at no cost to tens of thousands of participants. This Fabianist-tinged venture, inspired by Kellner's encounter with Toynbee Hall in London, grew out of his interest in social reform and the provision of welfare. He had already been drawn into a kind of small-scale welfare work soon after completing his studies in Vienna, devoting up to half a day each week to counselling a stream of young teachers, translators, writers, and students, many of whom were Galician Jews, who sought his advice and assistance. In Troppau, where many of his students were from peasant or lower-middle-class families of limited means, he took particular pride in persuading some of the school's wealthier families to assist students in need, whether in the form of tutoring, financial aid, or occasional hospitality.[89]

Issues of poverty, welfare, and social reform now also surfaced in his essays, which even as a full-time teacher he published at regular intervals, in these years mostly in Vienna's *Neue Freie Presse*. In the summer of 1893 he wrote a vivid portrayal of poverty in London's Whitechapel, full of 'squalor' and 'pitiable creatures', setting his account against the background of William Booth's *In Darkest England* and the work of his Salvation Army.[90] For the most part, though, he continued to craft elegant and informative snapshots of London's cultural life, taking in literature (such as novels by women), theatre (the reception by local critics and audiences of Norwegian playwright Henrik Ibsen), and contemporary poetry (complementary postscripts to his earlier series).[91] He had by now amassed a considerable body of work in this vein, using his outsider–insider vantage point to convey

[87] *WZ*, 23 Apr. 1884, 4; *NFP*, 17 June 1887, 4; 23 Nov. 1894, 6; 24 Mar. 1896, 22; *Freies Blatt*, 3 May 1896, 5; *NWT*, 1 Dec. 1897, 6. [88] See below, ch. 4.

[89] A. Kellner, *Leon Kellner*, 29–30, 54–6. See also Kellner, *Meine Schüler*, 151–60. On the social profile of Austrian secondary schools, see Cohen, *The Politics of Access to Higher Education*, n.p.

[90] *NFP*, 2 Sept. 1893, 1–3 (p. 1); 5 Sept. 1893, 1–3; Booth, *In Darkest England*.

[91] On novels, see *NFP*, 6 July 1894, 1–4. On Ibsen, see *NFP*, 10 Aug. 1893, 1–3. On poetry, see *NFP*, 16 July 1892, 1–3; 12 Oct. 1892, 1–3; *AZ*, 2 Oct. 1891, Suppl. 230, 5–6; 6 Nov. 1891, Suppl. 260, 3–6.

44   THE MAKING OF AN INTELLECTUAL

to a German-speaking readership a sense of the light and shade of British society and of the idiosyncrasies of its culture. He pressed ahead with his scholarship, too, despite an already punishing work regime. Having lost his post as Dozent at the University of Vienna as a result of relocating to Troppau, he laboured to maintain a scholarly profile as one of the new generation of Anglicists. His journal of choice remained *Englische Studien*, where he published an investigation of the principles of variation and of tautology in grammar and phrasing in Old and Middle English, an article on the Middle English romance *Ipomadon*, and where his 1892 book (noted above) on the historical development of English grammar was 'warmly recommended as a convenient introduction for German philologists to the history of English syntax'.[92] At the same time, while in Troppau he completed the companion volume to his work on historical grammar (see above), along with a reworked edition for Austrian schools of a textbook on English grammar published thirty years earlier in Germany.[93] Troppau was a way station for Kellner. Vienna remained an irresistible magnet for an ambitious intellectual, and in the summer of 1894, three years after he had left, he returned to take up a post teaching language and literature at a secondary school in the capital.[94]

[92] For the review, see *Englische Studien*, 18 (1893), 220–3 (p. 223). See also Kellner, 'Syntaktische Bemerkungen zu Ipomadon'; id., 'Abwechslung und Tautologie'. He also published a good number of reviews; see *Englische Studien*, 15 (1891), 424–5; 17 (1892), 242–3, 254; 18 (1893), 460–1; 19 (1894), 261–8.

[93] Kellner, *Historical Outlines of English Syntax*; Baudisch and Kellner, *Sonnenburgs Grammatik der englischen Sprache*. (For a glowing review of the latter, see *NFP*, 6 June 1896, 8.) He also put in an appearance at the biennial congress of German philologists, held in Vienna in 1893, to speak about the novelist Mary Ward: Kellner, 'Mrs. Humphrey Ward und der englische Roman der Gegenwart'.

[94] On this appointment to the Realschule in Währing, see OS, AV/PUW, Zl. 8729/1895 (Apr.); *WZ*, 11 July 1894, 3.

THREE

※

HERZL AND ZIONISM

IN EARLY MARCH 1896 Theodor Herzl, editor since the previous summer of the feuilleton section of the *Neue Freie Presse*, wrote to Kellner,
whom he had not met, with a 'presumptuous request': would he be willing
to 'thoroughly check' the English translation of a 'brochure' Herzl had written and 'quickly' return it to him? When it came to English, Herzl added a
couple of days later, he was an '*amhorez*' (ignoramus) and so would have
little to add to Kellner's commentary.[1] The two men knew one another only
by reputation and correspondence, although they had attended university
in Vienna at the same time. Herzl had not long before asked Kellner to join
the roster of contracted regular contributors to the *Neue Freie Presse*, where
Kellner had been publishing occasionally since 1888, but Kellner had already
committed to such an arrangement in 1895 with the *Neues Wiener Tagblatt*.[2]
Kellner had not been impressed by Herzl's early feuilletons ('light chit-chat'
and 'contrived chic') but had come to appreciate his more recent 'inimitable
masterpieces'.[3] This new work, though, was of an entirely different order.
The 'brochure' was Herzl's *Der Judenstaat* (*The Jewish State*), which had been
published in mid-February. Kellner read it almost in one sitting, enthralled
and inspired, and upon finishing work the next day sought out Herzl at his
office. They fell into animated conversation: as Kellner later recalled, 'the
English translation was forgotten; there was so much of importance to discuss'.[4] That they were not well acquainted was evident in Herzl's suggestion
soon after that Kellner forgo afternoon coffee at the Café Griensteidl—a
fashionable coffee-house in the town centre frequented by writers, artists,

[1] Herzl to Kellner, 4 Mar. 1896 and 6 Mar. 1896, CZA, H1/2605.

[2] A. Kellner, *Leon Kellner*, 59; Kellner to Herzl, 12 Jan. 1899, in Arnold, 'Herzl and Kellner'
(Heb.), 137.

[3] See Kellner, 'Herzl und Zangwill', 112, for his opinions on Herzl's writing. In early February
Herzl had asked Kellner for an article on Joseph Chamberlain, the British Secretary of State for
the Colonies; see Herzl to Kellner, 3 Feb. 1896, CZA, H1/2605.

[4] Kellner, 'Herzl und Zangwill', 113; Arnold, 'Herzl and Kellner' (Heb.), 120.

and intellectuals—and instead visit him at home, noting that he would not be in his office at the newspaper as he was 'ailing' (his doctor diagnosed a 'heart condition' a few days later).[5] Even had Kellner wished to do so, neither his teaching duties at school—a considerable distance from the city centre —nor his Stakhanovite work habits would have allowed him to while away his afternoons at a coffee-house. He spent much of the next three weeks working intensively on the translation and discussing revisions of language and style with Herzl, who promptly sent the finished product in instalments to the waiting translator in London. As the work drew to a close towards the end of March, Kellner candidly told Herzl that although as a rule he was not given to fantasy, he was 'moved' by the bold proposal to establish a Jewish state; whether or not the plan came to fruition, the book's publication nonetheless represented an 'event' in and of itself, a kind of 'redemption'. Herzl quickly replied that 'to have won such a friend as you is a great satisfaction'.[6] Kellner's role as editor of this first English version of *Der Judenstaat* has gone unrecognized, since he neither asked for nor received formal acknowledgement. This was not modesty. Rather, the Ministry of Education —his employer—made it clear to him that, publicly at least, he ought to refrain from too close an association with an outlandish scheme of this sort, with its potentially explosive political and social consequences.[7]

Leon and Anna's return to Vienna had been a welcome resumption of the life they had established in the second half of the 1880s. Thanks to Leon's stable, although modest, income as a full-time state-employed teacher—he later described it as 'voluntary penury'—the family could afford a larger apartment with a garden, some 2 miles from the school.[8] Within a few months he had applied for reinstatement as a Privatdozent at the university, and he resumed lecturing in 1895, beginning with a series on the history of English literature in the Victorian era, a theme on which

---

[5] Herzl to Kellner, 11 Mar. 1896, CZA, H1/2605; Bein, *Theodor Herzl: Briefe und Tagebücher*, ii. 315. On the Café Griensteidl, see Carr, 'Time and Space in the Café Griensteidl'.

[6] Kellner to Herzl, 26 Mar. 1896, in Arnold, 'Herzl and Kellner' (Heb.), 122; Herzl to Kellner, 27 Mar. 1896, CZA, H1/2605.

[7] York-Steiner, 'Leon Kellner', 4; Arnold, *Memoirs* (Heb.), 44; id., 'Herzl and Kellner' (Heb.), 117.

[8] See Kellner, *Meine Schüler*, 185, for the quotation. See also Arnold, *Memoirs* (Heb.), 18; A. Kellner, *Leon Kellner*, 57. The apartment was in Döbling, the city's nineteenth district; the Oberrealschule was in Währing, the eighteenth district.

he was later to publish a book.[9] Relocation, of course, briefly interrupted his writing and research, but before long he began to publish feuilletons in the *Neue Freie Presse* once more.[10] He made his first foray into a new field with an appreciation of the recently deceased Oliver Wendell Holmes, marking the beginning of a long interest in American literature fuelled in part by an imagined affinity with the New England Puritan tradition, which he associated with the 'almost ascetic simplicity of life' practised by his parents.[11] This, too, would eventually result in a book which incorporated the piece on Holmes, who, a reviewer noted, 'has probably never been so thoroughly read as he has been by Professor Kellner, nor so enthusiastically applauded'.[12] More scholarly was a pioneering study that drew attention for the first time to the influence of Volney's *Les Ruines* (*The Ruins of Empires*) of 1791 on Shelley's poem 'Queen Mab' of 1813, a point subsequently taken up by others.[13] In early 1896 Kellner was contracted by the long-established Braunschweig publisher Friedrich Vieweg to produce a new edition—the eighteenth—of Friedrich Wilhelm Thieme's English–German dictionary, first published in the 1840s. This became a lexicographical marathon, six long years, as he later recalled, of 'gruelling work . . . and the most profound emotional upset'.[14] Having re-established his familiar routine as an over-committed teacher, essayist, and scholar, he was suddenly swept up in something radically new, one of a select few participants in the birth of a revolutionary political movement that would transform the Jewish world.

[9] Kellner to Professoren-Collegium, 17 Oct. 1894, AUW, PUW/2172, Zl. 78; Ministerium für Cultus und Unterricht, 2 May 1895, OS, AV/PUW, Zl. 8729; *WZ*, 16 May 1895, 5; 26 Sept. 1895, 444. The book was Kellner, *Die englische Literatur im Zeitalter der Königin Viktoria*.

[10] *NFP*, 5 June 1895, 1–3; 12 July 1895, 1–5; 12 Oct. 1895, 1–3; 4 Jan. 1896, 1–2; 9 Apr. 1896, 1–3; 10 Apr. 1896, 1–2.

[11] Kellner expressed his sympathy for Puritanism in a letter to the Viennese-born American writer Gustav Pollak. See Pollak's 'Preface' in Kellner, *American Literature*, p. ix. See also Kellner, 'Oliver Wendell Holmes'. Holmes Sr was the father of United States Supreme Court judge Oliver Wendell Holmes Jr.

[12] *The English Journal*, 4 (Nov. 1915), 618. The book was Kellner, *Geschichte der nordamerikanischen Literatur*.

[13] Kellner, 'Shelley's "Queen Mab" und Volney's "Les Ruines"' (*Les Ruines, ou méditations sur les révolutions des empires*). See also Duffy, *Shelley and the Revolutionary Sublime*, 44: 'Since Kellner first marked the relationship—more than a century ago—critics have repeatedly pointed up Shelley's numerous structural, thematic and verbal borrowings'; Cameron, *The Young Shelley*, 391 n. 36. Volney's full name was Constantin-François de Chasseboeuf, Comte de Volney.

[14] Kellner, 'Englische Wortforschung', 28.

The publication of *Der Judenstaat* proved to be, as Kellner had predicted, an 'event', provoking surprise, fascination, and scepticism in equal measure from London to Moscow. Kellner's response was not untypical; the book's effect on nationalist-inclined groups and individuals scattered across the continent was electrifying. Ardent expressions of support began to flow in from all points of the compass, and a political movement began to take shape around Herzl, built on the foundations of an inchoate pan-European Jewish nationalist sentiment that had developed in the previous few decades without establishing itself as a significant political force. Herzl's charismatic leadership and single-minded pursuit of the vision of a Jewish state wrought a dramatic change, catapulting the 'Jewish Question' onto the international diplomatic stage in unexpected and startling fashion. In the first half of 1896 he embarked on a frenetic series of diplomatic sorties, hoping to win the backing in the first instance of the powerful and wealthy. With no organization to support him and representing little more than an idea, he travelled to Germany in April to meet with the Grand Duke of Baden, met with the papal nuncio in Vienna in May, and headed to Constantinople in June hoping to be granted an audience with Sultan Abdul Hamid II (he met the sultan's secretary and the grand vizier, but not the sultan). In July he was in London, where he not only met with Anglo-Jewish notables but also spoke to a reportedly enthusiastic crowd at the Jewish Working Men's Club in Whitechapel. From London he travelled to Paris to meet with—and be disappointed by—Edmond de Rothschild.[15]

Among the notables Herzl met in London, during this visit and a previous one in November 1895, was the writer Israel Zangwill, author of the 1892 novel *Children of the Ghetto*, a runaway success in Britain and the United States that had made Zangwill 'the preeminent literary voice of Anglo-Jewry'.[16] When Zangwill informed Herzl that he would be passing through Vienna briefly at the end of May 1896, en route from Venice to London, Herzl, keen to earn Zangwill's sympathy for the cause, offered to

---

[15] Vital, *The Origins of Zionism*, ch. 11; Pawel, *Labyrinth of Exile*, 279–308.

[16] Rochelson, *A Jew in the Public Arena*, 51. The novel is a colourful account of Jewish life in the East End of London. For the 1895 visit, see Vital, *The Origins of Zionism*, 256–7; Pawel, *Labyrinth of Exile*, 258–61.

play host—'to make you the "Honneurs" in the capital of Anti-Semitism'.[17] Herzl's English was evidently not as fluent as he wished, nor had he read *Children of the Ghetto*. Since his new friend Kellner, however, spoke excellent English and naturally had read the novel, Herzl invited him to lunch with Zangwill at the Herzls' home.[18] The encounter was not without incident. Kellner later recalled that Herzl's wife Julie, expecting a 'tall, blond, fashionably attired Englishman with consummate manners', was 'visibly disappointed' when confronted instead with 'a man of medium height in an ill-fitting suit, of grotesquely Jewish appearance, and truly gauche demeanour'. 'Startled' to be served a large crayfish, Zangwill required guidance on how to eat the 'monster'. Julie remained with the men only as long as etiquette demanded. Herzl, though appreciative of Zangwill's intellect and eloquence, recoiled from what he regarded as his slovenliness and informality; he was taken aback, for example, by Zangwill's 'nonchalance' in reposing at full stretch on a chaise longue. Kellner brought relief by spiriting the guest away to the horse races.[19]

For his part, Kellner was grateful for the opportunity to meet the celebrated writer, and the two struck up a friendship. Two weeks later, Herzl asked Kellner to write a piece for the *Neue Freie Presse* on *Children of the Ghetto*, which was published at the beginning of September.[20] This was probably the only occasion on which Kellner openly broached Jewish matters in the *Neue Freie Presse*, whose editors pointedly ignored Herzl's Zionist campaign. Continental writers thought ghetto a 'ghastly term', wrote Kellner, but for the English it conjured up something 'curious, archaic, and unfamiliar'. Zangwill cannily appealed to this English sensibility by casting his 'masterpiece' as a form of 'ghetto romanticism' that tried to capture 'the spirit, the idealism, the poetry' of the ghetto.[21]

Kellner smuggled in an oblique reference to Herzl's book in passing, in a manner that Herzl himself could not. He took aim at the view expressed by the former British prime minister William Gladstone on *The Jewish State*, a copy of which Gladstone had received from the Jewish banker and

---

[17] Herzl to Zangwill, 30 Mar. 1896, Bein, *Theodor Herzl: Briefe und Tagebücher*, iv. 85.
[18] Herzl to Kellner, 22 May 1896, CZA, H1/2605.
[19] Kellner, 'Herzl und Zangwill', 113–14. See also Herzl's unflattering remarks about Zangwill in November 1895 in Bein, *Theodor Herzl: Briefe und Tagebücher*, ii. 280–1.
[20] Herzl to Kellner, 8 June 1896, CZA, H1/2605.   [21] *NFP*, 1 Sept. 1896, 1.

philanthropist Samuel Montagu (Baron Swaythling), the Liberal MP for Whitechapel from 1885 to 1900, whom Herzl had met in London. Gladstone's comment was brief, disappointingly so for Herzl's supporters, noting merely that Herzl's ideas were 'most interesting'. Avowing that he was 'naturally' opposed to antisemitism, he instead recommended for those with an interest in the 'Jewish Question' an 'idiosyncratic and rather compelling' novel, *The Limb: An Episode of Adventure*, by X.L. (Julian Osgood Field). The *Neue Freie Presse* printed a small item relaying Gladstone's opinion, although only after Herzl had pressed the reluctant editor.[22] Kellner was scathing about Gladstone's 'unfounded recommendation' of the book by Field, a well-connected writer and convicted fraudster. For Kellner, the novel was an 'unappetizing story' replete with anti-Jewish stereotypes. Foremost among these was its 'reprobate' protagonist, an 'unscrupulous Jew' filled with 'furious hate' towards his own people who escapes the confines of the Pale of Settlement and joins forces with a Polish count and a Russian general to rid Russia entirely of Jews. That even the 'most intelligent' of men such as Gladstone could praise such a 'worthless book' was evidence not only of how little the ghetto was understood but also of how 'an unscrupulous, publicity-seeking writer could achieve easy success with a novel about Jews'. Kellner interpreted Gladstone's praise for *The Limb* as a veiled dig at Herzl rather than the approbation the Zionists hoped for, noting that the novel's Jews are duped en masse by a messianic pretender. The message, thought Kellner, was clear.[23]

In December 1896 Zangwill sought Kellner's advice for a piece he was writing on the Baal Shem Tov, the founder of hasidism, and suggested they travel together to Galicia and Jerusalem: 'If you could be with me for a couple of days in Galicia it would be enough for you to show me the most characteristic features of Jewish life.'[24] Although nothing came of these plans—Kellner was unable to find time for Jerusalem and Zangwill cancelled the Galician trip at the last minute—Zangwill was sanguine. 'I rely chiefly on my artistic imagination', he had written to Kellner, and later sent him a draft of the work, which was to constitute a chapter in his book

---

[22] Gladstone's comment is in Bein, *Theodor Herzl: Briefe und Tagebücher*, ii. 351–2.

[23] *NFP*, 1 Sept. 1896, 1. On Field, see Greene, *Edith Sitwell*, 82–3, 90–6.

[24] Zangwill to Kellner, 23 Dec. 1896, CZA, A74/9. See also Kellner to Zangwill, 28 Dec. 1896, CZA, A120/423.

HERZL AND ZIONISM

Dreamers of the Ghetto.[25] Kellner approved, responding (in English) that the story read 'as if you had lived for years among the Chassidim'.[26]

Kellner's friendship with Zangwill was one of a number that he forged in the first months of his involvement with Zionism. He found kindred spirits in the inner circle of local Zionists, a small 'band of loyalists' who had gathered in Vienna around Herzl, among whom were current and former members of the student nationalist association Kadimah.[27] Meeting weekly in a coffee-house, these activists and enthusiasts came to constitute a kind of 'general staff' for Herzl, who formally became their leader in September 1896.[28] As a result of Herzl's presence, Vienna became Zionism's hub in its first years, even as it spread internationally. Kellner was part of the 'inner sanctum', one of a select group 'responsible for day-to-day management of affairs in the world Zionist movement', but much of his work was not in the public eye; the watchful eye of the Ministry of Education mandated that discretion was the better part of valour when it came to overt political activism.[29] (He published almost all his Zionist writing as Leo Rafaels, a pseudonym with obvious paternal resonance.) For his colleagues, self-employed or professionals, there was no such constraint. The Odessa-born Johann Kremenezky, for example, was a pioneering electrical engineer and a successful industrialist, the first manufacturer of electric bulbs in Austria and one of the founders of the Jewish National Fund. He and Kellner first met in the course of their work with Herzl and became firm friends. In 1914 Kremenezky described himself as Kellner's 'most devoted and warmest friend', and the two men remained close until Kellner's death.[30] The same was true of his long friendship with the publisher

[25] Zangwill to Kellner, 23 Dec. 1896, CZA, A74/9.

[26] Kellner to Zangwill, 13 July 1897, CZA, A120/423. Cancelling the trip to Galicia, Zangwill sent Kellner a copy of his book *Without Prejudice* 'as compensation for the loss of my company'; Zangwill to Kellner, 9 Feb. 1897, CZA, A74/9. At Herzl's request, Kellner reviewed *Dreamers of the Ghetto*; Herzl to Kellner, 20 Mar. 1898, CZA, H1/2605. For the review, see *Die Welt*, 25 Mar. 1898, 11–12. For Kellner and Zangwill's continuing friendship, see also Kellner to Zangwill, 20 Apr. 1899, CZA, A74/9; Zangwill to Kellner, 24 Apr. 1899, CZA, A74/9; Kellner to Zangwill, 9 July 1899, CZA, A120/423.

[27] See Vital, *The Origins of Zionism*, 322, for the quotation. See also Wistrich, *The Jews of Vienna*, 372–6.

[28] See Pawel, *Labyrinth of Exile*, 309, for the quotation. See also Vital, *The Origins of Zionism*, 321–2.   [29] See Wistrich, *The Jews of Vienna*, 375, for the quotations.

[30] Kremenezky to Kellner, 28 Mar. 1914, CZA, A72/9. On Kremenezky, see Hoff, *Johann Kremenezky*.

and writer Heinrich York-Steiner, whom he also met in this first phase of Zionist work. Another of the 'old guard', as Kellner later called them, was Moritz Schnirer, a prominent publisher of medical handbooks who became the Kellner family physician.[31]

These few months in the first half of 1896 marked a decisive turning point for Kellner. Herzl's Zionist vision, he later wrote, was a 'redemptive message' that 'struck like lightning'.[32] His conversion to the cause was abrupt and comprehensive; he became one of Herzl's earliest and closest confidants, and his commitment to Zionism remained steadfast until the end of his days. In June 1896 he wrote to a friend in Troppau that the normal routines of his life had been upended: 'In the past few months I have been occupied in earnest with only one thing: the Jewish Question ... I am with heart and soul a Zionist, and have sacrificed much time and money for a pure and ideal cause.'[33] He was a likely recruit: Herzl offered a clear, radical solution to a problem, antisemitism, with which Kellner had struggled for years. His initial prescription of faith in liberalism and a measure of ethnic defiance (first articulated to Anna in 1880) now appeared outmoded in the light of two decades of ever-increasing anti-Jewish sentiment.[34] In his first years in Vienna, the Kadimah-style nationalism emerging at the university had not dovetailed with the more immediate concerns of a young man recently emerged from the world of traditional Judaism and dazzled by the glitter of new cultural, social, and professional opportunity. He never entirely lost this sense of wonder, but he came to believe that as a Jew he faced undue impediments in establishing himself in the academic world and toyed more than once with the notion of emigration. 'If I continue to be treated this way in Austria', he wrote to Anna in 1888, 'I will need to seek out a livelihood in England.'[35] More than thirty years later, in a book written together with his daughter, he remarked that, in professions such as schoolteacher or university lecturer, 'the Jew, if exceptionally gifted, attains the same as his perfectly average gentile colleague, only it takes him twice the time to do it'.[36]

[31] On Schnirer, see A. Kellner, *Leon Kellner*, 44; *Österreichisches Biographisches Lexikon 1815–1950*, x. 405. For 'old guard', see *JC*, 9 Oct. 1908, 14.　　[32] *Die Welt*, 18 Aug. 1899, 1.

[33] A. Kellner, *Leon Kellner*, 59–60.　　[34] Arnold, 'Herzl and Kellner' (Heb.), 117.

[35] A. Kellner, *Leon Kellner*, 136. He also considered Germany: see Herzl to Abraham Salz, 12 Feb. 1897, in Bein, *Theodor Herzl: Briefe und Tagebücher*, iv. 187.

[36] Kellner, Arnold, and Delisle, *Austria of the Austrians*, 27.

Emigration was a last resort, as his emotional and ideological ties to Austria were deep-seated. His attachment to the Austrian empire and to German culture did not, however, preclude a commitment to Zionism.

I am a good Austrian in every respect, ready to rejoice and suffer with the fatherland ... I live and work with Christians, I teach Christian children, and every day as I set foot in my classroom I am filled with pride and satisfaction that I have been permitted to breach the barriers of prejudice, despite all the impediments of birth, education, and the malevolent zeitgeist [i.e. antisemitism].[37]

Moreover, he was not just an Austrian but also, in cultural terms, a German. 'I feel entirely German: the German language has become for me a second fatherland, a spiritual homeland, and despite everything I am a German writer.' But, he asked, how many Jews were so fortunate? 'They spend the first half of their life preparing for a profession, and—behold!—all professions are closed to them ... How can I know what the future holds for my children?'[38] This was his preoccupation and was at the core of his Zionism: how was it possible to secure the future of the Jews? The answer, he said, was ownership of land. 'We have not conquered the soil with sword or plough, so we Jews enjoy everywhere only the rights of guests; we are not intrusive or burdensome guests, but, rather, are sought after and in demand, and have transformed many economically fallow and broken lands into flourishing emporiums.'[39] He felt, though, that Jews metaphorically 'pay extortionately high interest for land which is lent to them only in the short term'.[40] He wished to channel 'the unified strength of thousands ... to create something great and permanent for our grandchildren and great-grandchildren'.[41] This remained the leitmotif of his Zionism. The claim of Zionism is 'quite simple', he said in a speech in Lemberg in 1907: 'The Jewish people lack a territory and they must win one.'[42] At a commemoration of Herzl's death earlier that year, he struck a similar note:

There is only one way to solve the Jewish Question ... We who worked with Herzl—David Wolffsohn, Johann Kremenezky, Max Nordau, Heinrich York-Steiner, yours truly—might not make it to Palestine ... but if we do not, our children will; and if not our children, then I know with certainty that our grandchildren will.[43]

---

[37] A. Kellner, *Leon Kellner*, 60–1. [38] Ibid. [39] *Die Wahrheit*, 1 Apr. 1904, 8–9.
[40] *Die Welt*, 10 June 1898, 2. [41] *Die Welt*, 27 Aug. 1897, 7.
[42] *Jüdische Volksstimme*, 20 Dec. 1907, 4. [43] CAZ, 6 July 1907, 3.

His Herzlian insistence on land and sovereignty never wavered, although in practice, as will become evident, he exemplified the dual-track approach of Austrian Zionism first developed in Galicia: the goal remained Palestine, but the political and cultural problems of the here and now demanded immediate attention.[44] In the first years of the movement, one of Kellner's particular concerns was religion. Zionism helped him to refine his perspective on the function of religion in Jewish society and, in addition, on the loss of the religious faith that had shaped his early years and left a lasting imprint on his character and thought. In 1891 Herzl's bitter critic Ahad Ha'am, for whom Jewish settlement in Palestine was more a source of cultural renewal in the diaspora than the necessary basis for a Jewish state, had described the condition of emancipated Jews as 'slavery within freedom'. Kellner levelled a similar reproach against them: 'You have won the entire earth, but have thereby lost your soul . . . You speak of Jewish distress, alluding to the persecution by our enemies that damages our livelihoods, wounds our honour, and on occasion threatens life and limb. But there is a much greater Jewish distress—the decay of all authentic, spiritual life.' Unchecked, this would lead to 'moral destitution'.[45] In a series of articles in the movement's newspaper *Die Welt*, written between 1897 and 1900 to mark religious festivals such as Passover, Hanukkah, or the Jewish new year, he drew on his own experience to suggest the ways in which Zionism's drive for Jewish regeneration could forge a mutually reinforcing relationship between religion and nationality. For the Zionist movement, religion was a minefield: traditionalists rejected Zionism's conception of Jews as a modern and secular nation, objected to its claim to represent Jews in the political arena, and scorned the purported ignorance of many Zionists of Jewish norms and practices.[46] Unlike Herzl, Kellner had an insider's grasp of the problem. As he wrote to Herzl, semi-ironically: 'You need a ghetto Jew who can speak the ghetto's language. You're not one. But I am . . . I can speak and write in that ghetto spirit that you don't understand.'[47] His interest in formulating a modus vivendi between religion and nation, which he used as placeholders for tradition and modernity, was therefore personal and political.

[44] On what in the Zionist lexicon was called *Landespolitik* or *Gegenwartsarbeit*, see Shanes, *Diaspora Nationalism*, 49–50, 192–6; Gaisbauer, *Davidstern und Doppeladler*, 451–523.

[45] *Die Welt*, 8 Sept. 1899, 3. On Ahad Ha'am's essay, see Zipperstein, *Elusive Prophet*, 73–5.

[46] Almog et al., *Zionism and Religion*.   [47] Kellner to Herzl, 2 Feb. 1899, CZA, H1/1455-17.

In this, of course, he was hardly unusual. It was 'the curse of Jews', he wrote, that 'modern society in its parochialism' reduced them to living 'partial and constrained' lives.[48] The cost could be considerable, as he made plain in a *cri de cœur* written in London in the late summer of 1898, during the Jewish new year, describing a 'dark tumult of emotions':

in the midst of five million people in London, I feel more abandoned than a shipwrecked survivor on a rocky island in the Atlantic . . . consumed by a profound, powerful, and insatiable yearning, like the pain of lost youth, lost home . . . My pain is the yearning for God . . . I have not suddenly lost all logic and consistency . . . The slow spiritual process, which took place within me half a lifetime ago, is just as valid now as it once was: the existence of God could be proved neither by Bahya or Maimonides, nor their successors. The painful effort to manage without God remains vivid in my memory, as though it were yesterday. It was like an amputation . . .

As a young man, without knowing Goethe's formula, I tried on the basis of art and science to build my life anew.[49] . . . My views have not changed; from the standpoint of logic I have precisely the same relationship to God as ever, and yet—when the week comes to an end, my work, otherwise my life's joy and purpose, loses its allure . . . I want to flee my unsatisfactory present, my unsatisfactory self—but to where? . . . It is quite illogical, but . . . like an irresistible enchanted melody I hear the ancient song: Come, let us sing to the Lord [Ps. 95].[50]

A visit to a local synagogue provided no relief (a 'sham service'); a packed church, however, offered surprising consolation, the congregation heartily singing Psalm 95:

Call it an atavistic relapse, call it childish sentimentality, explain it how you will, but I could barely hold back my tears . . . We work, eat, and sleep, we acquire and waste, we scurry and speed through one day after another, one week after another, year in, year out—not a day of composure and reflection remains.

Is this, he asked, the price of 'enlightenment and liberation'? Must political emancipation bring 'a rupture with the religious past'? How is it that,

despite all scientific knowledge, despite all enlightenment, the church has not lost its hold on the soul . . . while among us only the poor, in spirit and means,

[48] *Die Welt*, 4 June 1897, 13.

[49] A reference to Goethe's aphorism in *Zahme Xenien* (9): 'He who possesses science and art has religion; he who has neither, let him have religion.'   [50] *Die Welt*, 30 Sept. 1898, 13–15.

preserve the old God in their hearts? . . . Have we alone among the earth's peoples drawn the most extreme logical consequences of modern enlightenment? Or, after all, has abstract thought deposed only the God of Abraham, Isaac, and Jacob? . . . I make no claims and wish to prove nothing: the lament has no design, no goal. But those, like me, who can compare life without Shabbat and the new year to what they once knew will understand.[51]

Notwithstanding his disclaimer, he did have a goal in mind. Extrapolating from his own situation, he suggested that Zionism could become the synthesis of the religion/nation antithesis. 'The rebirth of the pan-Jewish idea', for example, showed the Jewish new year 'in a new light', revealing 'its proper significance . . . Even the formulaic catalogue of sins recognises no "I": it is "we" from beginning to end . . . The fears and hopes of the individual are subsumed in the yearnings and expectations of the entire people.'[52] Like it or not, Jews were part of a collective, and religion and its rituals could act as a reminder of this:

One does not forget Jewish descent, and the will to forget has little bearing on this. It is a secret but undeniable law: whoever has belonged to Judaism can never be alien, cold, or indifferent to it. Hatred or love; perhaps burning hatred or burning love, according to temperament and circumstance . . . [But] Jewish indifference towards Judaism is, consciously or not, a lie.[53]

Orthodoxy could not help a modern rationalist, since it was not 'as though a scientific theology could ever exist'.[54] Traditionalists had reduced their heritage to a form of 'self-torment'; they 'eagerly and with serene submission subordinate all impulses to fossilized, codified laws'. Here, too, he used a Zionist prism: this obsessive obedience—'from the first moment out of bed to the last moment before bed, everything is determined and codified'—was the problematic means to a worthy end: Jewish 'solidarity'. The 'fence of law' that Jews had built around themselves was effective: 'we remain, despite different languages and fates . . . a united people'.[55] His critique embraced the diluted Judaism of the reformers:

---

[51] *Die Welt*, 30 Sept. 1898, 13–15.   [52] *Die Welt*, 24 Sept. 1897, 1.

[53] *Die Welt*, 4 June 1897, 13. The writer Arthur Schnitzler made a similar point in 1912: 'It was not possible, especially not for a Jew in public life, to ignore the fact that he was a Jew; nobody else was doing so, not the Gentiles and even less the Jews.' Cited in Wistrich, *The Jews of Vienna*, 595.   [54] *Die Welt*, 4 June 1897, 13.   [55] *Die Welt*, 10 Mar. 1899, 4–5.

How misguided and myopic our enlightened Jews are to represent the Day of Atonement as an exclusively personal matter . . . How perverse that our so-called idealists divest our festivals entirely of their collective character, transforming them instead into 'ethical institutions' . . . No, the Yom Kippur Jews attend synagogue once every year not to be edified by homilies and song; rather, despite the folderol of reform, they attend because the synagogue is a house of assembly, where Jews congregate in order to be persuaded of their existence in the diaspora.[56]

For Kellner, religious rites and rituals were moments in which the individual merged with the collective, a supposition that enabled a reconciliation between religion and nation, or tradition and modernity, that appealed to him both personally and politically. By addressing the twin sources of Jewish distress—land and culture—Zionism could heal both body and soul: 'We are a people rooted not in space but in time . . . This is our weakness but also our strength . . . The soil in which our peoplehood is rooted is our past [and] the memory of no other people reaches back as far.' At the same time, 'we have never lost sight of the connection with the mother soil of our peoplehood'.[57]

Given Kellner's predisposition to reflection, it is no surprise that meeting Herzl and plunging headlong into Zionism—both the messenger and the message had a magnetic appeal—acted as a catalyst for him to reconsider issues that had long preoccupied him, although this entailed a refashioning rather than a wholesale restructuring of his thought. Zionism was now the intellectual and emotional ether in which he organized and articulated his ideas about the Jewish future, antisemitism, the nation, and religion.[58] Recast in a Zionist mould, these ideas would underpin his political and cultural work for the following decades. As a young man, he had written that he wished to be 'a helper to his people'; Zionism proved the ideal vehicle.[59]

In January 1897 Herzl suggested to Kellner that he stand as a Zionist candidate for an east Galician constituency in the imperial parliamentary elec-

---

[56] *Die Welt*, 28 Sept. 1900, 2.   [57] *Die Welt*, 24 Mar. 1899, 3.
[58] A number of his essays on these themes were later published in book form; see Kellner, *Jüdische Weihestunden*. See also *CT*, 3 Oct. 1913, 4.   [59] A. Kellner, *Leon Kellner*, 80.

tions to be held in March. A 'wary' Kellner declined, telling Herzl that the 'entire movement was merely noise'. True enough, replied an irritated Herzl, but 'the whole of world history is nothing but noise' and noise should not be discounted: 'In truth, noise is a great deal . . . and a sustained noise is in itself a striking fact.'[60] The prospect was not greatly appealing to Kellner, already busy with his full-time teaching post, writing for the press, and research. He was in any case not temperamentally inclined to political activism. 'I am no politician', he wrote in 1901; 'I am, and have always been, far removed from the political and agitational work of the Zionist movement.'[61] This was not strictly true, although he preferred to remain behind the scenes. His work was no less valuable for that. Although not a formal member, he was a frequent attendee at meetings of the so-called Engeres Aktions-Comité (Inner Actions Committee), the movement's supreme executive council.[62] A regular speaker at Zionist events, he presided ('splendidly', said Herzl) over what Herzl called the 'first public Zionist meeting' in March 1897, and in October 1897 the *Österreichische Wochenschrift* called him 'one of the leading spirits of the Zionist movement'.[63] Herzl often sought his advice and assistance on political and cultural matters; Kellner's daughter recalled that in these early years their contact was almost daily, whether in person, by telephone, or by letter.[64] By March 1898 Herzl went so far as to call Kellner 'my best and most beloved friend, whose visits are glimmers of light amid all the troubles', and in May of that year he confided to his diary that in the event of his death he wanted 'dear Kellner' both to take care of publishing his diaries and to take over as chief editor of *Die Welt*: 'he is the most familiar with my intentions'.[65]

Although he once affectionately chided him as an 'impractical scholar', Herzl valued Kellner's political and diplomatic skills.[66] In London for a year-long research stay from the summer of 1898, Kellner offered Herzl help with 'our cause'; he confidently predicted that in the course of the year, he

---

[60] Bein, *Theodor Herzl: Briefe und Tagebücher*, ii. 584. On the parliamentary candidacy, see ibid. 480–1 and iv. 187.   [61] *Die Welt*, 8 Mar. 1901, 6.

[62] Arnold, 'Herzl and Kellner' (Heb.), 126; Herzl to Kellner, 28 Sept. 1897, CZA, H1/2605.

[63] *OW*, 1 Oct. 1897, 802; Bein, *Theodor Herzl: Briefe und Tagebücher*, ii. 490.

[64] Arnold, 'Herzl and Kellner' (Heb.), 124.

[65] Bein, *Theodor Herzl: Briefe und Tagebücher*, ii. 575, 587.

[66] Herzl to Kellner, 21 Nov. 1898, CZA, A74/33-4.

would 'certainly speak with the most important politicians'.[67] Herzl needed no further prompting. In the quest for a Zionist anthem to rally the troops, for example, Herzl looked to Kellner, along with the composer Ignaz Brüll, a friend of Brahms, for inspiration. In October 1898 Kellner composed and recited a poem, *Psalm*, to an estimated crowd of 7,000 at a meeting addressed by Herzl in the East End ('a German professor broke out into poetry', wrote an observer).[68] Set to music by Brüll, *Psalm* was for some years a quasi-official Zionist anthem, standard morale-raising fare at Zionist meetings, until superseded by Naftali Herz Imber's 'Hatikvah'.[69] In December 1898 Herzl asked Kellner and the journalist Jacob de Haas, Herzl's first private secretary and one of his most trusted lieutenants, to investigate in the strictest confidence the acquisition for the movement of the English weekly *Jewish World*, of which de Haas was editor. (Nothing came of this.[70]) Kellner's principal purpose in London was to complete his edition of Thieme's English–German dictionary, on which he had been labouring since 1896; he had promised the Ministry of Education and his publisher that he would finish it while abroad.[71] Behind schedule largely due to his Zionist commitments, he redoubled his efforts in the first few months of his stay.[72] He nevertheless found time to work with local and visiting Zionist leaders such as Moses Gaster, the Romanian-born scholar and leader (*hakham*) of the Spanish and Portuguese Congregation, and David Wolffsohn, later to succeed Herzl as head of the Zionist movement; he also took part in the founding meeting of the English Zionist Federation in January 1899.[73]

---

[67] Kellner to Herzl, 12 Jan. 1899, in Arnold, 'Herzl and Kellner' (Heb.), 137. For his offer to help, see Kellner to Herzl, 26 July 1898, CZA, H1/1455-5.

[68] *JC*, 7 Oct. 1898, 11. See also *Die Welt*, 14 Oct. 1898, 2–5; Pawel, *Labyrinth of Exile*, 370.

[69] *JC*, 23 Jan. 1948, 13, 19. See also *Die Welt*, 19 Jan. 1900, 13–15.

[70] Herzl to Kellner, 14 Dec. 1898, CZA, H1/2605. See also Cesarani, *The Jewish Chronicle*, 68–9; *New York Times*, 22 Mar. 1937, 23.

[71] Kellner to Herzl, 11 Apr. 1899, in Arnold, 'Herzl and Kellner' (Heb.), 145.

[72] On being time-poor, see Kellner to Herzl, 20 Mar. 1899, in Arnold, 'Herzl and Kellner' (Heb.), 144–5; Kellner to Herzl, 5 Dec. 1898, ibid. 133.

[73] On Gaster and Wolffsohn, see e.g. Bein, *Theodor Herzl: Briefe und Tagebücher*, ii. 626; Kellner to Herzl, 9 Nov. 1898, in Arnold, 'Herzl and Kellner' (Heb.), 130; Kellner to Herzl, 5 Dec. 1898, ibid. 133; Gaster to Kellner, 18 Feb. 1898, CZA, H1/1264-2. For the English Zionist Federation, see *Die Welt*, 10 Feb. 1899, 10; Goodman, *Zionism in England*, 17–18.

In March 1899 Herzl approached Kellner with further 'strictly confidential' tasks. Could he build and direct (anonymously) a 'vital' English- and French-language Zionist news service, collating and distributing news from the 'Orient' to Europe and the United States?[74] Could he also 'render the movement a great service' and make contact with the Conservative MP Sir Ellis Ashmead-Bartlett, a former civil lord of the Admiralty, with a view to 'winning' him for the cause? Herzl had reason to believe that Ashmead-Bartlett, a zealous advocate of British imperial interests and a noted popular orator, was 'often in Constantinople as a guest of the sultan' and might therefore be a valuable conduit to the Sublime Porte (one of many such leads that Herzl pursued).[75] Ashmead-Bartlett enthusiastically declared to Kellner that he was ready to plead the Zionist case to the sultan but stipulated that a loan of between £1 million and £2 million would be needed to facilitate any political 'concessions' regarding Palestine.[76] Kellner also met with the Conservative MP George Wyndham, Under-Secretary of State for War and formerly private secretary to Arthur Balfour. Smoothing Kellner's path was the fact that Wyndham was also an author with an interest in Shakespeare; as Kellner reported to Herzl, he 'has a high opinion of me as a philologist'.[77] Herzl hoped that Wyndham might provide entrée for him to Prime Minister Salisbury and asked Kellner to 'prepare' the ground for such a meeting.[78] In June, planning a trip to London, Herzl asked Kellner: 'whom should I see in London and how can I get an interview with Lord Salisbury? How can you help to arrange such a meeting?'[79] (There was to be no such meeting.)

In addition to discreet diplomacy, at which the articulate and personable Kellner was adept, Herzl liked to call on his friend's intellectual and literary skills. He suggested that Kellner pen from London 'an interesting and stylish political "letter from England", or perhaps a character sketch of an

[74] Herzl to Kellner, 18 Mar. 1899; Herzl to Kellner, 13 Apr. 1899, both CZA, H1/2605.

[75] Herzl to Kellner, 18 Mar. 1899, CZA, H1/2605. On Ashmead-Bartlett, see Fewster, 'Ellis Ashmead Bartlett'. See also Isaiah Friedman, Germany, Turkey, and Zionism, ch. 6; Cohen, Theodor Herzl, 209.

[76] Kellner to Herzl, 21 and 22 Apr. 1899, CZA, H1/1455-24 and H1/1455-25.

[77] Kellner to Herzl, 11 Apr. 1899, CZA, H1/1455-22.

[78] Herzl to Kellner, 13 Apr. 1899, CZA, H1/2605; Kellner to Herzl, 8 June 1899, in Arnold, 'Herzl and Kellner' (Heb.), 149.   [79] Herzl to Kellner, 6 June 1899, CZA, H1/2605.

HERZL AND ZIONISM

important English politician' for the Viennese press.[80] For the Jewish press, Herzl urged: 'I need feature articles from you [for *Die Welt*]; the more, the better'.[81] In January 1900 he asked Kellner to draft a 'very clear letter' with a 'presentation of our aims' for Herzl to send to Leo Tolstoy, in the hope of persuading the Russian author to express support for Zionism. A 'similar letter, *mutatis mutandis*', was required in English for Rudyard Kipling, with whom Kellner was acquainted.[82] Herzl and the Actions Committee also wanted to approach 'eminent English scholars, artists, and politicians'; they asked Kellner if he would assist them, not just 'by drafting an appropriate circular' but also by 'forwarding the relevant names and addresses'.[83] Such examples could be multiplied.[84]

Herzl also sought Kellner's counsel and support in his literary endeavours. In the summer of 1898 Herzl's new play *Unser Käthchen* (*Our Cathy*), a satire about marriage, was accepted for production at Vienna's Burgtheater. First postponed and then cancelled, it was premiered at the less grand Deutsches Volkstheater in February 1899; it provoked a scandal.[85] Hoping for a London production, Herzl turned to Kellner for help. In his search for a sponsor, Kellner met with friends and colleagues such as Leonard Merrick, a Jewish writer and former actor; William Archer, a leading critic who pioneered the staging of Ibsen's work in London; and Charles Wyndham, a theatre owner and actor. None was persuaded of the merits of the play or of its suitability for London audiences. Archer told Kellner he thought the first act was 'very clever indeed' but the second was 'very much inferior. I am afraid it would not do on the English stage.'[86] Undeterred, Herzl hoped that Kellner might find interest in London for his

[80] Herzl to Kellner, 10 Jan. 1899, CZA, H1/2605.
[81] Herzl to Kellner, 5 Apr. 1899, CZA, H1/2605. For similar, see Herzl to Kellner, 20 Mar. 1898; 3 June 1898; 3 Dec. 1898, all in CZA, H1/2605.
[82] Herzl to Kellner, 3 Jan. 1900, CZA, H1/2605.
[83] Herzl and Actions Committee to Kellner, 15 Mar. 1900, CZA, H1/2605.
[84] See, for example, Herzl to Kellner, 28 Sept. 1900, CZA, H1/2605, where Herzl asks Kellner for his assessment of Education Minister Wilhelm von Hartel, a philologist and professor of classics at the University of Vienna, whom Kellner knew well. See also Arnold, 'Herzl and Kellner' (Heb.), 157.
[85] Objections were raised about the play's 'immorality and indecent language'. See Pawel, *Labyrinth of Exile*, 394. See also ibid. 355.
[86] Archer to Kellner, 5 Feb. 1899, CZA, H1/1455-39. See also Kellner to Herzl, 13 Oct. 1898; 30 Nov. 1898; 7 Feb. 1899, all in Arnold, 'Herzl and Kellner' (Heb.), 129–30, 132, 138.

62   HERZL AND ZIONISM

play *I Love You*, which was to receive a hostile response both from the audience and critics at its premiere at the Burgtheater the following January. Kellner sent it to George Robert Sims, a prolific and successful novelist, playwright, journalist, and social reformer, but to no avail.[87] Later, Herzl asked for Kellner's opinion on a draft of his novel *Altneuland* (*Old New Land*), in which a thinly disguised Kellner appears as 'Wellner', commenting that '[a] word from you will either uplift or devastate me'.[88]

Kellner's most demanding formal Zionist role was as editor of the movement's weekly newspaper *Die Welt*, launched in June 1897. As a newspaper man, Herzl was eager to acquire a tribune to broadcast the Zionist message far and wide, and had twice been tempted by an offer from Minister-President Kasimir Felix Badeni, casting about for a press organ that would support the government, to take over a daily paper.[89] Instead, he opted to create his own weekly, a time-consuming labour of love that further complicated his already difficult relationship with his employers at the *Neue Freie Presse*.[90] In May 1897 Herzl offered Kellner a post as *Die Welt's* first chief editor or publisher, a 'risk' that Kellner, about to head to London for the summer, was at that stage not prepared to take, given possible government disapproval and the incessant pressure of other work.[91] He was, though, a willing contributor, 'enthusiastically' agreeing to Herzl's suggestion that he write a series of portraits of writers in relation to Zionism. The first of these, on Disraeli, appeared in the inaugural issue, the only occasion he published in *Die Welt* under his own name. Herzl continued to press him to write and in the paper's first years he readily obliged.[92] Herzl was always generous in his praise. About one piece, for example, he gushed: 'I am simply enchanted. It is a masterpiece.'[93] On other occasions, he called Kellner's

[87] Herzl to Kellner, 18 Mar. 1899, CZA, H1/2605; Kellner to Herzl, 11 Apr. 1899, CZA, H1/1455-22. See also Penslar, *Theodor Herzl*, 129.

[88] Herzl to Kellner, 26 July 1900, CZA, H1/2605. Kellner's daughter recalled that he was not impressed with *Altneuland*; Arnold, 'Herzl and Kellner' (Heb.), 154.

[89] Pawel, *Labyrinth of Exile*, 252–5, 311–12; Toury, *Herzl's Newspapers*, 159–65.

[90] Pawel, *Labyrinth of Exile*, 323–6; Avineri, *Herzl*, 146–9; Toury, *Herzl's Newspapers*, 168–9. A final offer, from Prime Minister Ernest von Koerber, came in 1901. See Pawel, *Labyrinth of Exile*, 434–6; Toury, *Herzl's Newspapers*, 170–1; Penslar, *Theodor Herzl*, 104, 128–9.

[91] Bein, *Theodor Herzl: Briefe und Tagebücher*, ii. 510–11; Arnold, 'Herzl and Kellner' (Heb.), 125.

[92] For Herzl's requests, see e.g. Herzl to Kellner, 18 Sept. 1897, in Arnold, 'Herzl and Kellner' (Heb.), 125; Herzl to Kellner, 20 Mar. 1898; 3 June 1898; 3 Dec. 1898, all in CZA, H1/2605.

[93] Herzl to Kellner, 31 Dec. 1899, CZA, H1/2605.

articles 'magnificent' and 'sublime', and upon reading Kellner's new year thoughts in September 1900, he told Kellner happily that he 'had heard the great shofar'.[94]

As previously noted, Herzl had tried to recruit Kellner as a regular contributor for the *Neue Freie Presse* even before they had met. In January 1899 he came to Kellner with a much more substantial proposal: he had secured the agreement of the *Neue Freie Presse* to install him as the paper's editor for English literature and politics. 'Your feuilletons are already known', he told Kellner, but to press the case that Kellner was also a political expert Herzl suggested that for one of his regular contributions to the *Neues Wiener Tagblatt* he write an 'interesting political letter from England, *de grand allure*, perhaps a character sketch of an important English politician. It must be clear that you are writing from London.' Knowing where Kellner's true ambition lay, he added an inducement: 'from here, via political connections, you can move your way into a professorial chair at the university'.[95] Kellner, though, knew the politics of university appointments for Jews better than Herzl. Already a Privatdozent for nearly ten years, a chair in Germany, which he had once contemplated, was now 'out of the question. I will remain in Vienna no matter what. But here a professorship would now be a miracle.'[96] As to the *Neue Freie Presse*, Kellner was briefly tempted. His arrangement with the *Neues Wiener Tagblatt*, he told Herzl, was reasonable—he was paid well for his three monthly essays and the editors were lenient if he failed to fulfil his quota—and he had considered taking on editorial responsibility there, but he felt a stronger attachment to the *Neue Freie Presse*, where the 'moral value of feuilletons was something else entirely'.[97] Upon reflection, though, he felt himself unsuited to the task: 'If it were just a matter of thinking and writing it would be child's play; but you journalists are a special breed. I doubt very much that I would be a good fit in an editorial team. When it comes to practical matters, I am a novice. There's the rub.'[98]

---

[94] Herzl to Kellner, 30 Sept. 1900, H1/2605; for 'magnificent' and 'sublime', see Herzl to Kellner, 28 July 1900 and 28 Sept. 1897, CZA, H1/2605.

[95] Herzl to Kellner, 10 Jan. 1899, CZA, H1/2605.

[96] Kellner to Herzl, 12 Feb. 1899, CZA, H1/1455-17.

[97] Kellner to Herzl, 12 Jan. 1899, in Arnold, 'Herzl and Kellner' (Heb.), 136–7.

[98] Kellner to Herzl, 12 Feb. 1899, CZA, H1/2605.

In the midst of negotiations with the *Neue Freie Presse*, Herzl further muddied the waters. He proposed—'by the way'—that Kellner assume the role of chief editor at *Die Welt*. 'Your "by the way"', exclaimed Kellner, 'is giving me a headache!' Even free of regular teaching duties, he was working at the limits of his endurance. He admitted candidly that, once he had finished his English–German dictionary and returned to Vienna, he still faced a 'threefold burden that at times weighs heavily upon me, reminding me disagreeably of my waning powers, particularly with my sleepless nights'. In order to take on *Die Welt*, he asked, 'which part of my threefold burden can I shed: school, university, or *Neues Wiener Tagblatt*?' Herzl's thinking was that a well-remunerated position at the *Neue Freie Presse* would allow Kellner to set aside both school and the *Neues Wiener Tagblatt*, enabling him to take over at *Die Welt*. For his part, Kellner was willing but had reservations, writing to Herzl that:

Die Welt was conceived as a worldly paper . . . and should, as it has to date, primarily serve political ends. But a Jewish paper, Dr Herzl's paper, which speaks to all Jews, cannot neglect or treat the Jewish past and a large part of the Jewish present with disdain. The spirit of the old ghetto often hovers at the doors of *Die Welt*, and you need a ghetto Jew who can speak its language, even if he must, if need be, close the door to it. Neither Dr Herzl, nor Dr Werner, nor Rosenberger [members of the editorial staff] is such a Jew, but Kellner is.[99]

Knowing Herzl as he did, Kellner was alive to what this 'dangerous' job might cost him; it had the potential, he fretted,

to imperil our friendship, which I would not do for all the world. I was for many years satisfied with a single friend, my wife; Zionism brought you to me, and I am already too old and worn out to take such a loss lightly . . . If I belong to *Die Welt*, I will sometimes want to speak with that ghetto spirit in a language that you do not understand, just as the modern ghetto no longer understands the old. Let me say something difficult. First, you are very, very grand and superior; second, you are very suspicious. We have spent a great deal of time together and you know that I am not dogmatic or vain or petty. I yield very easily if I am persuaded of something. But I am much more independent than you perhaps believe, more jealous of my freedom and individuality—*such as it is* [in English]. How much of this freedom will you permit me, you enlightened despot?

---

[99] Kellner to Herzl, 12 Feb. 1899, CZA, H1/1455-17. On Werner and Rosenberger, see Fränkel, *Dr. Sigmund Werner*; Rosenberger, *Herzl as I Remember Him*.

I have spent precious hours in your company, but do you know how often I have said to myself: to help and be of service to this man is a joy; to be a true and genuine friend is difficult?[100]

Despite these misgivings, Kellner was prepared to take the post, telling Herzl in February 1899: 'If you need me, I am at your disposal.' He stipulated, however, that under no circumstances was he prepared to receive payment from Herzl's own pocket. Until the paper turned a profit—it had not yet done so—he would work without salary. 'I have unconditional faith in Dr Herzl both as employer and leader. But you must not be my employer, because I would pay too great a price for that; perhaps thegreatest.'[101]

Herzl was pleased: 'You're taking over the editorship of *Die Welt*. The agreement is that you can do everything you wish. That is to say: *you*! I am handing it over to *you* . . . When do you want to begin?'[102] The question of timing proved difficult to resolve. Herzl, typically, pressed repeatedly for quick action, but Kellner, with too much on his plate, resisted: 'In the name of God, yes! But not until December.'[103] In August Herzl invited Kellner to spend a week as his house guest, as the families of both men were holidaying out of the city. Kellner declined: 'My sister-in-law [with whom he was staying] would eat me alive were I to accept your kindness!'[104] In October, having resumed his 'threefold burden', the prospect of the editorship once more caused him 'sleepless nights and restless days'.[105] Despite this, he took over as chief editor in December. His worst fears about working with Herzl, who remained intimately involved with every phase of the paper's production, were not realized. 'I salute you', Herzl wrote in June 1900, 'this issue of *Die Welt* is just brilliant. I have always known that you are the man.'[106] More in this vein followed: '*Die Welt* is better every week', he wrote a month later.[107] Kellner's tenure as editor, if successful, was relatively brief.

---

[100] Kellner to Herzl, 12 Feb. 1899, CZA, H1/1455-17.

[101] Ibid.　　　　　　　　　[102] Herzl to Kellner, 15 Feb. 1899, CZA, H1/2605.

[103] Kellner to Herzl, 25 Feb. 1899, in Arnold, 'Herzl and Kellner' (Heb.), 143. See also Kellner to Herzl, 11 Apr. 1899, ibid. 145–6.

[104] Kellner to Herzl, 31 Aug. 1899, CZA, H1/1455-28; Arnold, 'Herzl and Kellner' (Heb.), 149. He accepted a similar invitation from Herzl in January 1900; A. Kellner, *Leon Kellner*, 148.

[105] Kellner to Herzl, 24 Oct. 1899, CZA, H1/1455-29.

[106] Herzl to Kellner, 22 June 1900, CZA, H1/2605.

[107] Herzl to Kellner, 26 July 1900, CZA, H1/2605. See also Herzl to Kellner, 28 July 1900 and 25 Aug. 1900, CZA, H1/2605; Arnold, 'Herzl and Kellner' (Heb.), 142.

The cumulative effects of work on a number of different fronts took a toll on his health, and by the summer he was struggling. In August, unable to attend the Zionist Congress in London, he told Herzl that he had hardly slept for six nights and needed a break in order to undergo a 'cold water cure'.[108] Insomnia was a chronic problem for Kellner; in tandem with his unforgiving work habits, it led to the occasional collapse.[109] The result in this instance was that he relinquished his post at *Die Welt* at the end of summer 1900.[110] With his strength quickly restored, he almost immediately threw himself into yet another taxing Zionist-related project that by the end of the year consumed much of his time and energy, the Jewish Toynbee Hall.

For all that Herzl demanded of Kellner, Zionism was of necessity a part-time pursuit, and he continued with his research and writing at a barely reduced pace. The sabbatical year in London, like his lengthy stay ten years previously, proved to be of great professional and personal importance. He had first broached the idea with the Ministry of Education in 1895, looking for an opportunity to concentrate on his research for an extended period, free of his day job; granting permission a couple of years later, a ministry official told him the dictionary would be a 'credit to the fatherland'.[111] For the most part, his plan was realized. The family settled quickly into life in London; their funds were sufficient to afford a 'nursery governess' and a cook, and the two girls, Paula (13) and Dora (8), were home-schooled, just as they had been in Vienna, and also took lessons at the Royal College of Music.[112] (Their third child, Viktor, was just over 2 years old.) As was his custom in London, Kellner spent the great majority of his days in the library of the British Museum. Intent on completing the dictionary, he nonetheless also found time not only to begin work on a popular illustrated

---

[108] Kellner to Herzl, 27 Aug. 1900, in Arnold, 'Herzl and Kellner' (Heb.), 156.

[109] See Arnold, 'Herzl and Kellner' (Heb.), 133; Kellner to Herzl, 12 Feb. 1899, CZA, H1/1455-17; Arnold, 'Leon Kellner', 179.

[110] Arnold, 'Herzl and Kellner' (Heb.), 142; *Die Welt*, 8 Mar. 1901, 5.

[111] A. Kellner, *Leon Kellner*, 143. On planning the sabbatical, see also Kellner to Zangwill, 10 July 1896, CZA, A120/423; Kellner to Herzl, 21 Aug. 1896, CZA, H1/1455-2.

[112] A. Kellner, *Leon Kellner*, 65–6; Arnold, *Memoirs* (Heb.), 18–19.

biography of Shakespeare but also to write regular essays for the Viennese press and for *Die Welt*, and to give occasional lectures (at the London Goethe Society, for example).[113] True to form, he also managed to gather material for more than thirty essays of 'observations, impressions, and short stories' exploring the highways and byways of English life, which he published in late 1900 as a book.[114]

Anna too spent a good deal of time at the British Museum library. She was by now not only a collaborator in, and facilitator of, Leon's research but was also earning a respectable income as a translator, a career path she had embarked upon in the mid-1880s. Initially working in French and English, she developed a true expertise in the field of English literature. For example, together with Leon she translated and edited a collection of English fairy tales for use in schools, published in late 1898. This was unusual on two counts: German translations of fairy tales and children's literature lagged behind other genres, as did translations from English.[115] If not for the English names and idiosyncratic humour, one reviewer marvelled, the reader could well imagine that these stories—not in fact just English but also Scottish, Welsh, and Irish—were a continuation of *Grimms' Fairy Tales*; one 'barely noticed' they were translations.[116] Samuel Singer, a philologist at the University of Bern, similarly admired the translation, which he thought 'struck just the right tone', and noted approvingly that the volume included 'sagas, farces, and anecdotes' along with more conventional fairy tales, making it suitable fare for children and adults alike.[117] Anna's translations of novels were particularly well received. The feuilletonist Johannes Ziegler found her rendering of Leonard Merrick's *The Actor-Manager* 'quite exquisite', and by 1905 a newspaper in Czernowitz could comment that her translations of novels, sometimes appearing in

---

[113] A. Kellner, *Leon Kellner*, 68. See also *JC*, 23 Dec. 1898, 25; 10 Mar. 1899, 14.

[114] Kellner, *Ein Jahr in England*, p. vii.

[115] Wolf, *The Habsburg Monarchy's Many-Languaged Soul*, 156–7. Kellner compiled and edited another collection in 1917, *English Fairy Tales*. [116] *Prager Tagblatt*, 16 Mar. 1902, 10.

[117] *NFP*, 26 Nov. 1899, 35. That the book (Leon and Anna Kellner, *Englische Märchen*) received a complimentary passing mention in the *Neue Freie Presse* (20 Dec. 1898, 2) soon after publication, and thus free publicity, was assumed by Kellner to be a favour on Herzl's part: Kellner to Herzl, 31 Dec. 1898, in Arnold 'Herzl and Kellner' (Heb.), 135. For reviews, see also *Die Nation*, 14 Jan. 1899, 234; *Englische Studien*, 27 (1900), 302–3; *Wiener Hausfrauen-Zeitung*, 25 Dec. 1898, 426.

68

serialized form in the German and Austrian press, had earned her a 'distinguished reputation'.[118]

Leon and Anna mixed with an impressive array of literary, cultural, and academic figures in London, often building on relationships established on earlier visits. Merrick, Archer, and Furnivall were close friends, but there were others too: the novelist Lucy Clifford (to whom Kellner dedicated his *Ein Jahr in England* (A Year in England)), a friend of Henry James and Rudyard Kipling; Mrs Humphry Ward (Mary Augusta Ward), a popular writer, social reformer, advocate for women's education (but later an opponent of women's suffrage), and niece of the poet Matthew Arnold; Sidney Lee (born Solomon Lazarus Lee), Shakespeare scholar and the second editor of the *Dictionary of National Biography*; John Mackinnon Robertson, a radical Scottish writer, Shakespeare enthusiast, avowed secularist, and later a Liberal MP; Cicely Hamilton, writer, actor, and feminist; James Fullarton Muirhead, a Scottish writer and translator long associated with the Baedeker guidebooks; and Elizabeth Robins, a writer (as C. E. Raimond), suffragette, theatre manager, actor, and friend of Oscar Wilde and Henry James.

Their list of friends and acquaintances was long indeed, and remarkable for a visiting foreign couple. Others were Robert Priebsch, philologist and professor of German at University College London; Frederick Pollock, Oxford Professor of Jurisprudence; the writer and activist Karl Blind, a comrade-in-arms of Mazzini, Marx, and Louis Blanc, who had fled Germany after 1848; Mary Jeune, essayist, philanthropist, and salon hostess; the political scientist and Fabianist Graham Wallas, part of a group involved with the founding of the London School of Economics; Oscar Levy, a writer and translator with a passion for Nietzsche's ideas; Ernest Rhys, poet and later the editor of the Everyman's Library series, and his wife Grace, also a writer; Edmund Gosse, essayist, poet, translator, critic, and later House of Lords librarian; and Walter Besant, writer, social reformer, onetime secretary of the Palestine Exploration Fund, and founder of the Society of Authors (to which Kellner was elected in 1925). Through contacts of this sort they were afforded the opportunity to meet luminaries such as

---

[118] *CAZ*, 29 Dec. 1905, 4. See also *CAZ*, 14 Jan. 1906, 4. For Ziegler, who mistakenly noted that her style in German 'betrayed' her Viennese origins, see *NWT*, 2 Sept. 1902, 1. See also A. Kellner, *Leon Kellner*, 40, 128, 130.

HERZL AND ZIONISM

the future prime minister Ramsay MacDonald and the influential French anarchist Louise Michel. Immersion in this milieu was both privilege and pleasure for Kellner; he was, wrote Anna, 'in his element' and his work plainly benefited.[119]

Such was the breadth of subject matter of *Ein Jahr in England*, commented a reviewer, that it could be read with equal profit by 'the literary historian, sociologist, economist, teacher, and tourist. Not to mention the politician ... The author combines an observational gift with an appealing and captivating artistry of characterization', his descriptions of people so clear that 'it is as though we had seen them ourselves'. Of particular note was the portrait of the celebrated author Rudyard Kipling, at whose home on the south coast Kellner spent a long afternoon on a 'cloudless day' discussing literature, translation, imperialism, and race: 'He has rendered Kipling more vividly than anyone previously.'[120] Notably absent from the book is any mention of Jews; as an essayist, he operated in two distinct spheres. In his more generalist writings, as already noted, he touched on Jewish themes only in passing and with a certain reserve. This was a pragmatic and aesthetic decision; attuned to his readership, Kellner tailored his message accordingly.

Kipling was not the only author of note he encountered during the year. George Bernard Shaw, upon meeting Kellner, described him as a 'strong-minded ... well-informed ... man of infinite resource. He talked English literature (about which he knew more than any of us).'[121] Kellner's appraisal

---

[119] A. Kellner, *Leon Kellner*, 68; see also 65–8; Arnold, *Memoirs* (Heb.), 18–28; id., 'Leon Kellner', 173–4. Among acquaintances from previous trips were Mathilde Blind (Karl's stepdaughter), a prominent poet and feminist; William Ernest Henley, poet, critic, and editor; and W.P. (William Paton) Ker, a fellow of All Souls College, Oxford and professor of English language and literature at University College London. For Leon and Anna's correspondence with a number of the above-mentioned people, see CZA, A74/29. On Kellner's election to the Society of Authors, see *The Author*, Jan. 1926, 64; *NFP*, 31 Jan. 1926, 6.

[120] *NFP*, 6 Jan. 1901, 32. See also Kellner, *Ein Jahr in England*, 261. First published in *NWT* on 10 Nov. 1898 (1–3) and 11 Nov. 1898 (1–2), the Kipling piece was 'widely noticed and much reprinted'; *AZ*, 30 Nov. 1900, Suppl. 275, 8. See also Kellner, *Ein Jahr in England*, 259–75. He also received warm praise for an illustrated Shakespeare biography, written for a series on 'Writers and Performers' and published at almost the same time as *Ein Jahr in England*; it was described as a 'thoroughly readable' and 'very commendable resource for the study of the poet and his time'. See *AZ*, 4 June 1901, Suppl. 126, 5. For reviews, see *NFP*, 11 Nov. 1900, 34–5; *AZ*, 24 Jan. 1901, Suppl. 20, 8; *NFP*, 11 Nov. 1900, 34–5; *Die Welt*, 8 Feb. 1901, 8–9.

[121] Shaw, 'A Devil of a Fellow', 249.

of Shaw as an 'essayist, agitator, music critic, and comic dramatist' was instrumental in bringing Shaw's work to notice on the continent; the author himself called Kellner 'one of the first German Shawites'.[122] That Shaw valued Kellner's critical acumen was apparent in his advice to his first German translator, Siegfried Trebitsch, whose translations had been gently ridiculed by Kellner in 1903, leading to a public spat. Trebitsch received little consolation from Shaw, who was well aware of Trebitsch's inadequacy as a translator: 'Do not think me unfeeling—but I have laughed myself almost into hysteria over Kellner's onslaught . . . A reply to Kellner is impossible, because he is perfectly right . . . The truth is, you are very lucky to get off so easily.' He suggested that Trebitsch add a preface to the next edition of his translations: 'I am indebted to Dr Leon Kellner, who was the first to draw the attention of German readers to the works of Bernard Shaw, and whose knowledge of English local life and political organization is unrivalled . . . Dr Kellner is an expert in English sociology as well as in English literature.'[123] In the spring of 1899 Kellner spent the better part of a long day discussing literature and politics with W. B. Yeats, to whom he was introduced by Ernest and Grace Rhys. 'Never before or since have I listened to such an outpouring so curious, so captivating, so repellent, so contradictory . . . One yields to the magic of his marvellous personality, although reason, affronted, objects.'[124]

This second prolonged stay in London, with its whirlwind of social, intellectual, and political activity, was a key juncture in Kellner's career. It was a period of sustained and varied stimulation that not only enabled him to further his research and expand his academic and cultural networks but also yielded abundant inspiration for essay writing, the net result of which was to consolidate and burnish his reputation as an academic and writer at home and abroad. The Zionist work in London, meanwhile, usefully honed his political instincts, which would in time stand him in good stead as a regional political leader in Czernowitz. Last but not least, his experiences in London helped to crystallize his thinking about the links

[122] Shaw to Trebitsch, 26 Jan. 1903, in Weiss, *Bernard Shaw's Letters to Siegfried Trebitsch*, 38. For Kellner on Shaw, see *Die Nation*, 18 Mar. 1899, 358–61 (p. 359). See also *NWT*, 12 Apr. 1900, 1–3; Kellner, *Die englische Literatur der neuesten Zeit*, 381–97.

[123] Shaw to Trebitsch, 26 Jan. 1903, in Weiss, *Bernard Shaw's Letters to Siegfried Trebitsch*, 38. For Kellner on Trebitsch, see *NWT*, 22 Jan. 1903, 1–2; 6 July 1911, 1–3.

[124] *Die Nation*, 8 Aug. 1903, 714. See also *NWT*, 23 Apr. 1903, 1–3.

HERZL AND ZIONISM

between social reform, political activism, cultural work, and educational opportunity, all of which were to come together the following year in Vienna in the shape of the Jewish Toynbee Hall.

The first volume of the English–German dictionary, on which he had toiled so long and which had furnished the basis for his London sabbatical, was finally published in 1902 to a warm reception. It was 'exemplary', a testament to his

knowledge of the land and people (gracefully and enthrallingly displayed in 'Ein Jahr in England'), his intensive personal contact with Englanders of high intellectual calibre, his sensitivity to the most subtle shades of a language's meaning, and, finally, his bee-like diligence . . . Leon Kellner's distinction as an English philologist is acknowledged not just in Austria, but—perhaps even more importantly—also in England itself.[125]

His painstaking attention to detail was on full display here. The dictionary was compact but comprehensive, with an astonishing wealth of new lexicographical, literary, and practical information about the English language and its use in British and North American societies—contemporary idioms, technicalities of pronunciation and transcription, weights, measures, currency, honours, titles, Celsius and Fahrenheit conversion, and much more. 'One could scarcely demand more vigilance from a lexicographer'; it 'should soon become established in all German schools that teach English'.[126]

Even before the dictionary's appearance, Kellner had published a textbook for teaching English to girls at secondary school, a 'thoroughly practical' work that continued to be used in Austrian schools until the First World War.[127] As this was a primer designed for school use, Kellner adhered to the Ministry of Education's requirements and catered to the

---

[125] *Prager Tagblatt*, 7 Dec. 1902, 17. The work's title is *Neues und vollständiges Handwörterbuch der englischen und deutschen Sprache von Dr. F. W. Thieme.*

[126] For the first quotation, see *NWT*, 11 Jan. 1903, 24. For the second, see *Wiener Abendpost* (*Beilage zur Wiener Zeitung*), 4 June 1903, 6. On the German–English volume, 'an indispensable manual for Englanders learning German' published three years later, see *WZ*, 25 Nov. 1905, 8. See also *NWT*, 22 Nov. 1905 (Abendblatt), 4.

[127] *NWT*, 4 Jan. 1903, 24. On use of the *Lehrbuch der englischen Sprache für Mädchen-Lyzeen*, see Labinska, *Die Entwicklung des Fremdsprachenunterrichts in der Bukowina und in Wien*, 201–2; *Jahresbericht des Privat-Mädchen-Lyzeums . . . 1908/1909*, 24; *Jahresbericht des Privat-Mädchen-Lyzeums . . . 1909/1910*, 13; *Jahresbericht des Privat-Mädchen-Lyzeums . . . 1910/11*, 23.

HERZL AND ZIONISM

book's audience. This entailed, for example, incorporating texts—as a reviewer approvingly noted—'relating to the life of women. The most enchanting is the autobiography of a needle. The reading passages "How to Dress" and "Don't" are very instructive; "A Cheap Dinner" and "The National Dish" introduce us to the life of the kitchen.' Beyond this, Kellner did his utmost 'to inculcate the spirit of a foreign language into the pupils', paying 'due attention to the geography of England', adding a number of historical and biographical sketches, and concluding with a 'rich reading passage' on 'The Voyage of Life'.[128]

The pace of Kellner's work in the years around the turn of the century was, as always, intense. In addition to the books already noted, he published academic articles and reviews, and wrote regularly in the press on English, and sometimes American, culture and politics, along with his own occasional fictional pieces.[129] It should be kept in mind that he was all the while holding down a full-time teaching post, creating and then presiding over the Jewish Toynbee Hall in Vienna (which demanded almost daily attention for some four years), lecturing at the university and in more popular forums, and travelling frequently to inspect schools in Galicia as a Zionist delegate on the board of the Baron Hirsch Foundation (on this last, see below). By late 1901 such was his academic and public profile that the Franz-Joseph University in Czernowitz recommended him to the Ministry of Education as the ideal candidate to fill its new chair in English philology. It was a surprise, remarked the university's proposal, that Kellner had not been appointed to a chair in Austria or Germany long ago, as his scholarly record, his 'pedagogical gift', his 'extensive circle of friends and his relationships with writers and journalists in England', and 'his familiarity with the living language' were 'unequalled among his contemporaries'.[130] Pro-

---

[128] *NWT*, 4 Jan. 1903, 24. See also the review in *Beiblatt zur Anglia*, 17 (1906), 59–64.

[129] For a sample of research and reviews, see Kellner, 'To Suggest: Ein Beitrag zur neuenglischen Lexikographie'; *Die Nation*, 28 Mar. 1903, 416 and 8 Aug. 1903, 713–15; *Englische Studien*, 26 (1899), 262–3; 32 (1903), 315–16. For essays, see *NWT*, 31 Oct. 1899, 1–3; 10 Nov. 1899, 1–3; 25 Jan. 1900, 1–3; 17 Feb. 1900, 1–3; 12 May 1900, 1–3; 13 June 1901, 1–2; 23 July 1901, 1–2; 26 Sept. 1901, 1–2; 7 Nov. 1901, 1–3; 12 Feb. 1902, 1–2; 21 June 1902, 1–3; 6 Aug. 1902, 1–2; 7 June 1903, 2–4; 29 Dec. 1903, 1–3; 29 Mar. 1904, 1–3; *Bukowinaer Post*, 12 Nov. 1899, 1–3; *Die Welt*, 18 Apr. 1902, 2–4; 15 Aug. 1902, 1–3. For stories, see *NWT*, 17 Aug. 1900, 1–3; 12 Feb. 1901, 1–2; 22 Oct. 1901, 1–2; 23 Oct. 1901, 1–2.

[130] Dekanat der philosophischen Fakultät [Prof. Carl Zelinka] an das k. k. Ministerium für Kultus und Unterricht, 12 Dec. 1901, OS, AV/PCK, Zl. 47189.

fessorial appointments required agreement from the relevant crownland and the ministry in Vienna, and were signed off by the emperor himself; more than two years were to elapse between the university's suggestion and Kellner's appointment.[131]

Kellner's friendship with Herzl remained strong, even as his involvement in day-to-day Zionist politics necessarily diminished.[132] In the years immediately after 1900, his principal commitments to the movement were in the nominally apolitical fields of education and culture, tied together by a concern for social reform and aligning neatly with his professional and intellectual interests. Both also dovetailed with Herzl's wish to make Zionism as broad a church as possible. The Jewish Toynbee Hall was Kellner's idea; Herzl suggested another, seeing Kellner as an asset in the quest to spread Zionist influence among the non-Zionist upper echelons of Jewish society. One such target was the Baron Hirsch Foundation, a pre-eminent welfare institution and 'development agency' that operated a network of some fifty schools in Galicia and Bukovina with nearly 10,000 pupils.[133] Hoping to reduce the sway of the *heder* in the empire's eastern provinces, the schools offered a broader and more secular curriculum, including Hebrew and religious instruction in Polish. The foundation also promoted a programme of economic and cultural reorientation not unlike that of the Haskalah, investing heavily in vocational and agricultural training. In December 1900, just after Kellner had launched the Jewish Toynbee Hall in Vienna, Herzl persuaded the industrialist and philanthropist David Ritter von Gutmann, president of the Hirsch Foundation, of Kellner's suitability to sit on its board of trustees (as 'our representative', wrote Herzl to Kellner).[134] His fellow trustees, a number of whom were government appointees, were not natural allies but rather 'bankers, industrialists, rabbis, and lawyers . . . who believed that the Ostjuden of Galicia must be retrained, productivized, and gradually assimilated to their gentile environment'.[135]

---

[131] On appointment procedures, see Surman, *Universities in Imperial Austria*, 114–19.

[132] Arnold, 'Herzl and Kellner' (Heb.), 151–2.

[133] Wistrich, *The Jews of Vienna*, 78. See also Lehmann, *The Baron*, 174--81..

[134] Herzl to Kellner, 31 Dec. 1900, CZA, H1/2605. See also Bein, *Theodor Herzl: Briefe und Tagebücher*, iii. 180.

[135] Wistrich, *The Jews of Vienna*, 78, 80. See also Grunwald, 'A Note on the Baron Hirsch Stiftung', 230; Grill, *Der Westen im Osten*, 229–32.

74 HERZL AND ZIONISM

Herzl had hoped to keep the plan under wraps, but in early March 1901 it became the subject of polemics in the Jewish press, with opponents decrying it as a 'betrayal' of Baron Hirsch's intentions and a 'shameful concession' to the Zionists.[136] Professing to be unconcerned, Kellner thought the 'abusive articles' to be 'pitiful gossip, obnoxious misrepresentation, [and] . . . deplorable invective'.[137] Kellner was familiar with Hirsch's work. Almost a decade earlier, in 1892, he had asked Hirsch, one of the empire's wealthiest industrialists and most generous philanthropists, whether he could be of service in the Argentinian agricultural colonies established by the baron's Jewish Colonization Association; Hirsch declined the offer, calling him (as Herzl later did) an 'impractical scholar'.[138] After meeting with Kellner and Herzl, Gutmann agreed that Kellner should join the board.[139] Kellner took his responsibilities seriously, travelling extensively throughout Galicia for the next few years to report on and work with the foundation's schools.[140] Scorned as *goyishe* by hasidim, who mounted a concerted and sometimes violent campaign against them, the schools became a fixture of the Galician Jewish landscape, lauded by the Viennese social reformer Bertha Pappenheim and the Russian activist Sara Rabinowitsch in 1904 as 'an oasis in the desert . . . bringing light and air into the life of Galician Jews'.[141] No sooner had Kellner become a board member than he proved his utility by helping to negotiate the co-optation of three Zionist representatives to the board of another major philanthropic organization, the Israelitische Allianz zu Wien (Israelite Alliance of Vienna), of which David Gutmann was also president.[142]

Herzl hoped, too, that Kellner would aid in his El-Arish venture. At the beginning of March 1903, anticipating that Zionists were 'on the threshold of founding a city and a country' in the northern Sinai around the coastal town of El-Arish, he asked Kellner to write a book on the history of the area. This might, he thought, furnish evidence of the project's viability.

---

[136] For 'betrayal', see *OW*, 22 Mar. 1901, 199. For 'shameful concession', see *OW*, 8 Mar. 1901, 171. See also *OW*, 1 Mar. 1901, 147; 29 Mar. 1901, 219; 6 Sept. 1901, 595.

[137] *Die Welt*, 8 Mar. 1901, 6. [138] *Jüdische Volksstimme*, 10 Apr. 1909, 5.

[139] *Bericht des Curatoriums der Baron Hirsch-Stiftung*, 25–6, 45–6; *Die Welt*, 3 Apr. 1901, 30.

[140] Arnold, 'Herzl and Kellner' (Heb.), 152, 158–9.

[141] Pappenheim and Rabinowitsch, *Zur Lage der jüdischen Bevölkerung in Galizien*, 11, 96. See also Tenenbaum, *Galicia: My Old Home* (Yid.), 129–30; *Die Welt*, 11 Sept. 1903, 11–12.

[142] Bein, *Theodor Herzl: Briefe und Tagebücher*, vi. 103–5, 203.

With neither the time nor the inclination, Kellner agreed only if he were paid a princely sum, telling Herzl, 'I no longer want to be foolish.' Having imagined Kellner as 'secretary general' of the new polity, Herzl was 'disconcerted' by his friend's response.[143] At the end of March, Herzl spent nearly two weeks in Cairo attempting to persuade British and Egyptian officials of the feasibility and benefits of Jewish settlement. On the day of his return to Vienna in mid-April—a brief stay before heading to Paris—Herzl asked Kellner to read his draft proposal, written at the behest of the British, for a 'concession' (something short of a charter) that was to be put to the Egyptian government. He was to be disappointed once more. Kellner dismissed the entire idea as impractical and unwise, leading to a heated disagreement. Within a couple of months, the idea had in any case run aground, superseded by the 'Uganda' scheme.[144]

The recommendation in December 1901 to appoint Kellner to the new professorial chair in English philology in Czernowitz had meanwhile moved slowly through the machinery of government.[145] The emperor gave his assent in late February 1904 and received Kellner soon after for a brief ceremonial audience.[146] Among many others, Herzl was quick to congratulate him.[147] Herzl's death in July found Kellner on a family holiday in the Adriatic coastal resort town of Abbazia (now Opatija); he travelled day and night in order to attend the funeral, at which he served as a pallbearer.[148] At the beginning of October, the family left Vienna, their home for twenty years, to begin a new life in Czernowitz.

[143] Ibid. iii. 519–20.

[144] Arnold, 'Leon Kellner', 179–80; id., 'Herzl and Kellner' (Heb.), 159. On El-Arish, see Vital, Zionism: The Formative Years, 146–54; Avineri, Herzl, 204–16; Penslar, Theodor Herzl, 185–6. On 'Uganda', Herzl's proposal for a Jewish settlement in East Africa (today's Kenya), see Vital, Zionism: The Formative Years, ch. 9; Avineri, Herzl, 237–44.

[145] See the correspondence between the ministry in Vienna, the regional government in Bukovina, and the Lower Austrian police authorities: Ministerium für Kultus und Unterricht an den k. k. Statthalter in Wien, 4 Apr. 1903, OS, AV/PCK, Zl. 4891; K. K. Polizeidirektion Wien to k. k. n. ö. Statthalter, 25 Apr. 1903, OS, AV/PCK, Zl. 38601; Bukovina k. k. Landesregierung to k. k. Ministerium für Kultus und Unterricht, 28 Apr. 1903, OS, AV/PCK, Zl. 4891.

[146] WZ, 8 Mar. 1904, 1; NFP, 8 Mar. 1904 (Abendblatt), 1; A. Kellner, Leon Kellner, 70. On the audience, see NFP, 17 Mar. 1904 (Abendblatt), 3. Viennese mayor Karl Lueger was among others to be granted an audience that morning.　　[147] Herzl to Kellner, 11 Mar. 1904, CZA, H1/2605.

[148] Die Welt, 8 July 1904, 15–16; NFP, 7 July 1904 (Abendblatt), 3; Arnold, Memoirs (Heb.), 46–7.

FOUR

THE JEWISH TOYNBEE HALL

IN EARLY DECEMBER 1900 Herzl spoke to an audience of some 150 people crowded into a hall in Vienna's working-class district of Brigittenau, in the 'musty air' of a 'narrow, quiet street' where the 'glamour and affluence of the city had not yet penetrated'. Such was the interest in the event that, at Herzl's suggestion, the meeting was repeated twice more that evening. Herzl was lending his support to the opening of the Jewish Toynbee Hall, the first institution of its kind in Europe. Kellner, the Hall's prime mover and guiding spirit, spoke before Herzl. Here, he said, 'the prosperous and educated would devote a few hours of their time to those less fortunate and less educated in order to fortify them morally and spiritually for the struggle of the following day.'[1] He hoped the Hall would be an 'oasis in the desert' for the Jewish poor, the 'pedlars, junk dealers, and tradesmen [who] for a few hours might escape the terrible solitude of the big city and realize they were not alone in the world'.[2] Vienna's Jewish Toynbee Hall was an immediate popular success and launched a movement that spread quickly to other Habsburg lands—Bohemia, Moravia, Galicia, Bukovina—and also further afield to Germany, Romania, and the Netherlands. Its mixture of accessible lectures, musical and literary performances, adult education courses, children's entertainment, and food, all provided free of charge, proved a winning formula. For Kellner, the Jewish Toynbee Hall drew together his passions in an ambitious experiment, uniting his Anglophilia and liberal nationalism with his abiding interest in social reform, culture, and education.[3]

---

[1] *Die Welt*, 7 Dec. 1900, 12–13. See also *Die Neuzeit*, 7 Dec. 1900, 515; *NWT*, 4 Dec. 1900, 6–7; Kellner, *Eine jüdische Toynbee-Halle*, 7.

[2] Kellner, *Eine jüdische Toynbee-Halle*, 10–11.

[3] For partial accounts, see Oelschlägel, 'Integration durch Bildung'; Malleier, 'Die jüdische Toynbee-Halle'; Shanes, *Diaspora Nationalism*, 178–80; Hödl, *Als Bettler in die Leopoldstadt*, 162–5; Rozenblit, *The Jews of Vienna*, 66–7.

The idea was not new. He had written on several occasions in praise of the welfare and educational work of William Booth and the Salvation Army in London's East End, although he was less taken with the Army's 'religious bacchanalia' and its 'clamorous Corybant throngs wending their way through the streets with nerve-jangling music'.[4] He had visited Toynbee Hall in 1895, where he found much to like. Impressed by the diversity and quality of its programmes, the social composition of its clientele, and the 'enthusiasm and goodwill' of its youthful workforce, he thought it served the 'interests of the people' well.[5] He brought all this together with Zionism in the summer of 1900. Writing in *Die Welt*, he drew the attention of delegates attending the Zionist Congress in London to the Salvation Army as an 'exceedingly interesting example of a mass organization' founded on the principles of 'absolute equality and fraternity'. Zionists, he urged, would do well to study a movement 'that was built upon, and worked for, the people'. He recommended a visit, too, to Toynbee Hall, an institution that could 'pave the way for a solution to the social question in England'. Reiterating what he had written two years previously for the *Neue Freie Presse*, he added for this readership that one might see parallels between Toynbee Hall's pursuit of egalitarianism and access for all, regardless of social stature, and the practices of traditional institutions of learning in eastern Europe such as the *kloyz* or *beit hamidrash*.[6] Kellner now thought that it might be possible to transplant an appropriately modified version of Toynbee Hall to Vienna. This would not be straightforward, given that it was, in his own words, a 'peculiarly English' institution.[7]

Arnold Toynbee was an economic historian and Fabianist social reformer, commonly credited with popularizing the term 'industrial revolution'.[8] In the course of his political and social activism, he befriended Canon Samuel Barnett and his wife Henrietta, who had moved to London's East End in

---

[4] *NWT*, 16 Mar. 1897, 1. See also *NFP*, 2 Sept. 1893, 1–3; 5 Sept. 1893, 1–3.
[5] *NFP*, 12 July 1895, 1–5 (p. 4). See also Kellner, *Ein Jahr in England*, 225–48.
[6] For the Salvation Army, see *Die Welt*, 10 Aug. 1900, 4–5. For Toynbee Hall, see ibid., 27 July 1900, 3.   [7] *NFP*, 12 July 1895, 3.
[8] On Toynbee, see Kadish, *Apostle Arnold*. Toynbee's nephew was the historian Arnold Joseph Toynbee.

the early 1870s in order, as Henrietta later wrote, 'to work for, to teach, and learn of, the poor'. What they found, she recorded, was 'an Irish quarter and a Jews' quarter . . . [with] whole streets . . . given over to the hangers-on of a vicious population, people whose conduct was brutal, whose ideal was idleness, whose habits were disgusting . . . Robberies, assaults, and fights in the streets were frequent'.[9] This was William Booth's 'darkest England'; far from deterring the Barnetts, it suited their reforming zeal well. They wished to lead the way in improving an environment that Henrietta believed 'lent itself to every form of evil, to thriftless habits, to untidiness, to loss of self-respect, to unruly living'.[10] Toynbee enthusiastically joined the Barnetts in this work, spending extended periods in Whitechapel.

At the end of 1884 the Barnetts established their first 'settlement', a purpose-built house modelled on an Oxford college, in which university graduates lived. The aim of 'Toynbee Hall', as they called the house in memory of the recently deceased Arnold, was for the graduates, as Samuel Barnett wrote, to 'share themselves with their neighbours' and to be 'a club-house in an industrial district . . . where the residents may make friends with the poor'.[11] Forging friendships across the class divide was perhaps asking too much of both sides; nonetheless, the residents, all male and mostly Oxford and Cambridge graduates, threw themselves into local life, organizing an array of innovative educational, cultural, and social events, engaging with trade unions, schools, and boards of guardians, dispensing legal advice, and conducting pioneering research into social deprivation.[12]

News of the experiment spread fast. Within a few years it was noted in Baedeker's London guide, and a number of similar projects had been founded in the city. This was the beginning of the settlement move-ment, which spread first across Britain and then to the United States and Canada.[13] In the most general terms, a settlement aspired to bridge social difference and act as 'an outpost of culture and learning . . . where the men, women, and children of slum districts could come for education,

---

[9] Barnett and Barnett, *Towards Social Reform*, 241. The previous quotation is ibid. 252.

[10] Ibid. 240.   [11] Ibid. 270.

[12] See Meacham, *Toynbee Hall and Social Reform*; Scotland, *Squires in the Slums*, ch. 2.

[13] On the settlement movement, see Scotland, *Squires in the Slums*. For Baedeker, see Koven, *Slumming*, 244. The movement made fewer inroads on the continent; see Marriot, *English–German Relations in Adult Education*, 46–50; Dornseifer, 'Geschichte der Settlements', 235–6. For Jewish analogues, see Haustein and Waller, 'Jüdische Settlements in Europa'.

recreation, or advice'.[14] Toynbee Hall was often called the 'mother of all settlements' but was atypical in many respects. Most of the London settlements aligned themselves denominationally (Methodists, Quakers, Catholics), whereas Toynbee Hall, if imbued with a religious ethos, was non-denominational and open to all; it attracted 'seekers and doubters, not the men of faith'.[15] At work in Toynbee Hall and other settlements was an eclectic compound of late-Victorian ideas about religion, political reform, social service, education, and the power of culture to civilize and elevate morally.[16] Those of a more radical disposition were unimpressed by what they saw as paternalism and *noblesse oblige*; the anarchist Emma Goldman dismissed settlements as 'teaching the poor to eat with a fork'.[17] For their part, Toynbee Hall's residents hoped to blunt the worst excesses of the East End's overcrowding, poverty, unemployment, crime, and squalor; they wanted to ameliorate lives that were, in their eyes, tragically blighted.

Many of these lives were Jewish. By the early 1880s some 120,000 Jews lived in the East End, both east European immigrants and English-born. Whitechapel, where Toynbee Hall was located, had the greatest concentration and most rapid increase of immigrants; in 1901 some 37 per cent of its residents were 'foreign'.[18] From its inception, then, Toynbee Hall was surrounded by Jews, although this was not something that it addressed directly in its work or rhetoric. Barnett did comment in 1893, however, that because Toynbee Hall was 'unsectarian', its sole Jewish resident, Harry Lewis (later a Reform rabbi), worked 'among the general poor as well as his own'. Barnett regretted the 'absence of reverence' he detected among Jews, who ought, he believed, to 'cultivate higher ideals'. They were also, he felt, in need of more sanitary inspectors and physical education. 'The conditions of East End life contain many of the elements of a *Judenhetze* [Jew-baiting or anti-Jewish agitation]', he warned.[19] Toynbee Hall's muted religiosity made it a welcoming environment for Jews, who comprised a

[14] Scheuer, *Legacy of Light*, 50.

[15] Koven, *Slumming*, 250, and also 247–8. For 'mother of all settlements', see e.g. Scotland, *Squires in the Slums*, 27, 52.

[16] See Ginn, *Culture, Philanthropy and the London Poor*, chs. 2 and 4.

[17] Goldman, *Living My Life*, i. 160.

[18] Abel, 'Canon Barnett', 121–2; Feldman, 'Mr Lewinstein goes to Parliament', 138–9; id., *Englishmen and Jews*, 166–72.   [19] *JC*, 25 Aug. 1893, 9–10.

THE JEWISH TOYNBEE HALL

substantial proportion of students taking classes—perhaps a quarter by the first decade of the twentieth century—and who also provided financial support and assistance with teaching. The *Jewish Chronicle*, Anglo-Jewry's paper of record, commented in 1894 that Jews had 'derived much advantage' from it, so much so that the idea of establishing a Jewish analogue was soon raised by Samuel Montagu.[20] An Orthodox Jew who reportedly told Herzl in 1895 that he felt himself 'more an Israelite than an Englishman', Montagu was at the forefront of Jewish welfare work in the East End.[21] In 1890 he suggested that a new institution, modelled on Toynbee Hall, should be created to cater for the welfare, educational, and cultural needs of immigrant and poor Jews in the East End. The existing Toynbee Hall, for all its fine work, was neither equipped nor inclined to take on such a task.[22] Montagu found support from another communal notable, Chief Rabbi Hermann Adler, who saw a Jewish Toynbee Hall as an ideal instrument for tackling 'the pressing duty of civilising and anglicising our foreign brethren'.[23]

To civilize and to anglicize, conceived as two sides of the same coin, remained the key impulses behind the project. It promised to be a

centre of light in a gloomy district, a clearing in a forest, a fountain in a desert ... [These] are Oriental images which suggest the sort of work to be done by the settlement of a colony of active, benevolent and God-fearing persons, imbued with true Jewish piety, and genuine English enlightenment in the midst of a necessitous and backwards population.[24]

The *Jewish Chronicle* editorialized that a Jewish Toynbee Hall would 'bring brightness into cheerless homes, and infuse hope into dreary lives'.[25] The Hall was to be a central element of the so-called 'East End scheme', an ambitious plan to build an institutional hub and community centre for the Jews of the area. Hopes for this scheme, and for a Jewish Toynbee Hall as part of it, were dashed as the proposal became mired in factional disagree-

---

[20] *JC*, 16 Feb. 1894, 12–13. See also *JC*, 6 Jan. 1893, 6; Briggs and Macartney, *Toynbee Hall*, 28.

[21] Bein, *Theodor Herzl: Briefe und Tagebücher*, ii. 280.

[22] *JC*, 14 Nov. 1890, 6. On Montagu, see Gutwein, *The Divided Elite*, ch. 2; Black, *The Social Politics of Anglo-Jewry*, 14–19.

[23] *JC*, 13 Oct. 1893, 14. For Adler, see also *JC*, 2 Feb. 1894, 9. Montagu later turned against the idea in its original form; see *JC*, 17 Jan. 1896, 10; 31 Jan. 1902, 25.

[24] *JC*, 2 June 1893, 5.   [25] *JC*, 18 Aug. 1893, 9. See also *JC*, 16 Feb. 1894, 12–13.

ments among the London Jewish leadership.[26] The idea of a Jewish Toynbee Hall periodically resurfaced, even on occasion after the First World War, but nothing came of it. It was, however, to find an echo across the Channel.

In September 1900, soon after taking his cold water cure, Kellner proposed that the Zionist organization establish under its auspices a Jewish Toynbee Hall in Vienna.[27] For the Zionists, this offered an opportunity to reach out beyond their core support. Just as London's Toynbee Hall was the 'mother of all settlements', so too could Vienna's Jewish Hall act as a model for others. This was in keeping, as the long-time secretary of Vienna's Hall wrote, with a loose reading of Herzl's 1898 injunction to 'conquer the communities', in this instance working among and for the people rather than targeting the leadership echelon of the formal representative organizations.[28] Why a *Jewish* Toynbee Hall, rather than one without confessional or national constraints? Kellner acknowledged that 'many Jewish friends had pledged generous support' for a non-confessional project if only he would abandon his 'disastrous plan' and instead establish a 'People's Hall open to all'. But this, he was convinced, would be merely a 'misguided, sterile replica, sure to sink without trace'. It was also wilfully to ignore the greatest obstacle of all—antisemitism. Vienna was not London, Kellner wrote, and the relatively straightforward social mixing of Jews and others he had witnessed in the East End would represent an 'inconceivable gamble' in Vienna; the mere fact that Jews were the founders and sponsors would make such an institution 'suspect' to many Viennese. Given that similar 'altruistic' projects, nominally open to all, in fact excluded Jews entirely, it was preferable to focus on the needs of the Jewish underprivileged and poor.[29]

The goal was to help 'our tradesmen, hawkers, pedlars, clerks, brokers [who] crave to forget... the tragedy of isolation in the wasteland of the big city, to feel part of a whole for a few hours, and to satisfy the traditional

---

[26] On the East End scheme, see Gutwein, *The Divided Elite*, ch. 2.
[27] *Die jüdische Toynbee-Halle in Wien im zweiten Jahre*, 9. See also *Die Wahrheit*, 29 Nov. 1901, 3–4; Malleier, 'Die jüdische Toynbee-Halle', 105.
[28] *Die Wahrheit*, 29 Nov. 1901, 3–4. See also Almog, *Zionism and History*, 188–93.
[29] Kellner, *Eine jüdische Toynbee-Halle*, 5–7.

Jewish need for intellectual nourishment'.[30] He proposed a division of labour between the wealthy and the learned: 'the prosperous and educated should devote a few hours of their day to the poor and less educated, to fortify them morally and intellectually for the next day's struggle.' If the initial inspiration came from London, Kellner pointed also to Jewish antecedents: 'The need for sociability and intellectual stimulation is an age-old element of the Jewish character.'[31] His project was but a new link in a long chain of institutions that catered to this need. 'Long before Arnold Toynbee', the Jews of eastern Europe 'had established countless Toynbee Halls' in the form of the study house and synagogue. He depicted these, a touch fancifully, as oases of radical social equality, where the mundane distinction between rich and poor had been erased, an aspiration that lay at the heart of the Jewish Toynbee Hall.[32] Here, all men and women would be welcome and all 'should feel at home'.[33]

This was also, at least in part, a moral crusade. Echoing the paternalistic tones of the settlement movement, the idyll of the Vienna Hall would counteract 'one of the saddest aspects of life in the metropolis', the tendency of Jewish youth in Vienna to frequent cabarets, dance halls, and cafes, entertainments that had 'ruined more lives than tuberculosis or plague'. An alternative that combined edifying entertainment—classical music performances, literature readings, poetry recitals—with demanding but accessible intellectual fare could, Kellner hoped, draw Jews away from such 'toxic sites' of 'brazenness and frivolity'.[34] The settlement milieu was reflected too in the impulse to educate. Adult education (commonly called *Volksbildung*) had flourished since the 1870s in Vienna and elsewhere in Austria; it was a key instrument in the drive to reduce social isolation, bridge class divides, and promote cultural 'improvement', and had reached audiences of hundreds of thousands by the turn of the century. This was in turn part of a pan-European development, often embedded in socialist or nationalist

---

[30] *Die Welt*, 19 Oct. 1900, 2. See also Kellner, *Eine jüdische Toynbee-Halle*, 10–11.

[31] The first quotation is from *Die Welt*, 7 Dec. 1900, 13; the second from ibid., 19 Oct. 1900, 1.

[32] Quotation from *Die Welt*, 27 July 1900, 3. See also ibid., 16 Nov. 1900, 8; *Die Wahrheit*, 30 Nov. 1900, 4–5.

[33] *Die jüdische Toynbee-Halle in Wien im zweiten Jahre*, 21; Kellner, *Eine jüdische Toynbee-Halle*, 10.

[34] Kellner, *Eine jüdische Toynbee-Halle*, 12–13. See also Hödl, *Zwischen Wienerlied und Der Kleine Kohn*.

THE JEWISH TOYNBEE HALL 83

movements.[35] A small cog in this large wheel, the Jewish Toynbee Hall's determinedly unsystematic, and strictly apolitical, programme of popular education was a precursor to the expansion of Jewish adult education in the years following the First World War, particularly in Weimar Germany.[36]

Although a Zionist initiative, the Vienna Hall insisted on political neutrality in its programmes and self-presentation, and the Zionist organization, if happy to claim credit for the idea, provided little in the way of financial or institutional support. From the outset, the Hall was entirely reliant on volunteers for every facet of its work and dependent on the generosity of donors for survival. Its template for activities was simple and unvarying: on week nights from October to March a lecture and discussion was held, followed by a pause for refreshment and either a second lecture/discussion or a musical or literary recital. Friday evenings were reserved for a talk on biblical themes, Saturday evenings for concerts, and each fortnight a children's party was held on Sunday. From April to September, adult education courses were offered in English, Hebrew, French, German literature, mathematics, accountancy, shorthand, and typing. All of this was provided free of charge.[37] Success was immediate. The Hall, able to accommodate some 150 people, was regularly filled to capacity, and it was soon apparent that demand exceeded supply; overflow crowds were common, on occasion requiring a police presence to maintain order. Within a year, new and more spacious premises were found (still in Brigittenau) and attendance increased accordingly.[38]

The early years saw up to 200 lectures annually in the winter months, on medicine, natural sciences, history, literature, psychology, philosophy, economics, and legal affairs, as well as on a variety of Jewish-themed topics, complemented by up to sixty performances. The summer courses were similarly successful, with between twenty and fifty students enrolled in each; the children's parties drew 200 5- to 12-year-olds from across Vienna.[39]

[35] Altenhuber, *Universitäre Volksbildung in Österreich*, 15–21; Seitter, *Geschichte der Erwachsenenbildung*, especially ch. 6.

[36] Brenner, *The Renaissance of Jewish Culture*, ch. 3; Aschheim, *Brothers and Strangers*, 193–7.

[37] *Die jüdische Toynbee-Halle in Wien im zweiten Jahre*, 29–30; Kellner, *Eine jüdische Toynbee-Halle*, 22–3; *Jahresbericht der Jüdischen Toynbee Halle . . . 1904*, 6.

[38] *Die Welt*, 15 Feb. 1901, 11; 4 Oct. 1901, 13; 20 Feb. 1903, 4–5; *Die Wahrheit*, 8 Mar. 1901, 7; Kellner, *Eine jüdische Toynbee-Halle*, 7.

[39] *Die jüdische Toynbee-Halle in Wien im zweiten Jahre*, 24–37; *Jahresbericht der Jüdischen*

84 THE JEWISH TOYNBEE HALL

This amounted to a cumulative clientele of thousands, made up of equal numbers of men and women aged 20 to 70—commercial employees, small traders, pedlars, porters, day labourers, students, and the unemployed.[40] The scale of such an undertaking required a prodigious outlay of time and energy from a devoted voluntary workforce. Tasks were divided to some extent along traditional gender lines: men took charge of the lecture programme; culture, adult education courses, and publicity were shared; women were responsible for the children's events and for the catering. This last, it was often noted, was the glue that held everything together, demanding a greater degree of daily organization and effort than all else. Many in the audience, the 'poorest of the poor' as one of the founders described them, were in dire need of the complimentary tea, cake, and biscuits.[41]

The idea was quickly taken up elsewhere. In the months following the Vienna opening in December 1900, new Halls opened in Brünn (Brno), Moravia's largest city, in eastern Galician Drohobycz, and in Brăila in southeastern Romania. A year later, these had been joined by Prague, Bucharest, Lemberg, Amsterdam, and Czernowitz, and planning was under way in Berlin.[42] Testimony to the success of the Zionist insistence that the Halls were an apolitical undertaking was that the philanthropic association B'nai B'rith set up a community centre, a Jewish Toynbee Hall in all but name, in Hamburg in late 1901.[43] In fact, so persuasively 'non-Zionist' was the concept that in the following years B'nai B'rith—a self-styled ethical elite with

Toynbee Halle . . . 1904, 7–12, 21–23; Kellner, *Eine jüdische Toynbee-Halle*, 14–17, 22–3; *Die Welt*, 26 Apr. 1901, 12; 20 Feb. 1903, 5; 27 Feb. 1903, 9.

[40] Kellner, *Eine jüdische Toynbee-Halle*, 9–10; *Die jüdische Toynbee-Halle in Wien im zweiten Jahre*, 22.

[41] *Die jüdische Toynbee-Halle in Wien im zweiten Jahre*, 4, 22 (for quotation), 37–41; *Jahresbericht der Jüdischen Toynbee Halle . . . 1904*, 12, 17–20, 24–6. The mixed picture with regard to the role of women is discussed in Malleier, 'Die jüdische Toynbee-Halle', 106–8; id., 'Gegen den fremden Kontinent der Armut', 113–14.

[42] On Brünn and Drohobycz, see *Die Welt*, 25 Jan. 1901, 14; 1 Feb. 1901, 15; 8 Feb. 1901, 12. On Brăila, see *Die Welt*, 8 Mar. 1901, 14. On Prague, see *Prager Tagblatt*, 15 Feb. 1902, 5; 30 Mar. 1902, 7; *Die Welt*, 15 Feb. 1901, 11; 7 Feb. 1902, 12. On Bucharest, see *Die Welt*, 14 Mar. 1902, 14. On Lemberg, see *Die Welt*, 1 Nov. 1901, 12; *Die Neuzeit*, 15 Nov. 1901, 466–7; 18 Apr. 1902, 166. On Amsterdam, see *JC*, 22 Aug. 1902, 16; *Stenographisches Protokoll der Verhandlungen des V. Zionisten Congresses*, 17–18. On Czernowitz, see *Die Welt*, 1 Nov. 1901, 12; 14 Feb. 1902, 15. On Berlin, see *Die Welt*, 1 Feb. 1901, 14–15; *Israelitische Rundschau*, 17 Jan. 1902, 5; Otto Warburg, Kommission zur Vorbereitung einer Toynbee Hall in Berlin, 1902, CZA, A12/50.

[43] On the Israelitische Gemeinschaftshaus (Israelite Community House) in Hamburg,

a liberal, affluent membership devoted to good works and virtuous citizenship, and with little sympathy for Zionism—came to play a crucial role in developing and sustaining Jewish Toynbee Halls in Germany and Austria.[44]

The Prague Jewish Toynbee Hall, for example, was a joint venture of nationalists and liberals from its inception in 1902, directed initially by Ludwig Bendiener, a prominent German liberal and a leader of the local Jewish community, and then by Philip Falkowicz, at one time head of the city's Deutscher Kaufmännischer Verein (German Merchants' Club).[45] B'nai B'rith assumed sole responsibility in 1905, although little changed under the new ownership. On a more modest scale than its Vienna counterpart, the Prague Hall held weekly lectures (Franz Kafka gave a reading there in December 1913, describing the audience as 'exemplary'), ran a library and reading room, and offered adult education courses in shorthand, French, Czech, and modern Hebrew until 1915.[46] In Berlin, too, B'nai B'rith took over the Toynbee Hall in 1904, putting an end to two years of work with the Zionists that had yielded little. Cleaving to the Viennese model, B'nai B'rith hoped 'to bring a glimmer of light into the dismal lives of the poorest of the poor by offering them . . . the spiritual uplift vouchsafed by art and learning'.[47] The 'poorest of the poor' (a repeated refrain) was made up here of glaziers, upholsterers, house painters, tobacco workers (in particular young Russian women), seamstresses, locksmiths, tradesmen, clerks, milliners, cobblers, and pedlars. And, as in Vienna, it was hoped that the 'dignified and respectable setting' of the Hall would steer impressionable youth away from the 'moral perils of the metropolis'.[48] Traces of Kellner's ideas were also to be found in B'nai B'rith's characterization of Toynbee Hall as the heir to a long chain of venerable Jewish ideals

---

see Maretzki, *Geschichte des Ordens*, 241; Hirsch, *Jüdisches Vereinsleben in Hamburg*, 98–9; Oelschlägel, 'Integration durch Bildung', 114.

[44] On B'nai B'rith, see Čapková, 'Jewish Elites', 119–42; Reinke, '"Eine Sammlung des jüdischen Bürgertums"', 315–40.

[45] *Prager Tagblatt*, 30 Mar. 1902, 7; *Die Wahrheit*, 26 Dec. 1902, 7; Čapková, *Czechs, Germans, Jews?*, 89. On Bendiener and Falkowicz, see Cohen, *The Politics of Ethnic Survival*, 109, 131–2, 163.

[46] Haas, 'Toynbeehalle', 127; *Prager Tagblatt*, 28 Apr. 1906, 23; 1 July 1906, 46; 30 Mar. 1913, 34; Koch (ed.), *Franz Kafka: Tagebücher*, ii. 215–16.

[47] *Bericht über das erste Betriebsjahr*, 19. See also Stein, *Zur Eröffnung*, 3–4.

[48] *Bericht über das erste Betriebsjahr*, 19. On the social composition of the audiences, of whom one-third were women, see ibid. 22, 24; Stein, *Zur Eröffnung*, 7–8.

86   THE JEWISH TOYNBEE HALL

and institutions, suggesting a direct line between synagogue, study house, yeshiva, and their new 'institute for adult education'.[49]

This 'temple of social and ethical progress' in Berlin continued to grow steadily until the First World War.[50] By 1909, when it moved to a larger site, more than 700 lectures and 3,000 musical and literary performances had taken place.[51] The nightly diet of enlightenment and food in the winter months—in contrast to Vienna, there were no summer courses—was frequently received with gratitude. 'Only in the evenings here', wrote a 'poor and almost blind' Polish-born tradesman, 'can I find consolation, joy, and education.' For a Russian-born woman, abandoned by her husband and eking out a living as a florist, the Hall was a 'great comfort' and a 'priceless achievement'. A seamstress called it a 'great blessing, particularly for unmarried people . . . Toynbee Hall is my sole recreation in the long winter nights.' A furrier from East Prussia wrote simply, 'I have seen better days and have had happier times. At Toynbee Hall, I can find something of these again.' A tailor succinctly captured the sentiments of a good portion of the Toynbee Hall faithful: 'It is as though everyone here is part of a large family.'[52] This would have been music to Kellner's ears.

In Vienna the original Hall followed a similar route. Despite the considerable popularity and acclaim it enjoyed in its first years, its finances were always precarious. Neither the warm words of appreciation from community notables and religious leaders, the occasional donations from wealthy supporters such as the Rothschilds, nor subventions from the Vienna Kultusgemeinde were sufficient to keep it solvent, and by the time of Kellner's departure for Czernowitz in 1904 its survival was in doubt. It had been kept afloat to that point solely by the generosity of Kellner's friend Johann Kremenezky.[53] In late 1904 B'nai B'rith in Vienna stepped in

---

[49] Stein, *Zur Eröffnung*, 2–3; *Jahresbericht der Jüdischen Toynbee-Halle . . . über das achte Betriebs-Jahr*, 3. On Kellner's influence on the founding of the Berlin Toynbee Hall, see Stein, 'Zur Begründung einer jüdischen Toynbee-Halle', 147–8.

[50] Quotation in *Bericht über das erste Betriebsjahr*, 32.

[51] Stein, *Zur Eröffnung*, 5–6; *Bericht über das fünfte Betriebsjahr*, 3.

[52] Testimonies in *Jahresbericht der Jüdischen Toynbee-Halle . . . über das achte Betriebs-Jahr*, 4–5; *Jahresbericht der Jüdischen Toynbee-Halle . . . über das neunte Betriebs-Jahr*, 4–5.

[53] *Jahresbericht der Jüdischen Toynbee Halle . . . 1904*, 4, 14–15; *Die Welt*, 1 July 1904, 13–14. For examples of support, see *Die Neuzeit*, 28 Mar. 1902, 131; *Die Welt*, 26 Apr. 1901, 12; 6 Nov. 1903, 8–9; *Jahresbericht der Jüdischen Toynbee Halle . . . 1904*, 34.

decisively, rescuing the Hall by taking it over entirely.[54] The new management pushed aside the Zionists but was otherwise scrupulous in maintaining continuity, and B'nai B'rith's deep pockets allowed the Hall to flourish over the next decade. These were its most successful years. Annual visitor numbers increased to an average of 35,000 by 1910, an additional branch was opened in the city in order to reach a wider audience, and in November 1914 the Hall moved to its own premises.[55]

If in Germany, Vienna, and Prague it was B'nai B'rith that sustained and developed the Toynbee Halls—more were opened, for example, in Frankfurt, Mannheim, Breslau, and Munich—this was not the case further east, where the Zionist movement retained control.[56] But in east-central Europe, too, there was a B'nai B'rith dimension, albeit minor by comparison. Here it provided support rather than leadership, a function of the greater degree of mutual accommodation between Jewish nationalism and B'nai B'rith in this region than in Germany or Vienna. In Berlin and Vienna Zionists had expressed irritation at their exclusion from the Toynbee Halls following B'nai B'rith's takeover.[57] In eastern Europe, by contrast, personal and institutional links between the two movements were not uncommon. One of the founders of the Jewish Toynbee Hall in Iaşi, Romania, for example, a Zionist-run operation from its opening in 1906 until the First World War, was Jacob Niemirower, not only a committed Zionist but also in the interwar years the first Chief Rabbi of Romania and president of B'nai B'rith in the country.[58] In Galicia, which became the stronghold of the Toynbee Hall movement, Zionist sponsorship and leadership similarly remained clear, but in both Lemberg and Krakau, home to the two largest Halls in the

---

[54] Singer, 'Toynbee-Halle und Kinderhort', 72, 75–6; *Die Welt*, 11 Nov. 1904, 9; *Die Wahrheit*, 10 Nov. 1905, 7–8.

[55] Singer, 'Toynbee-Halle und Kinderhort', 79–80; *Jahresbericht der Jüdischen Toynbee Halle . . . 1907*, 6–7; *Die Wahrheit*, 5 Feb. 1909, 6–7; 9 Dec. 1910, 9–10; 20 Mar. 1914, 5–6. On B'nai B'rith in Vienna, see Klein, *Jewish Origins*, 75–84; Rozenblit, *The Jews of Vienna*, 149–50.

[56] On Frankfurt, see Wertheimer, *Unwelcome Strangers*, 154–5; *Frankfurter Israelitisches Gemeindeblatt*, Nov. 1931, 67. On Mannheim, see Maretzki, *Geschichte des Ordens*, 241–2. On Breslau, see *Jüdische Volksstimme*, 1 Nov. 1908, 5; 3 Nov. 1910, 6. On Munich, see Haas, 'Toynbeehalle', 126; *JV*, 14 Nov. 1913, 1–2. Zionists continued their work in Belgium, Copenhagen, and Cologne; see *Die Welt*, 1 Mar. 1907, 6; 27 Sept. 1907, 5–6; 4 Dec. 1908, 11.

[57] *Jüdische Rundschau*, 10 Nov. 1905, 588–9; *Die Wahrheit*, 10 Nov. 1905, 7–8.

[58] *Die Welt*, 23 Mar. 1906, 19; 13 Mar. 1908, 18; 21 Feb. 1913, 246–7; *Jüdische Volksstimme*, 27 July 1910, 1; 7 Sept. 1910, 2; Herşcovici, 'Iacob Isac Niemirower'.

province, there were significant links between Zionism and B'nai B'rith, particularly in the period of the Polish Republic. Rabbi Ozjasz Thon, for example, whose Yiddish-language pamphlet on the 'Jewish Question' was published by the Toynbee Halls, was a leader both of Zionism and B'nai B'rith in Krakau.[59] Despite irreconcilable ideological differences, the two movements—with their shared belief in Jewish unity, along with a profound sense of responsibility for the welfare of the less fortunate—found a modicum of common purpose in the neutral space of the Jewish Toynbee Hall. The Hall, said a Berlin B'nai B'rith leader in 1904, was the organization's 'favourite child', and B'nai B'rith in Prague later claimed exclusive patrimony, describing Toynbee Halls as the 'purest expression of the B'nai B'rith idea'.[60] For their part, Zionists celebrated *their* achievement in creating a 'model institution' that had enjoyed a 'triumphal march through the entire Jewish world'.[61] Success has many fathers.

This 'triumphal march' was most evident in Galicia, where the Zionists hoped to make each Hall a 'People's House', a focal point of the crowded landscape of libraries, reading rooms, and cultural venues. In Lemberg, home to one of the first Halls, this was proclaimed at the very outset.[62] The Hall was seen as the Jewish counterpart to the 'People's Houses' created by Polish and Ruthenian nationalists in Galicia, part of the process of carving out separate ethnic public spheres in the province.[63] From the Zionist perspective, as already noted, Toynbee Halls had a role to play in the movement's strategy of conquering the communities. Already in 1904 the Halls were described as 'the most important step' in this process, 'true People's Houses and nurseries of national life'.[64]

---

[59] Kargol, *Zakon Synów Przymierza*, 122–5; *Die Welt*, 21 Nov. 1913, 1598. On links between B'nai B'rith and Zionism in Lemberg, see Sroka, 'Stowarzyszenie Humanitarne "Leopolis" we Lwowie', 57–8. On Toynbee Halls and B'nai B'rith, see *Jüdische Rundschau*, 28 Oct. 1904, 360. In Prague, too, these links were evident; see Čapková, 'Jewish Elites', 134–6. On Germany, see Reinke, '"Eine Sammlung des jüdischen Bürgertums"', 333–4.

[60] For the Berlin leader's quote, see *Bericht über das erste Betriebsjahr*, 4. For Prague, see Haas, 'Toynbeehalle', 126. Kellner later considered opening a B'nai B'rith lodge in Czernowitz; see Kellner to Deutsch, 30 June 1909, AJA/GDP.

[61] *Die Wahrheit*, 10 Nov. 1905, 7. For 'model institution', see ibid., 29 Nov. 1901, 4.

[62] *Die Welt*, 1 Nov. 1901, 12. For similar in Krakau, see 'Eine jüdische Volkshochschule in Krakau'.

[63] Potoczny, *Oświata dorosłych i popularyzacja wiedzy*, 271–7; Hüchtker, *Geschichte als Performance*, 198–204, 235–44.   [64] *Jüdische Rundschau*, 28 Oct. 1904, 360.

THE JEWISH TOYNBEE HALL   89

This was not an entirely vain boast. The Lemberg Hall recorded some 10,000 attendees at its events in 1904 and branched out by publishing pamphlets on prostitution and tuberculosis (seen as issues of particular relevance for east European Jewry) and by supporting a gymnastic association and choir. By 1913 annual attendance had risen to more than 18,000.[65] Krakau's Hall opened in late 1905—four others already existed in Galicia, in Lemberg, Tarnopol (now Ternopil), Brody, and Zbarasż (Zbarazh)—and by 1913 had 3,000 members. During that year, its nightly lectures (in Polish and Yiddish) along with its concerts, children's parties, and adult education courses attracted more than 15,000 visitors.[66] An Association of Jewish Toynbee Halls in Galicia was created in 1907 to coordinate the work of its affiliates, most of which were in eastern Galicia. Three years later, the Association claimed an audience of 100,000 people annually and in 1913 reported that twenty of the twenty-five Halls in Galicia were members.[67] Still further east was the most successful of all Jewish Toynbee Halls, in Czernowitz. A Hall opened in the city in 1902, but soon ran aground. In early 1911 Kellner initiated a relaunch.[68] In Czernowitz he found the financial support that had been lacking in Vienna, and he succeeded in creating something close to the 'ideal type' of Toynbee Hall that he had always envisaged—'a hub', as he described it, 'of national and cultural life'.[69] In late 1913 he presided over the opening of purpose-built premises that soon housed a range of institutions and services: accommodation for apprentices, a day-care centre for children, a credit cooperative, an employment agency, a legal advice bureau, and newspaper and political offices.[70] This was indeed a People's House.

By 1914 Jewish Toynbee Halls were flourishing. If they had not, as an enthusiastic observer claimed, 'conquered the entire continent', they had

---

[65] Ibid.; *Die Neuzeit*, 18 Apr. 1902, 166. See also *Die Welt*, 29 Oct. 1909, 968; 21 Nov. 1913, 1598.

[66] *Die Welt*, 10 Feb. 1905, 11; 12 Dec. 1913, 1704; Shanes, *Diaspora Nationalism*, 179–80; 'Eine jüdische Volkshochschule in Krakau'. See also Gelber, *The History of the Zionist Movement in Galicia* (Heb.), ii. 501.

[67] Gelber, *The History of the Zionist Movement in Galicia* (Heb.), ii. 556, 586; Księga protokołów Zarządu głównego żyd. 'Toynbeehali' 1910/11, CZA, K2/19; *Die Welt*, 28 Mar. 1913, 411–12. For different figures, see *Die Welt*, 28 Apr. 1911, 390; 21 Nov. 1913, 1598.

[68] *CAZ*, 17 Jan. 1911, 4; *Die Welt*, 23 Feb. 1912, 241–2; *OW*, 23 Feb. 1912, 128. On the first attempt, see *Bukowinaer Post*, 5 Dec. 1901, 4; *Die Welt*, 14 Feb. 1902, 15.   [69] *JV*, 14 Nov. 1913, 1–2.

[70] *Die Welt*, 31 Oct. 1913, 1503; 5 Dec. 1913, 1667–8; *CAZ*, 15 Oct. 1912 (Abendausgabe), 3; 1 Nov. 1913, 4; 18 Nov. 1913, 3–4.

nevertheless established a secure niche in the cultural and social landscape of Jewish society in east-central Europe.[71] This proved, though, to be their zenith, as they were not able to withstand the catastrophic consequences of the First World War and its aftermath, either collectively or individually. Their trajectory in the radically changed circumstances of the 1920s and 1930s was one of instability and decline, as the educational, social, and welfare needs which they addressed were increasingly met in a more professional and systematic fashion, whether by states or political movements. What had worked well in 1910 was less effective in 1930.

Adult education, for example, expanded rapidly in interwar Austria and Germany, led by the state and by political movements, and philanthropic bodies like B'nai B'rith could not begin to match their resources.[72] Vienna's Hall operated on a much-reduced scale during the war years, its activity curtailed by the exigencies of war, severe restrictions on associational life, and the pressures imposed by an acute refugee crisis.[73] With the collapse of the Habsburg state and the chaos of the immediate post-war years of the new Austrian republic, marked by political instability, economic distress, and food shortages, the Hall subsided into inactivity. Resuming in 1921, it never fully regained its lost momentum and élan. The end came in the summer of 1939, when the Nazi authorities dissolved it and confiscated its assets.[74] In Prague similar wartime difficulties led to the suspension of the Hall's activity in 1915. A fresh start was made in 1923, with aspirations for expansion and for independence from B'nai B'rith, but it does not appear to have survived beyond the mid-1930s.[75] In Weimar Germany initiatives such as the Lehrhaus movement built on and surpassed the Toynbee Halls. Berlin's Hall, meanwhile, carried on, although no longer on the same scale as previously, eventually to be 'dissolved and prohibited' by the Nazi regime in 1937.[76] In Frankfurt B'nai B'rith restarted its Hall, closed before

---

[71] *Das interessante Blatt*, 28 Oct. 1909, 3.

[72] Dostal, 'Bildung zu "Volkstum und Heimat"'; Scheibe, '1919–1933: Weimarer Republik'; Dikau, 'Geschichte der Volkshochschule', 111–31.

[73] By early 1915 some 150,000 Galician and Bukovina Jews had fled to Vienna as the Russians advanced on the Eastern Front. See Hoffmann-Holter, *'Abreisendmachung'*.

[74] On the war and the 1920s, see Singer, 'Toynbee-Halle und Kinderhort', 80–4. On the closure, see WSL, Gelöschte Vereine, 2278/1926, M. Abt. 119, A32.

[75] Flusser, 'Die jüdische Toynbeehalle in Prag'; id., 'Die Prager Toynbeehalle'.

[76] Jüdische Toynbee-Halle für Volksbildung und Unterhaltung der Berliner Bnei-Briss-

the war, as part of a community welfare 'emergency campaign' in late 1931; it remained open until 1938.[77]

The Jewish Toynbee Hall was impressive testimony to Kellner's capacity for invention, his leadership qualities, and his remarkable energy. Beginning with nothing more than an idea formed by observation in London, he created a popular institution in Vienna and inaugurated a movement in central and eastern Europe that embodied his political, social, and cultural commitments. In its genesis the Jewish Toynbee Hall was unusual, a composite of late-Victorian British reformist enthusiasm, Zionism, and deep-seated Jewish traditions of education and sociability. Its historical trajectory, though, was familiar: it flourished in the first decade of the twentieth century, faded abruptly in the First World War and the immediate post-war years, and, in Germany and Austria, was destroyed by Nazism in the late 1930s. It was familiar also in its divergence between east and west. A nationalist initiative salvaged by anti-nationalists in western Austria and Germany, it remained in Zionist hands in Galicia, Bukovina, and Romania. In Berlin, Vienna, and Prague, the Halls became a valued part of B'nai B'rith's extensive philanthropic and educational network; in Galicia and Bukovina, they constituted a core element of the Zionist movement's cultural work. In both east and west, they were pioneers of secular Jewish adult education, attracting hundreds of thousands of women and men to lectures and courses, and acquainting them with the breadth and depth of Jewish history and culture. Nationalists and non-nationalists alike agreed that assimilation posed a mortal threat to Jewish life and were united in their wish to reinforce individual and collective Jewish consciousness on as broad a basis as possible.

The Toynbee Halls became a significant part of a kind of Jewish public

---

Logen, Circular, Dec. 1922, CAHJP, Berlin/DBe/4/497; *Die Stimme*, 29 Dec. 1937, 3; Oelschlägel, 'Integration durch Bildung', 117. On Jewish adult education in the Weimar Republic, see Brenner, *The Renaissance of Jewish Culture*, ch. 3.

[77] *Frankfurter Israelitisches Gemeindeblatt*, Nov. 1931, 67; Dec. 1934, 129–30; Sept. 1935, 513; *Jüdisches Gemeindeblatt für die Israelitische Gemeinde zu Frankfurt am Main*, Nov. 1937, 15; 15. Apr. 1938, 27. It was also known as Arnold Lazarus Hall, in memory of the B'nai B'rith leader and rabbi who had been head of the Hall prior to the First World War.

sphere, a dense web of associational life that tended to take religious or ethnic forms in western Europe and more overtly nationalist shape in eastern Europe. In the former, this has been called a 'subculture'; in the latter, it constituted one ethnic or national milieu among many.[78] In much the same fashion that other ethnic, national, and religious groups developed and sustained particularist traditions in this region, so too did Jews create a network of institutions that produced, consumed, and disseminated Jewish knowledge and culture. The Jewish public sphere was made up of adult education, literary and cultural societies, reading rooms, libraries, newspapers, and journals, all of which relied on Jewish society for their owners, operators, functionaries, activists, speakers, teachers, writers, performers, themes, and audiences. In and of itself, this kind of activity was not new. Whether in the first half of the nineteenth century in Germany or the final decades of tsarist Russia, Jews banded together socially, culturally, and economically in ways that went well beyond the ties of religion.[79] From the 1870s in the Habsburg lands the scope of associational life expanded quickly from the rather narrow bourgeois template that had been laid down in the decades before 1848. It was an expansion facilitated both by the greater freedom offered by a more liberal administration after the dissolution of neo-absolutism and by the nationalist wave that took hold from the 1880s, which was accompanied by a surge of activism.[80] Jews participated as individuals in this development but also carved out a collective domain of their own, an ethnic milieu powered by the addition of newer nationalist impulses to long-standing ethnic and religious bonds.

In both east and west, the extent and dynamism of this public sphere were a function of the coexistence, and sometimes the collision, of two forces. On the one hand, it was generated from within Jewish society by a will to collective self-assertion; on the other, it developed in response to the barriers to integration in the surrounding societies, where antisemitism and exclusion were a fact of life. The Jewish Toynbee Halls were characteristic of this ethnic milieu in that they adapted a model from surrounding

[78] For 'subculture', see Sorkin, *The Transformation of German Jewry*.

[79] On Germany, see ibid. On Russia, see Veidlinger, *Jewish Public Culture*.

[80] Judson, *Exclusive Revolutionaries*, 18–25 and ch. 5; Rumpler and Urbanitsch, *Die Habsburgermonarchie 1848–1918*, viii, pt. 1. More generally, see Trentmann, 'Introduction: Paradoxes of Civil Society'.

society to the particular needs of Jews. This was not a retreat into isolation or exclusivity. It was, rather, a form of partial self-segregation for the purposes of ethnic consolidation and comfort, the need for which arose both from developments internal to Jewish society and from external pressures. This is particularly clear in the Habsburg Austrian context out of which Kellner's idea for a *Jewish* Toynbee Hall emerged. It was made possible by a partially liberal state and a civil society with a measure of political and cultural pluralism. It was made necessary by that state's, and society's, powerful illiberal exclusionary tendencies and endemic ethnic and national frictions.

FIVE

❀

THE CZERNOWITZ YEARS

THE MOVE TO CZERNOWITZ, more than 440 miles east of Vienna and less than 20 miles from the Russian border, in October 1904 was a mixed blessing for the Kellner family. It certainly signified success and enhanced status, but it also brought a hint of social and professional exile, felt most keenly by Anna, whose career as a translator was now well established, with a number of English novels and newspaper serializations to her credit.[1] Their eldest daughter, Paula, remained in Vienna to continue her university studies in English and German philology, and Anna feared that neither her own mother, a regular visitor to Vienna, nor any of her many siblings would venture to Czernowitz. The prospect of managing a household in an unfamiliar city where she knew almost nobody gave her pause. Matthias Friedwagner, a long-time friend who had moved from Vienna to Czernowitz in 1900 to take up a post as professor of romance philology, found them an apartment but recommended they bring their own domestic help. Here, he wrote, they would find only poor Ruthenian girls with a bad work ethic. In short, the adjustment required of Anna was considerable; it is hardly surprising that she was for some time 'out of sorts and downcast'.[2] For both Leon and Anna, leaving Vienna was cause for regret. Save for three years in Troppau, Leon had lived in Vienna since 1880, Anna since 1884, and all three of their children had been born there. Having made their home and careers in the city, they had no wish to live elsewhere and were acutely aware that Czernowitz, even if sometimes known as 'Little Vienna', could not match the incomparable cultural, professional, and social attractions of the imperial capital.

[1] For example, of Leonard Merrick's *One Man's View* (*Eine persönliche Ansicht*) (1898) and *The Actor-Manager* (*Der Theaterdirektor*) (1902) and Elsa D'Esterre-Keeling's *Appassionata: A Musician's Story* (*Appassionata*) (1903). See also her translation of Samuel Gordon's story 'The Clothes-Prop of Grandmother Hindelah' ('Die wundertätige Megilla') throughout May and June 1903 in *Die Welt*.

[2] A. Kellner, *Leon Kellner*, 70–1. See also Arnold, *Memoirs* (Heb.), 83–4.

Czernowitz was a city in the throes of rapid growth, its population increasing from some 20,000 in the mid-nineteenth century to almost 70,000 by the early twentieth century.[3] It was also a strikingly Jewish city: by 1910, 33 per cent of its 86,000 residents were Jewish, with Ruthenians, Romanians, Germans, and Poles the other major groups. Ruthenians and Romanians comprised nearly 40 and 35 per cent respectively of Bukovina's population in 1910, Germans not quite 10 per cent, Poles almost 5 per cent, and Jews some 13 per cent.[4] This population diversity was a consequence of geography and politics. Upon seizing the area from the Ottoman Empire in the 1770s, Austria had embarked on a mission to 'civilize' this slice of north-western Moldavia, populated at the time mostly by Ruthenian and Romanian peasants. Aiming at nothing less than building a new society and economy, the Austrians imposed their norms of administration, justice, and culture, and encouraged large-scale immigration of Germans, Poles, Hungarians, and Jews. From the vantage point of the end of the nineteenth century, the Habsburgs believed they had succeeded in 'clearing away the Asiatic conditions of the new province and guiding it towards European civilization'.[5] Once a land neglected and mismanaged by the 'despotic' Ottomans, in Austrian hands it had become 'the jewel in the imperial crown'.[6]

Such sentiments were typical articulations of the long-standing myth that grew up quickly in and around the province and, in the second half of the nineteenth century, its capital: that in Bukovina a tangle of nationalities and faiths coexisted in a harmony enabled by the benevolent Habsburg state. It is a myth that has served various purposes. First and foremost it was a form of imperial boosterism, a cog in the machinery of Habsburg state formation and a reassuring cultural, social, and political aide-memoire to be invoked in times of political crisis or ethnic conflict. In the post-Habsburg era, it functioned as a nostalgic balm for the wounds inflicted on many—not least the Jews—by the loss of empire.[7] Reality did not, of course, align neatly with the myth. Czernowitz's primary drawback, from

---

[3] Kaindl, *Geschichte von Czernowitz*, 186–7.

[4] For statistics, see Rechter, *Becoming Habsburg*, 111–13, 148.

[5] *Die österreichisch-ungarische Monarchie in Wort und Bild*, 517.

[6] Polek, *General Spleny's Beschreibung*, 153; *Die Bukowina: Eine allgemeine Heimatkunde*, 5. More generally on Bukovina, see Scharr, 'Die Landschaft Bukowina'; Van Drunen, 'A Sanguine Bunch'. [7] For examples, see Rechter, *Becoming Habsburg*, 1–4.

the Kellners' perspective (and in this they were not alone), was that it was not Vienna. Described in the 1840s as 'a pleasant town, with streets wide, well-aired and clean' and 'avenues of poplars and linden trees', by the early twentieth century it had become the seat of regional government, a flourishing commercial and cultural centre that appeared as an 'oasis' of German culture at the eastern edge of the empire, home to a university, a German-language theatre, and the Greek Orthodox metropolitanate of Bukovina and Dalmatia.[8] Its heterogencity was proverbial: it was 'a Black Forest village, a Podolian ghetto, a small Viennese suburb, part deepest Russia and part most modern America'.[9] The writer Gregor von Rezzori, born and raised in Czernowitz, exaggerated only slightly in describing the city as 'a melting pot for dozens of ethnic groups, languages, creeds, temperaments and customs'.[10] Even if, as noted earlier, Joseph Roth was correct that the essence of Austria was its periphery, there was no escaping the fact that Czernowitz was a distant outpost of urban life, surrounded by an overwhelmingly poor and peasant population; at the beginning of the twentieth century, agriculture constituted some 75 per cent of Bukovina's economy, and around half of the province was covered in forest.[11] The city's infrastructure—sewerage, water pipelines, street lighting, transport—was notoriously poor, its streets and squares prone to flooding, and rain turned the many unpaved areas into 'bottomless black marshland'.[12] For those accustomed to Vienna, daily life here was not without its challenges.

The immediate benefits were more obvious to Leon than to Anna. Most obviously, his elevation to the exalted ranks of the professoriate represented, as Anna put it, 'release from the vassalage' of schoolteaching, although this was tinged with a hint of regret.[13] Contemplating an editorial position at the *Neues Wiener Tagblatt* in 1899, he had told Herzl that leaving his teaching post would be a 'tremendous relief'; nonetheless, he added, 'a piece of my heart would remain there'.[14] In Czernowitz he freely admitted to Anna that he 'missed' his school pupils.[15] This was more than compen-

---

[8] Bonar and M'Cheyne, *Narrative of a Mission Enquiry*, 431; Kohl, *Austria*, 428. For 'oasis', see Corbea-Hoisie, *Czernowitzer Geschichten*, 19.

[9] Beck, *Bukowina*, 22 (a description drawn from Franzos, *Aus Halb-Asien*, 160–4).

[10] Von Rezzori, *The Snows of Yesteryear*, 227.

[11] Buszko, *Zum Wandel der Gesellschaftsstruktur*, 32.

[12] Mischler, *Soziale und wirtschaftliche Skizzen*, 10.

[13] A. Kellner, *Leon Kellner*, 71.

[14] Kellner to Herzl, 12 Feb. 1899, CZA, H1/1455-17.

[15] A. Kellner, *Leon Kellner*, 72.

THE CZERNOWITZ YEARS

sated for by the opportunities and status—and the better salary—that his new position afforded. He was all too aware, of course, that the university in Czernowitz was in many respects the poor relation among the eight Austrian universities, its reputation neatly captured in a pithy, if not entirely fair, maxim: Austrian professors were 'exiled to Czernowitz, pardoned to Graz, promoted to Vienna'.[16] Established in 1875, it was the newest and smallest of the universities, with three faculties—law, theology, and philosophy (this last, in which Kellner taught, comprising humanities and natural sciences)—teaching some 400 students in 1900, compared with almost 7,000 in Vienna.[17] Its mission was clear: 'created as a political statement of the German spirit' to bring 'authentic Austrian character' to Bukovina, it was 'a stronghold of German culture and knowledge mediating between all the land's nationalities'.[18] As one of its history professors wrote in 1917, it had succeeded in 'spreading the seeds of German culture and education throughout the [monarchy's] far east, binding it more firmly to the other parts of the monarchy, [and] nurturing its non-German peoples to become faithful Austrians'.[19] Like many Austrian Jews, Kellner subscribed to this Josephinian composite of German culture wrapped in Austrian patriotism, celebrated by Karl Emil Franzos in the 1870s as 'not a German national state, but a German *Kulturstaat*'.[20] As already noted, Kellner had described himself in 1896 not only as a 'good Austrian in every respect' but also as 'entirely German' in a cultural sense (although how he reconciled this with his lifelong identification with Jewish culture remains an open question).[21] Philipp Menczel, founding publisher and editor of the leading daily paper the *Czernowitzer Allgemeine Zeitung* and a Herzlian Zionist, held fast to the same faith: Bukovina was home to the 'last true Austrians', the German language was 'the most trustworthy cultural and economic intermediary between Jews and other nations', and the university in Czernowitz was the 'last outpost of Josephinism in Austria'.[22]

---

[16] Surman, *Universities in Imperial Austria*, 341 n. 26.

[17] Staudigl-Ciechowicz, 'Zwischen Wien und Czernowitz', 223. By 1914 it had 1,124 students, compared to Vienna's 9,205. See Staudigl-Ciechowicz, 'Die österreichische Universitätslandschaft', 641.   [18] *CAZ*, 1 May 1918, 1.

[19] Staudigl-Ciechowicz, 'Die österreichische Universitätslandschaft', 646.

[20] Franzos, *Aus Halb-Asien*, i. 186.   [21] A. Kellner, *Leon Kellner*, 60.

[22] Menczel, *Trügerische Lösungen*, 22, 43, 36. More generally on the German language and Jews, see Volovici, *German as a Jewish Problem*, ch. 1.

If the university was Josephinian and German, it was also conspicuously Jewish, so much so that to Nicolae Iorga, the Romanian nationalist politician and historian (and Romanian prime minister from April 1931 to June 1932), it was little more than 'an Austrian university for Jews'.[23] Around 1900 just over 40 per cent of its students were Jewish, the highest percentage of any Austrian university, and Jews made up some 10 per cent of the professoriate, a proportion similar to Vienna but greater than elsewhere in Austria.[24] The professors in Czernowitz were by and large younger than in other universities and stayed for fewer years before moving on to another post.[25] Kellner was atypical in both respects, assuming his position—his first and only—in his mid-forties, having experienced the same frustrations as many other Jewish scholars in pursuit of a university career. In December 1907 Arthur Mahler, Privatdozent in archaeology at the German University of Prague and a Jewish nationalist deputy in the imperial parliament, decried in a parliamentary debate on universities 'the invisible ghetto walls that are everywhere rising ever higher'.[26] On the very same day, Eugen Ehrlich, professor of Roman law and rector of the university in Czernowitz (and a Jewish convert to Catholicism), wrote in the *Neue Freie Presse* that 'for Jews and those of Jewish background an academic career in [Austria's] German universities has been as good as closed for some ten years'.[27] In this climate Kellner had reason to be pleased with his appointment, which was the fifth chair in English language and literature to be established at an Austrian university, following those in Vienna, Prague, Graz, and Innsbruck.[28] As the inaugural occupant of his chair, he was expected to establish, develop, and 'win renown' for his field, as the university told the Ministry of Education in Vienna.[29] In Czernowitz this posed a particular challenge, as the turnover of faculty and the dearth of Privatdozenten—there was no locally trained pool and the limited opportunities

[23] Corbea-Hoisie (ed.), *Jüdisches Städtebild Czernowitz*, 122.

[24] For student numbers, see Thon, *Die Juden in Oesterreich*, 104 (table LXVII); Lichtblau and John, 'Jewries in Galicia and Bukovina', 147 (table 1.6). For professors, see Surman, *Universities in Imperial Austria*, 237.   [25] Staudigl-Ciechowicz, 'Zwischen Wien und Czernowitz', 226.

[26] *Stenographische Protokolle des Abgeordnetenhauses des Reichsrates*, 3 Dec. 1907, 2898.

[27] *NFP*, 3 Dec. 1907, 1. See also Surman, *Universities in Imperial Austria*, 233–41.

[28] Klein, 'Austrian (and some German) Scholars of English', 245–6.

[29] Dekanat der philosophischen Fakultät [Prof. Carl Zelinka] an das k. k. Ministerium für Kultus und Unterricht, 12 Dec. 1901, OS, AV/PCK.

in Czernowitz deterred those from outside—hampered the development and maintenance of the subject.[30]

Kellner's adjustment to Czernowitz was relatively straightforward, as he was able to slip into a familiar and hospitable professional setting that allowed him to resume his work without delay. Anna's initial misgivings also gradually receded, without disappearing entirely, as life in Czernowitz became 'more tolerable and more palatable'.[31] She explored the city, Dora and Viktor began school, her mother arranged for one of the family cooks from Bielitz to join them, thus easing management of the household, she befriended the wives of a number of Leon's colleagues, and, most importantly, she resumed her work.[32] Soon after the move to Czernowitz she published a translation of Mary Cholmondeley's *Diana Tempest*, followed before long by two Leonard Merrick novels, a Kipling short story and another of Cholmondeley's novels, *Red Pottage*, in serialized form in the *Czernowitzer Allgemeine Zeitung*.[33]

Kellner's first major undertaking was to develop an idea that had been in gestation for some time. English–German lexicography, he believed, was in an unsatisfactory state, 'unable to meet the demands of research and praxis'.[34] Years of almost solitary labour on his edition of Thieme's English–German dictionary had confirmed for him that, as James Murray —the power behind the *Oxford English Dictionary*—had written, a dictionary should be 'the creation of no one man'.[35] 'With the best will in the world', wrote Kellner, 'an individual can achieve only partial results.' Better to enlist the service of 'hundreds of collaborators', each using specialist knowledge 'to translate the vast expanse of English vocabulary with expertise'.[36] Specialist knowledge was indispensable, he believed, because it was

---

[30] Surman, *Universities in Imperial Austria*, 162. [31] A. Kellner, *Leon Kellner*, 72. [32] Ibid.
[33] The translation of Mary Cholmondeley's book appeared as *Diana* (1904), Merrick's as *Liebe und Ruhm* (1904) and *Die Sünde* (1906); the latter was serialized in the *NWT* between September and November 1902. For Kipling's 'Three and—an Extra' ('Frauenkrieg'), see *CT*, 24 Dec. 1905, 11; Cholmondeley's *Red Pottage* (*Um ein Linsengericht*) began in *CAZ*, 14 Jan. 1906, 5, and finished on 25 Nov. 1906, 12. [34] Kellner, 'Englische Wortforschung', 29.
[35] Murray, *The Evolution of English Lexicography*, 6.
[36] Kellner, 'Englische Wortforschung', 28.

not enough to know just the obvious meaning of a word; rather, a translator 'must recognize the concealed essence and complexity' of all words. 'It should be the ideal of the English–German lexicographer to render an English term into German such that the two fit like two congruent triangles'—a goal beyond reach, he admitted, but the effort should nonetheless be made.[37] German speakers should not be content merely 'to intuit the sense of a Shakespearean verse and a phrase from Spenser', but needed a better guide 'for the eyes and ears to the immense wealth of words that seek to represent the world of emotion and intellectual labour' (the latter also encompassing the great variety of 'technical expressions from natural sciences and engineering'). An adequate and comprehensive dictionary that met this need was 'an urgent desideratum', requiring an expansive cooperative venture. 'If in the foreseeable future we wish to master this almost infinite subject, we need hundreds of dissertations and programmatic works, and we need our own journal to educate about lexicography.'[38]

This was the gist of the proposal he put in December 1902 to the Neuphilologische Verein (New Philological Society) in Vienna, an association set up by his teacher Jakob Schipper in 1894 to promote the study of modern philology.[39] Kellner suggested that the Verein establish a journal that, with the help of like-minded Anglicists from across Germany and Austria, would lay the foundation for an improved dictionary by building an inventory of words and acting as a clearing house for information and exchange. The primary focus of the journal was to be contemporary English literature, and in particular 'the semantics of contemporary English vocabulary'.[40] Kellner had long believed that lexicographical neglect of contemporary English had left German speakers without adequate English vocabulary and, consequently, comprehension. In his own teaching and scholarship, therefore, he made sure to pay careful attention to contemporary language practice in English.[41] As so often, his inspiration came in part from London. Kellner was well acquainted with the city's Philological Society and with its flagship project, the *Oxford English Dictionary*.

---

[37] Kellner, 'Englische Wortforschung', 30–1.   [38] A. Kellner, *Leon Kellner*, 74.

[39] Kellner, 'Englische Wortforschung', 29. On the Verein, see Reiffenstein, 'Zu den Anfängen des Englischunterrichts', 179.   [40] A. Kellner, *Leon Kellner*, 74.

[41] Kellner, 'Englische Wortforschung', 29. See also *NWT*, 4 Jan. 1903, 24; 11 Jan. 1903, 24; 22 Nov. 1905 (Abendblatt), 4; *Prager Tagblatt*, 7 Dec. 1902, 17.

He had been much impressed by meetings of the society, where he found the relaxed and convivial atmosphere a welcome change from academic gatherings in Vienna. Even in the presence of grandees from Oxford, Cambridge, Berlin, Paris, and St Petersburg, discussion flowed easily, light refreshments were served, 'the boredom normally inseparable from the very concept of philology was banished', and everyone was made to feel 'at home'.[42] His close friend Frederick James Furnivall was the society's long-serving secretary (from 1853 to 1910) and had been one of the *Oxford English Dictionary*'s founding fathers in the late 1850s, as well as its 'presiding genius' in the 1860s and 1870s; the Philological Society had shepherded the dictionary through subsequent decades of publication in instalments.[43] The practice of the *Oxford English Dictionary* of drawing on the wisdom of the crowd, gathering its raw material from multiple contributors, reinforced Kellner's hard-won conviction that lexicography was best pursued collectively and furnished a template for his proposal to the philologists in Vienna.

The Neuphilologische Verein was not unsympathetic, but in Vienna Kellner could find neither the time nor resources to carry the idea to completion. In Czernowitz, however, his new status provided both. By July 1905 he was able to launch his journal *Bausteine*, the name—'building blocks'—clearly signalling his intent to construct a library of English and German terms which in time could be consolidated into a dictionary. It was a way, too, for Czernowitz to begin to establish an international presence in the field of English philology. A degree of cross-border cooperation was evident, as *Bausteine* was published in Berlin, enjoyed the formal sponsorship of Vienna's Neuphilologische Verein, and was edited by Kellner along with Gustav Krüger, a Berlin colleague whose magnum opus *Schwierigkeiten des Englischen* (The Difficulties of English) took over thirty years to write and ran to nearly 4,000 pages.[44] The journal, however, was short-lived, running aground after one year due to a dearth of subscribers and to what Kellner called the 'indifference' of the field towards contemporary, as distinct from classical, philology.[45] This indifference was most apparent in the disap-

---

[42] *NWT*, 27 Sept. 1889, 1–2.
[43] Gilliver, *The Making of the* Oxford English Dictionary, ch. 2 (p. 59). See also chs. 3 to 6.
[44] Opitz, 'Specialized Bilingual Dictionaries of the Past', 244–5. See also *Bausteine*, 1 (1906), 242–3, 444–5. [45] Kellner, 'Englische Wortforschung', 28.

pointingly thin roster of contributors, a fatal flaw for what was by definition a collective effort. The problem was not one of quality but of quantity. Authors included Kellner's friends and colleagues from across Germany, Austria, and Belgium, and the journal was warmly greeted in the *Neue Freie Presse*.[46] But Kellner alone accounted for nearly a quarter of the year's content. He wrote succinctly, for example, on the theory and practice of lexical categories in contemporary English, and at length on the usage and meanings of the 'weighty' words 'suggest', 'suggestion', and 'suggestive'.[47] He tackled the 'assorted gaps and inaccuracies' that marred translations in German dictionaries of British parliamentary language, offering definitions for terms such as 'appropriation bill', 'borough constituencies', 'catch the Speaker's eye', 'Hansard Debates', 'heckle', 'lobbying', 'Question Time', and 'substantive motion'.[48] Using examples from prose literature, he suggested multiple alternative German renderings of the words 'abject', 'aggressive', 'baffle', 'besetting', 'bewildering', 'blatant', 'casual', and 'crude' in order to supplement current dictionary definitions.[49] Finally, he wrote miscellaneous notices, comments, responses, and book reviews. This was obviously an unsustainable level of commitment. He later reflected that, although his *Bausteine* 'had been reduced to a pile of rubble', he would gladly participate in rebuilding it should the opportunity present itself.[50] It did not, and he instead shifted his attention away from lexicography and towards literary history, with a view to completing what would be his

[46] *NFP*, 17 June 1906, 38. Contributors included (besides Kellner's daughter Paula) his longtime friend Helene Richter, a pioneering independent Viennese scholar; Rudolf Brotanek, who followed in Kellner's footsteps as a student of Schipper and a Privatdozent at the university in Vienna, and was from 1908 a professor in Prague; Roman Dyboski, a Schipper student and Privatdozent in Vienna who in 1911 became a professor at the Jagiellonian University in Krakau; Gustav Reiniger, a professor at the Handelsakademie in Prague; Willi Bang-Kaup, a professor at the University of Louvain; Otto Luitpold Jiriczek, later a professor in Würzburg; Francis Curtis of the Akademie für Sozial- und Handelswissenschaften in Frankfurt; and legal scholars Julius Hatschek, a professor at the Prussian Verwaltungsakademie in Posen and later in Göttingen, and Professor Eugen Ehrlich in Czernowitz.

[47] For the first, see *Bausteine*, 1 (1906), 432–5; for the second, ibid. 1–28. 'Suggest, Suggestion, Suggestive' was a revision of Kellner's article 'To Suggest', written for a Festschrift dedicated to his teacher Schipper; the *Neue Freie Presse* commented on the original that Kellner demonstrated an 'uncommonly refined feeling for language'. See *NFP*, 7 June 1903, 42.

[48] *Bausteine*, 1 (1906), 420–31 ('assorted gaps' quotation on 420).

[49] Ibid. 85–9, 308–19, 396–419.   [50] Kellner, 'Englische Wortforschung', 28, 35.

THE CZERNOWITZ YEARS   103

largest work to date, a history of nineteenth-century English literature for which he had been accumulating material for well over a decade.

Even before *Bausteine* had seen the light of day, the university, with the 'full support' of the Bukovina government, had asked the Ministry of Education in Vienna in the summer of 1905 to promote Kellner from *außerordentlicher* to *ordentlicher* professor (akin to the distinction between associate and full professor) 'in recognition of his outstanding academic and scholarly activity'. The ministry was unwilling, pleading financial constraints, a refusal that held firm over the next few years despite repeated requests from the university.[51] He was 'aggrieved' at this, he told Anna in June 1907: 'I feel like a man who has suffered a shipwreck.'[52] Vienna did, however, approve a substantial salary increase in 1907 to reward his 'fruitful work'.[53] This 'fruitful work' extended beyond the university; Kellner lectured regularly in public and semi-academic settings, just as he had previously done in Vienna.[54] In his new position in a smaller city, he was in great demand, delivering talks, for example, on the Salvation Army, pedagogy, American literature, the Bible, Goethe, and Gladstone.[55] He helped to develop further education courses for women to learn English and was a fixture in the annual adult education 'Popular University' courses, where his lectures on topics such as Shakespeare, English literature, and the British parliament were enthusiastically received.[56]

Although Kellner had quickly established his presence in the university and the city, the pull of Vienna remained powerful for the family, even as they learned to appreciate Czernowitz. In the summer of 1905 he wrote a paean to the latter in the *Neue Freie Presse*, saturated with the rhetoric of the above-noted myth. It was, he wrote,

[51] Karl von Stürgkh [Minister of Education] to Emperor Franz Joseph, 8 Apr. 1909, OS, AV/PCK, Zl. 4781. See also K. K. Landesregierung to K. K. Ministerium für Kultus und Unterricht, 16 Jan. 1906, OS, AV/PCK, Zl. 1336.   [52] A. Kellner, *Leon Kellner*, 160.

[53] Karl von Stürgkh to Emperor Franz Joseph, 8 Apr. 1909, OS, AV/PCK, Zl. 4781.

[54] For Vienna (and elsewhere), see e.g. *NFP*, 9 Dec. 1899, 2; 12 Jan. 1900, 5; *JC*, 10 Mar. 1899, 14; *OW*, 7 Mar. 1902, 164; 15 Jan. 1904, 46; *Die Welt*, 31 Dec. 1897, 13; 23 Mar. 1900, 3–4; 4 May 1900, 12; 14 Dec. 1900, 14; 8 Feb. 1901, 12; 8 Mar. 1901, 14; 15 Nov. 1901, 12; 27 Dec. 1901, 13. He was also a regular speaker at the Jewish Toynbee Hall.

[55] *CAZ*, 22 Jan. 1905, 4; 14 June 1906, 3; 5 Dec. 1908, 4; 19 Feb. 1911, 4; 22 Mar. 1912, 4; *Bukowinaer Post*, 13 Nov. 1910, 5.

[56] *CT*, 5 Nov. 1904, 3–4; *CAZ*, 22 Nov. 1906, 4; 20 Jan. 1907, 4; 4 Oct. 1907, 4; 29 Sept. 1908, 3; 23 Oct. 1909, 4; 9 Nov. 1910, 4; A. Kellner, *Leon Kellner*, 76.

the most singular of all the monarchy's cities. For the observer of human behaviour, it is an undiscovered, unexploited El Dorado ... a youthful, hustling, pristine community, heir to a future of unimagined possibilities. For the Austrian, who as we know does not suffer from a surfeit of self-awareness, Czernowitz is a vivid, conspicuous symbol of what the skill and honesty of Austrian administration can accomplish: out of a desolate, remote, abandoned backwater, in a hundred years Austria has conjured up a grand city with a degree of prosperity, modern social services, and auspicious potential for development.[57]

The city 'can boast of a virtue that makes it the crown jewel of Austria: it is the monarchy's most peaceable and perhaps thus most politically mature city ... Undisturbed by the waves of world-historical storm tides, a whole host of scattered peoples, divergent in language, nature, and tradition, live side by side.' And the key to this harmony? 'German culture, which in the east is coterminous with Austrian culture and to which Bukovina owes so much. All the heterogeneous elements of this ambitious province merge willingly into a higher unity if German zeal and German civic spirit are at the heart of this crystallization.' The university was equally the beneficiary of German culture, he added. Part of his purpose in bathing the city in such a warm (if German-imbued) Habsburg glow was to make the point that Austria had much to lose if nationalist aggression, making its presence felt there too, was not kept in check.[58]

In this discussion of relations between national groups he made no mention of Jews, some 30 per cent of the city's population. As already noted, as a rule he kept Jewish and general themes at arm's length from one another in his writing for the general press, calibrating content to audience and vehicle. The *Neue Freie Presse*, as Herzl had learned, was not the place to bring Jews into a discussion of national groups.

This was the only occasion on which he wrote about Czernowitz for the Viennese press. He otherwise stayed true to his brief, bringing an informed, critical perspective on British culture and society to the readership of both the *Neue Freie Presse* and the *Neues Wiener Tagblatt*, albeit at a reduced pace due to the new demands on his time in Czernowitz. He reviewed, for example, a three-volume biography of William Pitt the Elder by the German historian Albert von Ruville; compared child poverty in Britain and Austria; assessed the treatment of female characters by contem-

[57] *NFP*, 31 July 1905 (Abendblatt), 1. [58] Ibid.

THE CZERNOWITZ YEARS

porary British and Irish novelists; wrote an admiring sketch of George Eliot (recommending in passing his friend Helene Richter's new book on her); drew a portrait of the author George Meredith on the occasion of a new German edition of his 1859 novel *The Ordeal of Richard Feverel*; and explained to German readers how they might learn to appreciate the poet Robert Browning.[59] Whether as professional critic or erudite enthusiast, he articulated his views on authors, works, and cultural movements with clarity and with generosity of spirit, assuming a knowledgeable and cultured readership and making few concessions to middlebrow taste. His discussion of critic and essayist Walter Pater's theory of aesthetics and his advocacy of 'art for art's sake' is a case in point, touching on Epicureanism, the Renaissance, the relationship between art and nature, Max Nordau's *Entartung (Degeneration)*, Joris-Karl Huysmans's novel *À Rebours (Against Nature)*, the Irish novelist George Moore's *Confessions of a Young Man*, Maurice Barrès, Charles Baudelaire, Théophile Gautier, Symbolism and the Decadent movement in France, Late Latin poetry, and the philosopher and author Apuleius.[60] Kellner's intent was not to dazzle the audience with his learning; rather, he wrote in the service of a larger cause. Reviewing a history of Indian literature, he allowed that he was straying from his usual path: 'How is it', he asked, 'that I am writing for the readers of this newspaper about the treasures of ancient India?' His answer amounted to a credo: 'the love of literature, the longing for acquaintance with the spirit of those far removed in time and place, the inextinguishable faith in the equivalence of the heartbeat of all civilized peoples—these give me the right.'[61] These sentiments were always the animating impulse of his writing.

[59] On Pitt, see *NFP*, 5 Mar. 1905, 34–5. On child poverty, see *NWT*, 20 July 1905, 1–3. On female characters, see *NWT*, 16 June 1906, 1–3. On George Eliot, see *NFP*, 4 Aug. 1907, 31–2. On Meredith, see *NFP*, 22 Jan. 1905, 34–7 (see also *AZ*, 12 Feb. 1889, Suppl. 43, 633–4). On Browning, see *NFP*, 4 Mar. 1906, 32–5.

[60] *NFP*, 6 Jan. 1907, 33–4. He also wrote for other publications: see e.g. *CAZ*, 1 Nov. 1905, 1–2, marking the death of the theatre manager/actor Henry Irving (about whom he had written previously in *AZ*, 14 Apr. 1889, Suppl. 104, 2–3), and *CAZ*, 15 Apr. 1906, 1–2, a meditation on the post-graduation careers of his school pupils (later published in Kellner, *Meine Schüler*, 161–8). He continued to write occasionally for *Die Welt*; see e.g. 3 Mar. 1905, 14–16; 26 Jan. 1906, 11–13; 9 Feb. 1906, 21; 13 Apr. 1906, 12.

[61] *NWT*, 24 Sept. 1906 (Abendblatt), 6. The author of the book—*Geschichte der indischen Literatur* (*A History of Indian Literature*)—was Moriz Winternitz, professor of Sanskrit in Prague; Kellner and Winternitz had studied Sanskrit together in Vienna in 1880.

Anna wrote about their new home too, in her case with a mixture of affection and condescension, publishing a feuilleton in the *Neue Freie Presse* that recounted a summer spent in southern Bukovina. On the one hand, she sang the praises of its landscape, peoples, towns, and potential; on the other, she gently mocked its quaint customs and costumes. For a city dweller it was remote and parochial, a far cry from the summer holiday destinations with which she was more familiar, such as the Alps in South Tyrol or the Salzkammergut.[62] What was true of rural Bukovina was, *mutatis mutandis*, also true of Czernowitz, and the lure of the imperial capital proved too strong to resist. In early 1907 the family decided that Anna and the children should return permanently to Vienna, a decision, Anna wrote, that 'cost the sleep of an entire winter'.[63] For a number of reasons this appeared the most practicable and desirable option. Anna's ambivalence about Czernowitz had abated but not disappeared, and her translation work was based in Vienna; the distance from Paula, an aspiring writer and now a part-time teacher, had proved painful for both sides; Dora had graduated from the girls' Lyzeum in Czernowitz and wished to attend Gymnasium in Vienna; Viktor was in his first year at secondary school and could transfer without difficulty. University terms occupied barely half the calendar year, enabling Leon to spend long periods in Vienna (more than half the year, according to Paula).[64] That summer, after three years in the empire's far-eastern reaches, the family headed west, to resume, as far as possible, the life they had left.

Kellner now split his time between Czernowitz and Vienna. With *Bausteine* defunct, he turned to completing a book on which he had been working for some time, which was published in 1909 as *Die englische Literatur im Zeitalter der Königin Viktoria* (English Literature in the Time of Queen Victoria). In the Victorian era, he wrote:

---

[62] *NFP*, 2 Sept. 1907 (Nachmittagblatt), 1–3. Anna published a similar piece in *NFP*, 15 Nov. 1910, 34–5.   [63] A. Kellner, *Leon Kellner*, 81.

[64] Arnold, *Memoirs* (Heb.), 86; A. Kellner, *Leon Kellner*, 81–2. Anna's serialized translations of English novels began to appear regularly in the Viennese press. See, for example, a series beginning in *NFP*, 23 Apr. 1911, 31–2, and others beginning in *NWT*, 5 Nov. 1910 (Abendblatt), 1; 24 July 1911, 1–3; 18 May 1912 (Abendblatt), 1–2; 29 Oct. 1912 (Abendblatt), 1–2; 9 May 1914 (Abendblatt), 1–2. She also published translations in 1909 of a collection of Leonard Merrick's short stories (*Ein Bombenerfolg und andere Novellen*, drawn primarily from *The Man who Understood Women, and Other Stories*) and in 1914 an adaptation of Cicely Hamilton's play *Diana of Dobsons*, as *Der Ruf des Lebens*.

the soul of the nation searched for a new relationship with the other peoples of the world, for a new political and social order, for a new accord with foreigners in its midst and in its colonies, for a new god and a new moral code . . . [Literature] was a faithful expression of these internal crises in England, which are nothing more than the struggles to adapt . . . to a new national, moral, social, economic, and local environment.[65]

Written in a scholarly but accessible style, it was his most ambitious and expansive work to date, a compendium and commentary arranged as a series of portraits of writers, a grand synthesis constructed from a wealth of detail. Teeming with information, analysis, opinion, and illuminating asides, the tone was not dissimilar to his high-register journalism, and in fact some of the material had appeared in the press in modified form over the preceding decades.[66] Kellner followed his established practice of treating author and work as closely related yet distinct, examining the life and work of each author in discrete sections, an approach that was not, he acknowledged, 'in keeping with current practice [that] . . . imposed the obligation to demonstrate at every turn the organic connection between life and literature'. That approach, he believed, too often succumbed to the 'temptation to inflict violence upon recalcitrant facts' in the service of a 'preconceived theory'.[67] Kellner had long thought it necessary to try to understand 'where literary physiognomy and biography meet', and believed the relationship between art and life—text and context—was more opaque than such a theory admitted.[68]

The book won generous plaudits, hailed as 'a guidebook for current and future friends of English literature' and 'a sturdy bridge between the intellectual lives of two great kindred nations'.[69] Kellner, wrote one reviewer,

unites qualities that are seldom found together: a feel for detail with the broad perspective of a cultural historian, an understanding of real life, sober judgement, and aesthetic sensitivity. That Kellner is himself quite the artist is demon-

---

[65] Kellner, *Die englische Literatur im Zeitalter*, 4.

[66] See, for example, *AZ*, 26 Sept. 1888, Suppl. 268, 3937–8; 12 Feb. 1889, Suppl. 43, 633–4; 12 Oct. 1892, 139; *NWT*, 10 Nov. 1898, 1–3; 11 Nov. 1898, 1–2; 25 Jan. 1900, 1–3; 13 June 1901, 1–2.

[67] Kellner, *Die englische Literatur im Zeitalter*, p. viii. On the positivist method, see also Pils, 'Disziplinierung eines Faches', 544–5; Stanzel, 'Erinnerungen an die Anglistin Helene Richter', 323.

[68] Kellner, 'Oliver Wendell Holmes', 418. See also his comments in *AZ*, 21 Aug. 1885, Suppl. 231, 3401–3.   [69] *NFP*, 4 July 1909, 33; *WZ*, 7 July 1910, 6.

strated by his own German prose... A philologist who thinks also as a psychologist... [he] understands the style of Swinburne or Tennyson just as he understands the philosophy of Herbert Spencer.[70]

There was praise for his 'conspicuously generous' treatment of women writers, for his portraits of Wilde, Ruskin, and Kipling, and for his 'exhaustive discussion of writers unfamiliar to the German public, such as Elizabeth Barrett Browning, Charlotte Brontë, Robert Louis Stevenson, Yeats, and the Celtic movement'.[71] He was 'the greatest authority on England today among German-language writers and scholars', enthused one critic.[72] Another commented a few years later that the book was 'in the unanimous opinion of German, French, and English critics not just a scholarly achievement of the first rank but also supremely enjoyable and stimulating to read. There is no better guide to nineteenth-century English literature.'[73]

The university had continued to press the case for Kellner's promotion, reporting that he was 'indefatigably busy'. In addition to *Bausteine* and *Die englische Literatur im Zeitalter der Königin Viktoria*, his lectures were increasingly well attended (although low attendance in his faculty was a perennial problem); he had founded a philology association, along the lines of Vienna's Neuphilologische Verein but not confined to modernists; and the second volume of his enormous edition of Thieme's dictionary had been published at the end of 1905. He had succeeded in 'establishing and consolidating interest in his discipline', the university argued, and had exerted an 'inspiring and nurturing influence on neighbouring philological disciplines'.[74] In 1909 the ministry agreed to promote him to full professor.[75]

---

[70] *NWT*, 7 May 1909, 23.

[71] On women writers, see *Germanisch-romanische Monatschrift*, 1 (1909), 653; for the second quotation, see *NWT*, 7 May 1909, 23. In 2013, his work was described as being of 'particular importance' in drawing the attention of German-speaking academia to Charles Dickens; Foltinek, 'Dickens in Austria', 249.   [72] *Germanisch-romanische Monatschrift*, 2 (1910), 517.

[73] *NWT*, 26 Jan. 1913, 26. See also *Englische Studien*, 41 (1910), 314–18, and *Das literarische Echo*, 12 (1909/10), 484–6.

[74] Karl von Stürgkh to Emperor Franz Joseph, 8 Apr. 1909, OS, AV/PCK, Zl. 4781; A. Kellner, *Leon Kellner*, 73. On attendance at lectures, see *NFP*, 20 June 1916, 1.

[75] 16 May 1909, OS, AV/PCK, Zl. 20781; *WZ*, 25 Sept. 1909, 1.

Kellner's move to Czernowitz coincided with a shift in the Zionist centre of gravity away from Vienna following Herzl's death in July 1904, marked by the transfer of the Zionist headquarters to Cologne in 1905. Even before that, Kellner had stepped back from day-to-day involvement at the heart of the burgeoning movement. As he later commented, this was due 'mostly to the force of personal circumstances', although as a pure Herzlian who believed in the redemptive qualities of land he was also wary of the movement's increasing tilt towards diaspora nationalist politics (so-called *Landespolitik*).[76] He was able, though, to work with post-Herzlian 'synthetic Zionism', a settlement between the conflicting wings of the movement—involvement in local politics versus single-minded pursuit of the goal of a Jewish Palestine—that enabled them to coexist (uneasily) under the Zionist umbrella.[77] This arrangement suited Kellner, as he came to accept that these were not mutually exclusive goals. Relocation from the imperial centre to the periphery had brought with it a change of perspective and new opportunities. Circumstances nudged him forcefully towards *Landespolitik* in Bukovina, and in time he became a central actor in the Zionist politics of Czernowitz and of the province as a whole. It also provided an outlet for his social reformist drive, which was still strong; besides the Jewish Toynbee Hall, adult education teaching, and the Baron Hirsch Foundation, he was active in the Czernowitz branch of the Israelitische Allianz.[78] For Kellner, this was not an either/or choice: both diaspora and Zion were necessary.

His reputation preceded him. The *Czernowitzer Tagblatt* reported breathlessly on a festive evening to bid farewell to Kellner held in March 1904 at Vienna's Jewish Toynbee Hall, describing 'the almost indescribable scenes that unfolded', the crowd spilling out into the street and demonstrating 'the extent to which Viennese Jews have taken this man to heart ... Envy and resentment of Czernowitz, which had taken a man so dear to them, rang out in every speech.'[79] In his first few years in Czernowitz, however, he rarely participated in Zionist events.[80] Bukovina Zionism was in

[76] *JC*, 9 Oct. 1908, 14.

[77] By 1907, synthetic Zionism had been adopted as policy by the Austrian and world movements. See Gaisbauer, *Davidstern und Doppeladler*, 451–9; Vital, *Zionism: The Formative Years*, 477–8. More generally, see Mendelsohn, *On Modern Jewish Politics*, 57–8.

[78] On the Allianz connection, see *JC*, 1 May 1908, 19; *Jüdische Volksstimme*, 1 June 1908, 9.

[79] *CT*, 30 Mar. 1904, 3. See also *Die Welt*, 1 Apr. 1904, 8.

[80] He attended very few meetings and confined himself to making occasional speeches. See *CT*, 30 Nov. 1904, 4; 4 Mar. 1906, 5; Reifer, *Menschen und Ideen*, 48.

110 THE CZERNOWITZ YEARS

disarray, unable in 1905 even to elect a leadership.[81] It was the poor relation in the federal structure of the Austrian movement, in which the Galician and Bohemian regions objected to Vienna's pretensions to the status of first among equals. In the years leading up to 1910, the Bukovina branch—dismissed by the Viennese leadership as 'stagnant' and 'extremely pitiful' —was almost in stasis, debilitated by lack of funds, a thin base of support, and poor organization.[82]

If formal Zionism was weak, Jewish nationalism was a potent force, a function of Bukovina's distinctive political culture in which nationality and ethnicity trumped all other claims in the decades prior to the First World War. Faithfully reflecting this reality, ethnic/nationalist politics superseded liberalism among Jews from the 1880s, and Jewish collective interests came to be explicitly articulated as distinct from those of Romanians, Ruthenians, Germans, and Poles. In the absence of a dominant national group (a category which generally included Jews), shifting alliances and an unstable balance of power were the norm, with the province's politics a kind of national 'chess'.[83] In this environment, autonomous Jewish politics—Bukovina's version of *Landespolitik*—flourished, manifested in Jewish representation, qua Jews, in chambers of commerce, in municipal and regional government and administration, and even in the imperial parliament, where the Jewish nationalist Benno Straucher (long-time president of the Czernowitz Kultusgemeinde) represented Czernowitz from 1897 to 1918. Jews were 'a decisive factor in Bukovina's politics'.[84] None of this, though, was in the hands of the Zionist movement.

Kellner made his first foray into the public arena on Jewish issues in the summer of 1906, writing a front-page opinion piece in the *Czernowitzer Tagblatt* in emphatic support of the demands of Jewish students at the university to register their nationality as Jewish. For government purposes, the ascription of nationality followed from the choice of mother tongue, and the authorities recognized neither a Yiddish language nor a Jewish nationality. Most Jewish students were native German speakers, but in the

[81] *CT*, 21 Mar. 1905, 4.

[82] Zionistisches Zentralbureau Köln to Akademische Verbindung Hebronia, 30 Aug. 1908, CZA, Z2/389; Zionistisches Landes-Komité für Österreich to Zionistisches Zentralkomitee für West-Österreich, 15 Sept. 1908, CZA, Z2/436.

[83] *CAZ*, 20 Dec. 1906, 1.   [84] *JZ*, 8 Nov. 1907, 2. See also *Neue Zeitung*, 20 Sept. 1907, 2–3.

nationally fraught atmosphere of Czernowitz, and with the increasing exclusion of Jews from German student fraternities, many Jews were reluctant to register as 'German'. The demand for the right to register as Jewish at university, initiated by students at the University of Vienna in 1902, was part of an unsuccessful campaign by Jewish nationalists to persuade the government to give formal recognition to Jewish nationality.[85] The article represented a departure for Kellner with regard to his public profile. He wrote here about his Zionist beliefs—as he had never done in the Viennese press—reaffirming his view that 'if we are a nation we must have that which constitutes the first attribute of all nations: our own home, our own land'. At the same time, he voiced his concern about the tone and content of the student demands, cautioning against the excessive 'fervour' and 'narrow horizons' that he thought an inescapable consequence of too close an involvement with local politics. 'We know today that the greatest error of liberal Jews was that they helped kindle the flames of national passion in Austria to boiling point.' Jews must not, he warned, make the same mistake in Bukovina. Instead, they should steer clear of the national conflicts of others and keep their eyes on the higher ideal of Zion.[86]

He had sounded a similar alarm a few months earlier, accusing Emil Byk, the anti-Zionist Jewish leader in Lemberg, of recklessness for impugning the loyalty of Galician Zionists who had advocated, in the context of debates around electoral reform in Galicia, that Jews should constitute a separate electorate (what was called a 'curia', such as urban dwellers or Chambers of Commerce), a proposal that would soon also be relevant in Bukovina. Byk had called this 'a declaration of war on Poles' and an attempt 'to build our own fatherland in Galicia', against which the Galician Poles would surely 'defend themselves with fire and sword'. The potential risks of Landespolitik—'enemies to fear, friends to lose'—were clear.[87] Kellner had been concerned about this since Herzl's death. As he explained (in English) to the *Jewish Chronicle* in London, 'In Herzl's time it was really a Zionist movement, aiming at Zion, at the creation of a Jewish settlement. What

---

[85] Rozenblit, 'The Assertion of Jewish Identity', 177–9. On the increasingly fraught atmosphere, see Corbea-Hoisie, 'Urbane Kohabitation in Czernowitz'.

[86] *CT*, 24 June 1906, 2. The university agreed in November 1906 that Jewish students could register both 'Jewish nationality' and their mother tongue, although this permission was later revoked. See *CT*, 4 Nov. 1906, 5; *Die Welt*, 9 Nov. 1906, 9; *JZ*, 27 Mar. 1908, 7; 3 Nov. 1911, 3; Van Drunen, 'A Sanguine Bunch', 220. [87] *Die Welt*, 26 Jan. 1906, 12–13.

it is aiming at now is political national equality. This striving is absorbing the whole of its activity.'[88] It was a shift in priorities that 'naturally makes many enemies', he believed. Rehearsing familiar arguments, he held this position responsible for 'the constant persecution of Zionists, their perpetual exclusion from all positions and offices, from private businesses, the press, and public works'.[89] Speaking at the opening of the Lemberg Jewish Toynbee Hall at the end of 1907, Kellner observed that:

'Slay all Zionists' . . . is the slogan which increasingly rings out around us . . . Zionism is no longer as pure as it once was and today we pursue tasks unrelated to the Zionist idea . . . I hear a great deal about Jewish-national obligations and duties but nothing about 'Zion'. Our goal is to acquire a homeland for the Jews. Woe betide us if we should bear the guilt of extinguishing the torch lit by Herzl.[90]

Diverting attention from Palestine led to discord in Zionist ranks ('the battle cries that I hear continually from Vienna') and provided ready ammunition for opponents: 'the anti-Zionist patriots assail us daily—"one is either a good Austrian or a Zionist"'.[91] In short, too much local politics and too little Zion had muddied the strategic and tactical waters; the movement's focus had blurred, its purpose had shifted, and internecine conflicts were sapping its energy.

Kellner had witnessed these changes at one remove. In the first post-Herzl years, he and his friends in what he affectionately called the 'old guard'—Kremenezky and Schnirer, for example—had 'kept aloof from the movement'. By 1908, however, they were ready to resume an active role. For Kellner this meant first and foremost in the Austrian movement. Rather than reverse recent developments, he wanted to create a shared sense of purpose between the bickering factions and achieve a workable form of synthetic Zionism. 'We are going to work together with the National Party', he told the *Jewish Chronicle*, 'with the object of uniting the old Zionists with the exponents of the new national aspirations.'[92] Zionists in Austria had established the Jüdischnationale Partei (Jewish National Party) in 1906 to contest the 1907 Reichsrat elections; the introduction of universal male

---

[88] *JC*, 9 Oct. 1908, 14.

[89] *Jüdische Volksstimme*, 20 Dec. 1907, 4.   [90] *Die Welt*, 13 Dec. 1907, 13.

[91] The first quotation is from *Die Welt*, 25 Sept. 1908, 8; the second from ibid., 13 Apr. 1906, 12.

[92] *JC*, 9 Oct. 1908, 14.

suffrage helped the Jewish nationalists win four seats (two in Galicia, one each in Bohemia and Bukovina), leading to the formation for the first time of a 'Jewish Club' in the imperial parliament. By April 1908 Kellner, Kremenezky, and Schnirer were meeting regularly with the Jewish Club, and by October Kellner was confidently predicting: 'a change for the better is likely to take place soon'.[93]

The issues that so disturbed Kellner were present in concentrated form in Bukovina, where Herzlian Zionism was overshadowed by a powerful diaspora nationalism and where ideological differences were intertwined with extraordinarily acrimonious personal rivalries that rendered collaboration impossible. The province's enormous Zionist potential was unrealized due to the debilitating conflicts generated by and around Benno Straucher, the self-described 'Jewish politician par excellence', a talented demagogue who occupied multiple Jewish, municipal, and regional offices. His opponents called him a Jewish Karl Lueger, a petty Caesar, a modern Herod; his supporters were grateful that he had made Bukovina's Jews 'a political power . . . with which the other nations in the land must reckon'.[94]

With electoral reform in Bukovina in 1910, the leaders of Austrian Zionism saw an opportunity not unlike that of the 1907 Reichsrat elections. One of a series of limited regional reforms, the 'Bukovina Compromise' was a latticework of intersecting class, geographical, and national interests. Crucially for the Zionists, it included national curias, one of which was to be Jewish, signifying recognition of Jewish nationality. Unsurprisingly, Vienna withheld approval of this unprecedented step, but the provincial authorities established a de facto Jewish curia within the German one.[95] To take advantage of this, Zionists attempted to revive their flagging Bukovina branch in order to bring some of the 'political power' of Bukovina Jewry under its aegis. To spearhead this revival and forge a workable form of synthetic Zionism in the province, they turned to Kellner, electing him as leader in March 1910.[96]

[93] Ibid. On Austrian Zionism's *Landespolitik*, see Gaisbauer, *Davidstern und Doppeladler*, 458–74; Shanes, *Diaspora Nationalism*, 192–6. On the Jewish Club, see Falter and Stachowitsch, '"Denn für uns Juden erhebt sich keine Stimme!"', 47–66; Binder, *Galizien in Wien*, 448–54.

[94] Rechter, *Becoming Habsburg*, 156–8; for his supporters' quotation, see *VW*, 20 Apr. 1911, 2.

[95] Leslie, 'Der Ausgleich in der Bukowina'; Rechter, *Becoming Habsburg*, 146–7.

[96] *JZ*, 11 Mar. 1910, 5.

114   THE CZERNOWITZ YEARS

Although he had indicated his willingness to re-enter the Zionist fray, this was indeed a step change for a man who just a few years earlier had asserted: 'I have always kept my distance from politics and . . . political ambition is entirely alien to me.'[97] But above all Kellner wished to be, as he had said many years before, 'a helper to his people'.[98] Even as he proclaimed his indifference to political ambition, he had maintained that only an 'ossi-fied mummy' could ignore the 'wanton acts' of a Jewish leader who oper-ated 'with innuendo, distortion, intimidation, and incitement'.[99] Straucher, he felt, was precisely such a morally indefensible leader and bore consider-able responsibility for what Kellner described as the 'intolerable condi-tions' in which much of Bukovina Jewry lived, buffeted by 'appalling . . . poverty and helplessness, neglect, and brutalization'.[100] He was correct about the depth and extent of Jewish poverty, which coexisted with a small, thriving urban professional and commercial class in a largely agricul-tural economy.[101] By 1910 Kellner was ready to move from commentary to activism.

He threw himself into a relaunch and reorganization of Bukovina Zionism, recruiting supporters, raising funds, and lecturing throughout the province. For nearly two years he laboured heroically but to no great effect. It was only the direct intervention of the central Zionist office in Berlin in mid-1912 that led to a modest improvement in Zionist fortunes in the region. This was as much as could be expected in the circumstances; the divide between the Zionist organization and the Straucher-dominated Jewish nationalists, along with overlapping personal animosities, was so entrenched as to be unbridgeable.[102] Kellner had no illusions about this, but taking the helm of the local organization was only one aspect of what for him was both a national and a social mission. Just as when he estab-lished the Jewish Toynbee Hall in Vienna a decade earlier, here too nation-alism and social reform went hand in hand. With the Zionist organization almost incapacitated, he instead tried to harness the power of local Jewish nationalism to achieve his goals. In October 1910 he called for the creation

---

[97] *Die Welt*, 26 Jan. 1906, 13.   [98] A. Kellner, *Leon Kellner*, 80.

[99] *Die Welt*, 26 Jan. 1906, 13.   [100] *JV*, 17 Mar. 1911, 2.

[101] On the economic profile of Bukovina Jewry, see Rechter, *Becoming Habsburg*, 117–25.

[102] *Bericht über die Tätigkeit des Bukowiner Landeskomitees in dem Jahre 1910 und 1911*, CZA, Z2/389; *Bericht des zion. Landes-Komitees an die Landeskonferenz, Mai 1912–Okt. 1919*, 1–4, CZA, Z4/0998. See also Rechter, *Becoming Habsburg*, 152–3.

THE CZERNOWITZ YEARS

of an entirely new institution, a Jewish Volksrat, or People's Council, which was to act simultaneously as a Jewish parliament and an executive and administrative body representing Bukovina Jewry in political and civic affairs.[103]

The People's Council was a reality by March 1911, constituted on the basis of Bukovina-wide elections. Its aspirations were grandiose: it was a political party that set up welfare and employment agencies, published its own newspaper, opened a library and a Jewish Toynbee Hall, and provided adult education, legal aid, economic assistance, and childcare. A bold experiment tailored to Bukovina's hyper-nationalized society, the Council—not formally a Zionist body but nevertheless conceived and steered by Zionists—styled itself as the government of a quasi-autonomous Jewish public sphere, with Kellner as its leader. As such, it was an open challenge to the Jewish status quo and precipitated what amounted to a 'civil war', the effects of which were felt throughout Bukovina Jewish society, in political organizations, communal bodies, professional, commercial, and trade associations, student groups and social clubs, at countless raucous public meetings, and in the Jewish and general press. Given the critical Jewish role in local political and economic life, particularly in Czernowitz, conflict also spilled over into parts of the public administration, drawing in municipal and regional authorities.[104]

Kellner was a somewhat reluctant politician. Anna was not keen that he 'plunge into politics'; nor was her mother, who wrote to Leon to warn him that politics would bring him only 'immense agitation . . . You, of all people, who loves nothing more than working quietly at your desk in tranquillity and peace, you want to wade into this battle?'[105] He knew full well that he would be perceived as a newcomer and an outsider, and that he was stepping into a political and social minefield by taking on a powerful local clique. For the next few years he was subjected to incessant insults from Straucher and his partisans. He was a 'bookish Englishman . . . a sanctimonious professor . . . a duplicitous scholar . . . a wretched dissembler', 'one of the greatest political impostors ever seen in Bukovina'.[106] 'Pussyfooting and

[103] *An die Juden der Bukowina*, CZA, Z2/390.

[104] On the Council and this 'civil war' (*VW*, 13 Apr. 1911, 1), see Rechter, *Becoming Habsburg*, 162–75. [105] A. Kellner, *Leon Kellner*, 79.

[106] For the first four phrases, see *VW*, 22 Feb. 1913, 2; for the final quotation, see *VW*, 14 June 1913, 1.

THE CZERNOWITZ YEARS

lisping', he was 'nothing more than an English-language teacher'.[107] 'A furious, ugly, and hate-filled battle rages among Jews throughout the land, and who is the instigator, the disturber of the peace, the fomenter of this hate? . . . Wherever Kellner goes, there you will find strife and hate, dissension and conflict, discord and division.'[108] Reluctant or not, Kellner proved an adept politician and leader, taking charge of the Council's campaigns in a series of bitter electoral contests—for the Kultusgemeinde, the Chamber of Commerce, the municipal council, and the regional and imperial parliaments. A charismatic and eloquent public speaker, he worked tirelessly to rally public support for the Council's reform crusade, the end result of which changed the Jewish political landscape in Bukovina.

In April 1911, following a campaign described in the local press as 'electoral war', Kellner was elected as a Council representative to the Landtag (the regional parliament), catapulting him onto a larger public stage.[109] The regional assembly, with its sixty-three deputies elected on a limited franchise and representing a mixture of collective interests (landowners, chambers of commerce, urban and rural communities) and the general electorate, had influence but limited power. Responsible for administration and oversight of the province's infrastructure, education, transport, finance, and health, it answered to the provincial governor, an imperial appointment, and to Vienna. Notwithstanding its limitations, it was an important political forum in which, particularly from the 1890s, the province's national, economic, and cultural fault lines—including antisemitism—were on display.[110]

By the early twentieth century the national principle dominated the assembly. This was as true of its standing committees, where most of the work was done, as it was of its parties and deliberations. Kellner saw himself principally as a representative of Bukovina Jewry, one of ten Jewish deputies who, if acting in concert, constituted a powerful bloc that the larger Romanian and Ruthenian groups could not afford to ignore. Here

[107] For the first quotation, see *VW*, 20 Apr. 1911, 2; for the second, see *VW*, 24 Dec. 1910, 2.

[108] *VW*, 6 Apr. 1911, 2.

[109] For the quotation, see *Bukowinaer Post*, 2 Apr. 1911, 3. See also *JV*, 28 Apr. 1911, 1–3; *CT*, 28 Apr. 1911, 1, 3–4.

[110] Ceauşu, 'Der Landtag der Bukowina', 2188–98; Hye, 'Die Länder im Gefüge der Habsburgermonarchie', 2455–64. On antisemitism in Bukovina, see Rechter, *Becoming Habsburg*, 142–4; Corbea-Hoisie, '"Wie die Juden Gewalt schreien"'.

THE CZERNOWITZ YEARS

too, though, the poisonous animosities of Bukovina's Jewish politics ensured that cooperation remained a pious hope. The Jewish deputies established a club, the only formal such grouping in any of the empire's regional parliaments, but it was paralysed by antipathy between Straucher and his colleagues. It existed 'only on paper', commented one of the disappointed deputies.[111] The club's dysfunction, Kellner lamented, too often left the Jewish deputies 'without knowledge of the facts, without information, without strategy, without a plan'.[112] As a consequence, the collective Jewish voice on the Landtag's most pressing issues was 'close to zero'.[113]

Nonetheless, Kellner and his colleagues played their part. They were active participants both in the assembly's brief formal sittings—between June 1911 and January 1913 it convened for only three sessions of between one and three weeks each—and in the regular business of committee work, such as preparation of legislation, lobbying, and oversight of public expenditure. Of the three principal issues that occupied the Landtag in these years, two touched on Jewish interests: electoral reform and a change in the system of alcohol production and distribution that threatened the livelihood of the tens of thousands of Jews who had long been a mainstay of the industry. The third, a controversial recovery package for Romanian, Ruthenian, and German agricultural cooperatives that had found themselves in dire straits due to questionable financial practices, was of less direct concern.[114]

In a parliamentary speech in October 1912, interrupted occasionally by antisemitic catcalls, Kellner castigated the 'invidious' and 'unjust' alcohol law, which imposed a crushing financial burden on innkeepers (most of whom were Jews), treating them purely as a source of revenue, rather like 'fiscally useful livestock'.[115] A few months later, he used a speech on electoral reform, again in the face of antisemitic interruptions, to plead the case for Jewish nationality to be recognized formally in the province's electoral system. In the 1910 compromise, as noted, the principle of a Jewish curia had been stymied by the government in Vienna. As part of a reform bill

[111] *JV*, 5 July 1912, 1.
[112] *OW*, 23 Aug. 1912, 563. See also *CAZ*, 14 July 1912, 3; 28 Oct. 1912, 2–3.
[113] *JV*, 5 July 1912, 1. See also *JV*, 1 Nov. 1912, 2–4.
[114] On this last, see Hensellek, *Die letzten Jahre der kaiserlichen Bukowina*, 88–92. See also Dobrshanski, 'Der politische Kampf in der Bukowina'.
[115] *Stenographische Protokolle des Bukowiner Landtages*, 17 Oct. 1912, 158; *JV*, 25 Oct. 1912, 2.

further refining the compromise, Kellner resurrected the idea of a separate Jewish electorate. 'The issue here', he told the parliament in January 1913, 'is to put into effect a clean separation between German and Jewish voters . . . Let Jews and Germans vote separately.' He was pessimistic about the prospects: 'The bill will be forwarded to the central government in Vienna, and one can anticipate that the government will reject it, alas.'[116] His proposal was unanimously adopted by the assembly but was not considered by Vienna before the outbreak of war in the summer of 1914. Mindful always of the larger picture, Kellner took the opportunity in these parliamentary debates to state the Jewish nationalist case in a Habsburg key: it was the Jews' 'greatest misfortune . . . to be a people without land. Not in the historical, political sense that we have no home; that is long since not the case. We are children of Austria; Austria is our home.'[117] The 'Jewish Question', however, was not confined to Austria. Jews were 'good Austrians and good subjects . . . [but] also feel the need to help a landless people, everywhere buffeted, despised, and trampled underfoot, to become settled . . . We want once more to have a land and be settled.'[118] Kellner's speeches expressed an unusual political stance: he was a patriotic regional parliamentarian, elected as the leader of a Jewish nationalist organization intensively engaged with local politics, but affirmed that the 'Jewish Question' could truly be solved only in Palestine.

Although he remained true to Herzl's vision of a homeland secured by international guarantee, he had always been equally invested in the parallel strategy of incremental gains in Palestine (disparaged by purist Herzlians as 'infiltration'). His enthusiasm for what he called 'practical Zionist work in word and deed' was on display, for example, in his regular lectures in support of Bezalel, the Jerusalem art and crafts school established in 1906 (on one occasion speaking alongside its founder Boris Schatz).[119] His most ambitious scheme as leader of Bukovina Zionism went well beyond the

---

[116] *Stenographische Protokolle des Bukowiner Landtages*, 13 Jan. 1913, 235–9; *CAZ*, 14 Jan. 1913 (Mittagsausgabe), 3–4.

[117] *Stenographische Protokolle des Bukowiner Landtages*, 17 Oct. 1912, 160.

[118] *Stenographische Protokolle des Bukowiner Landtages*, 13 Jan. 1913, 237. See also *CAZ*, 14 Jan. 1913 (Mittagsausgabe), 3.

[119] Quotation in *CAZ*, 24 Mar. 1909, 4. See also *Jüdische Volksstimme*, 10 Apr. 1909, 5. For his lectures, see *CT*, 30 Nov. 1907, 4; 28 Mar. 1909, 4–5; *CAZ*, 12 Feb. 1908, 4; *Die Welt*, 28 Jan. 1910, 79; *Jüdische Volksstimme*, 20 July 1909, 4.

THE CZERNOWITZ YEARS

promotion of educational and cultural institutions in Palestine. Soon after his election to the Bukovina parliament in 1911, he called for the creation of a settlement in Palestine to smooth the path of emigration for Bukovina's Jews. A little familiarity, he reasoned, might ease integration into a radically unfamiliar environment. 'We Jews, for all our national solidarity, nonetheless possess locally imbued idiosyncrasies . . . [and] local ties acquired in the diaspora that we preserve with pious tenacity . . . This not only has emotional value but is also of great social significance.' The settlement, to be called 'Bukovina', might attract 'those who believe that the regeneration of our people can only be achieved through the return to the soil and, indeed, to our soil'.[120] With the support of Johann Kremenezky he outlined a plan for a small agricultural colony adjacent to a village or town that could in time absorb the new settlement.[121] Student associations led the way in collecting funds, and the idea attracted attention from beyond Bukovina, including from the German Zionist Davis Trietsch, one of Zionism's leading experts on settlement, but the Bukovina Zionists, their scant resources stretched too thin, abandoned the scheme towards the end of 1912.[122]

Anna and Leon made their first visit (of three) to Palestine in March 1913, a trip of nearly three weeks for which they had long planned and saved.[123] Sailing from Trieste to Alexandria, Leon wrote a panegyric in the *Neues Wiener Tagblatt* to the *Helouan*, one of Austrian Lloyd's largest and newest ships. The voyage on this 'work of art' and 'most beautiful of all steamships' was a world away from the many ferries and ships on which he had travelled to and from England, 'the sole significant memento of which is retained by my nose. The odour with which one is confronted when boarding an English vessel, a diabolic *mixtum compositum* of tar, machine oil, and putrescent seaweed, set my teeth on edge even more than English coffee and English bread.' The *Helouan*'s 'precious illusion of an Olympian existence'—passengers were 'spared the sight of the toil' that created the illusion—was not just a wondrous 'fairyland' but also a monument to Austrian ingenuity. Citing the fulsome compliments of his well-travelled British dining companions, he noted dryly that although 'it is a crime, or at

[120] *JV*, 21 July 1911, 1.   [121] Kellner to Kremenezky, 29 June 1911, CZA, A72/9.
[122] *JV*, 14 June 1912, 2; 9 Aug. 1912, 2–3; *Die Welt*, 24 May 1912, 628–9; 31 May 1912, 664–6; 14 June 1912, 718–19; *Bericht des zion. Landes-Komitees . . . Mai 1912–Okt. 1919*, CZA, Z4/0998.
[123] A. Kellner, *Leon Kellner*, 42; *Die Welt*, 21 Mar. 1913, 379; *CAZ*, 13 Apr. 1913, 4.

least an offence against good taste, to praise an Austrian institution . . . I ask every Austrian: how often do we have the opportunity to hear such accolades about our much-maligned fatherland?'[124] Conspicuous by its absence from his account was any mention of the reason for his journey. Here, as usual, he elided Jewish themes when writing for a general audience.[125]

An overtly patriotic register was not a common feature of Kellner's writing for the press, although an undertone of appreciation for Austria certainly was, and his rare discussions of contemporary politics invariably concerned Anglo-Austrian or Anglo-German relations. Harsh criticism in the British press of Austria's October 1908 annexation of Bosnia, for example, prompted him to write (in English) an 'open letter' in exasperated protest to his friend John Mackinnon Robertson, now a Liberal member of parliament. Robertson asked the leading Liberal London weekly *The Nation* to publish this 'appeal to English Liberals' from 'a good Austrian Liberal'. 'Professor Kellner knows England as few foreigners do; he is actually one of our first philosophical authorities on early English; and every English Liberal will listen to him, I feel sure, with courteous attention.'[126] Kellner's letter, for foreign consumption but soon reprinted in the Viennese press, gave full voice to an unabashed Austrian patriotism, and his 'liberalism' in this instance had a decidedly chauvinistic streak.

'My Dear Robertson', he wrote, 'Mine is a most deplorable position. Till within a few weeks ago I was an Anglomaniac, and gloried in the title; today I am an Anglomaniac still, but have to hide my head in shame . . . my life as an interpreter of English culture in Austria is anything but easy.' Summoning the popular idea of Austria's higher purpose in the east, he insisted that Austria had a 'mission' in eastern Europe.

[124] *NWT*, 22 Mar. 1913, 1–2.
[125] He made exceptions when necessary. In his sympathetic assessment of the social scientist Ignaz Zollschan's book *Das Rassenproblem* (The Problem of Race), he pointed out that the 'Jewish Question' was the basis for Zollschan's 'shattering of Aryan and Germanic race theory', which Kellner thought 'a redemptive act', but he alluded only euphemistically to the fact that Zollschan was Jewish and did not mention that he was a Zionist. See *NWT*, 10 May 1910, 1–3.
[126] *The Nation*, 26 Dec. 1908, 506; *NWT*, 11 Jan. 1909, 1–2.

THE CZERNOWITZ YEARS

It is we Austrians who have wrested Hungary, Transylvania, and other wide provinces from the clutches of barbarism, it is we who . . . have spread order and civilization . . . Austria, whom the English Press preposterously accuses of oppressing race, nationality, and creed, actually stands for freedom of race, nationality, and creed in the East of Europe . . . Austria has been, and is still, the battleground where Poles and Ruthenians, Germans and Czechs, Magyars and Croatians fight it out, not in the old fashion, popular still in Serbia and Turkey, by barbarous bloodshed, and devastation, but according to the English method by ballot and parliamentary debate . . . I do not think there is a spot on God's earth where conflicting races enjoy as much freedom as do the Poles, Ruthenians, Czechs, Roumanians, Croatians, Armenians, in the Austrian Empire. In fact, thoughtful Austrians consider this mission the chief *raison d'être* of our much-tried Austrian Empire.[127]

This was an exceptional outburst on Kellner's part, stating in slightly grotesque form his profound faith in Austria and voicing the patronizing view of Austria's eastern territories that was common among the empire's elites.[128] As a parliamentarian in 1911 he described himself as:

a good subject, a vestige of that era, now almost gone, when every Austrian saw in an Austrian official the embodiment of state justice and in every representative of the emperor the incarnation of the law . . . The impeccable management of state power is the strongest pillar in this ancient edifice, storm-battered but fortunately still weatherproof, this historical necessity, Austria.[129]

This heartfelt belief in the benevolence and rectitude of the Habsburg state, which could lead on occasion to an excess of defensive fervour, was, as has often been noted, a widely shared sentiment among Habsburg Jews.[130]

Even in these years of political activism, he did not neglect his role as 'an interpreter of English culture in Austria'. Describing himself as 'the most suggestible, the most willing reader of novels', he explained why H. G. Wells was unjustly neglected by the German-speaking world; recommended John Galsworthy's recent work, where the reader would find 'more sociological instruction than a voluminous didactic work with historical analysis and statistical tables'; tackled an experimental novel by Olga Wohlbrück, a

---

[127] *NWT*, 11 Jan. 1909, 506–7. He made a less strident plea for Anglo-German reconciliation in a feature article in *NWT*, 10 Apr. 1909, 1–2.

[128] See, for example, Okey, *Taming Balkan Nationalism*, chs. 1 and 2.   [129] *JV*, 1 Dec. 1911, 2.

[130] See, for example, Wistrich, *The Jews of Vienna*, 175–81; Rechter, 'Kaisertreu'.

pioneering film director in Germany; and used James Lane Allen's *The Choir Invisible* to illustrate the pleasures of the American 'regional novel', a genre he thought deserved more attention in Europe.[131] He expounded on dramaturgy and translation in Shakespeare and Shaw; discussed the poetry of Browning and Yeats; argued for the importance of John Mackinnon Robertson's work on the question of Montaigne's influence on Shakespeare; explored the works of the Nietzsche expert Josef Hofmiller, the theatre critic Julius Bab, and the historian of modern drama Wilhelm Creizenach, in a piece on contemporary literary criticism; lauded the 'erudite, almost professorial' new volume on English Romanticism by his friend Helene Richter; and reflected on his own prejudices in recounting that the views of his novelist friend Elizabeth Robins, whose 'rare art . . . reveals vast expanses of uncharted inner life and so enticingly depicts unfamiliar experiences', had persuaded him of the justice of the suffragette cause.[132] Some of this was familiar territory but, careful 'to guard against intellectual sclerosis and ossification', he now and then ventured into less familiar terrain (race, politics, German and French literature). In doing so, he hoped to avoid the 'malignant affliction' of stale thought and prove himself 'able to leave the cherished and well-worn paths of one's own thinking and strike out in new directions'.[133]

This was a challenge he set for himself whatever the forum. When interpreting literature and writing literary history, for example, which he did both for the press and in his scholarship, he was unwilling to be constrained by the genre's 'cast-iron rules'.[134] He aspired to something more; he wished to take into account 'the entire complexity of life . . . to immerse oneself in another soul, to study the surroundings of another individual, to listen

---

[131] For the first quotation, see *NWT*, 17 June 1912 (Abendblatt), 4. On Wells, see *NWT*, 22 Oct. 1909, 1–3. For the quotation on Galsworthy, see *NWT*, 8 Mar. 1910, 2; see also *NWT*, 6 Sept. 1911, 1–2. On Wohlbrück, see *NWT*, 17 June 1912 (Abendblatt), 3–4. On Allen, see *NWT*, 22 July 1912, 1–3.

[132] On Shakespeare, see *NWT*, 28 Oct. 1911, 1–3. On Shaw, see *NWT*, 6 July 1911, 1–3. On Browning, see *CT*, 4 May 1912, 1–2. On Yeats, see *CAZ*, 26 May 1912, 8–9. On literary criticism, see *NWT*, 6 Oct. 1910, 1–3. On Richter, see *NFP*, 16 July 1911, 33–4; 19 Oct. 1913, 31. 'Professorial' was a compliment: Helene Richter did not receive an academic appointment, doubly handicapped as a Jew and a woman. Her sister Elise, also a long-time friend of Kellner, was the first woman to be appointed as a Privatdozentin in a humanities field in Austria. See Freidenreich, *Female, Jewish, and Educated*, 14–15. On Robins, see *NFP*, 21 Sept. 1913, 31.

[133] *NWT*, 6 Oct. 1910, 1.   [134] Kellner, *Geschichte der nordamerikanischen Literatur*, 40.

THE CZERNOWITZ YEARS

in on their emergence and development with devoted, attentive sympathy'. He had tried to apply this 'most difficult and exacting of all methods' in *Die englische Literatur im Zeitalter der Königin Viktoria*.[135] He did so once again in his second major synthetic work, the *Geschichte der nordamerikanischen Literatur* (History of North American Literature), published in 1913 as a kind of companion volume to the previous work. Working from the assumption that literature is an expression of the national soul, the two books used the same template, building an argument about the development of a nation's literature through a series of biographical portraits of its writers, arranged according to chronology and theme. For the second volume, though, Kellner could not claim first-hand experience with the place itself. He had long been fascinated by the United States (it will be recalled that already in the 1890s he had written about Oliver Wendell Holmes and Puritanism) and had read copious amounts of its literature, but he had never visited.

As an introduction and guide for readers without deep knowledge of either the literature or the history of the United States (despite the title, Canada was ignored), the book was warmly welcomed for the most part, and an English-language version was published (as *American Literature*) in New York in 1915. Surveys of this sort were few and far between. The Viennese-born American writer and editor Gustav Pollak remarked in the introduction to the English edition that 'American letters have hitherto received but scant justice at the hands of German scholars'.[136] Of 'histories devoted wholly to American literature', wrote another American reviewer, Kellner's was 'the most pithy and vigorously written of them all . . . [and] has more worth perhaps than any other German survey of the subject'.[137] Particularly valuable was his perspective as an outsider and his independence of judgement: 'To the American the book is especially interesting as showing us ourselves as others see us.'[138] Kellner read American literature 'through the eyes of a European at once sympathetic, intelligent, [and] learned . . . Here, one feels, is practically no echoing of other critics.' The outsider's perspective, though, was a double-edged sword, as the reader was aware throughout that Kellner is 'a foreigner, consciously estimating

---

[135] *NWT*, 6 Oct. 1910, 3.   [136] Kellner, *American Literature*, p. vii.
[137] Nelson, 'Some German Surveys', 154, 160. See also *NFP*, 23 Nov. 1913, 34–5.
[138] *The Mississippi Valley Historical Review*, 2 (Mar. 1916), 594.

the accomplishments of a people and land not his own'.[139] The book was not unlike the 'photograph album of a tourist, filled with scenes from American letters and with the faces of more than a hundred writers', although this reviewer tempered his assessment by allowing that 'many of these studies are careful, accurate, and loving' and adding that Kellner was 'unusually gracious toward woman writers'.[140] H. L. Mencken, notoriously caustic and no great friend of the Jews, appreciated Kellner's attention to Puritanism—which Mencken famously defined as 'the haunting fear that someone, somewhere may be happy'—and thought his work 'an excellent little history of American literature' (although he described Kellner as a man of 'half-European, half-Oriental culture').[141] One of Kellner's central premises, however, met with a measure of scepticism. 'In comparing the history of the United States with its literature', Kellner wrote, 'one is struck with great force by the contrast between word and deed, between experience and representation . . . When has the human will achieved more in so brief a time? . . . [But] American literature lags far behind American history.' It lacked, he believed, the 'epic' qualities to match the epic scale of its accomplishments and its 'immense power'.[142] Reviewers looked askance at this suggestion. 'The whole book is a stimulus', acknowledged one, but its 'main thesis—the inadequacy of our literary expression—is not sustained . . . Our literature has a spiritual unity—which Professor Kellner somehow has missed.'[143] Decades later, no less a critic and writer than Alfred Kazin, in his landmark study of American literature, saw Kellner's book as a 'sophisticated' work that had been part of the 'spirit of a new interpretation of American literature'.[144]

In the years following the demise of *Bausteine* in 1906, Kellner had focused his scholarly energies on his two expansive works of literary his-

[139] Nelson, 'Some German Surveys', 159–60.

[140] *The Mississippi Valley Historical Review*, 2 (Mar. 1916), 594.

[141] Mencken, 'Puritanism as a Literary Force', 197, 205. The *New York Times* approved of Kellner's treatment of Oliver Wendell Holmes and Mark Twain (6 June 1915, Book Review section, 212). See also Fulton, who observes that Kellner's 'insightful discussion' enhanced Twain's 'international reputation' ('Contemporary and Early Reception', 297–8).

[142] Kellner, *Geschichte der nordamerikanischen Literatur*, 5–7.

[143] *The English Journal*, 4 (Nov. 1915), 618. See also *The Mississippi Valley Historical Review*, 2 (Mar. 1916), 594. For a rare negative American review, see *The Nation*, 20 July 1916, 64–5.

[144] Kazin, *On Native Grounds*, 155. Shurr called it 'one of the more interesting and eloquent formulations of American literary culture' (*Rappaccini's Children*, 10–11).

tory.[145] With these now complete, he turned once more to Shakespeare. From the very beginning of his career he had been perplexed by the textual ambiguities and challenges in Shakespeare's drama and poetry, by the many 'opaque passages' in need of 'clarification', as Anna expressed it. Convinced that the problem lay with the process of transcription and transmission of the manuscripts, he embarked upon a grand project—some might call it a folly—of elucidation and 'correction', aiming to produce a kind of Masoretic Shakespeare text. He began in earnest in the summer of 1913, using a generous grant awarded by the Academy of Sciences in Vienna to finance a long stay in London from November 1913 to April 1914, where, with Anna's invaluable help, he immersed himself in the systematic examination of Elizabethan handwriting.[146] The close philological and palaeographical study of Shakespearean texts was to be at the heart of his scholarship for the remainder of his life.

He first needed, however, to discharge another debt. For some years he had been working intermittently on a biography of Herzl, commissioned by the Zionist leadership in Cologne. At their request he had earlier edited a collection of Herzl's Zionist writings, published in the summer of 1905. It had not been an entirely happy experience, as he had been obliged to bow to pressure from Max Nordau and David Wolffsohn (the latter now president of the World Zionist Organization) to omit material they wished to keep out of the public domain.[147] For the biography, too, he did not have an entirely free hand. Wolffsohn was adamant that he would not consent to publish anything 'that diminished Herzl's reputation or painted him as a schlemiel'.[148] Chafing at the restrictions and pressed for time, Kellner

[145] Supplemented by occasional brief essays and reviews; see e.g. the pieces on English Romanticism in *Das literarische Echo*, 14 (1911–12), 310–11; on Shakespeare, ibid. 15 (1912–13), 469–75 and in *Englische Studien*, 46 (1912–13), 130–3; on English 'suffragette literature' in *Das literarische Echo*, 16 (1913–14), 155–63; and on Nietzsche in England, ibid. 1174–5. He also contributed to a book outlining Austrian history and society for an English-reading audience, written in the main by his daughter Paula; Kellner, Arnold, and Delisle, *Austria of the Austrians*.

[146] A. Kellner, *Leon Kellner*, 88–90; *Die Welt*, 1 Aug. 1913, 998.

[147] For example, Herzl's address to the Rothschilds and selections from his mania-induced jottings of June and July 1895, written as *Der Judenstaat* took shape in his imagination. These 'dubiously rational aphorisms' (Penslar, *Theodor Herzl*, 74) constituted in Kellner's view the 'best annotations' to *Der Judenstaat*. See Kellner, *Theodor Herzl's Zionistische Schriften*, ii. 292. See also *NWT*, 11 June 1905, 32–3; *Die Welt*, 21 July 1905, 29–30; 3 July 1914, 660–3.

[148] Wolffsohn to Kremenezky, 7 Jan. 1914, CZA, A74/7.

126 THE CZERNOWITZ YEARS

recruited his friend Felix Salten, later best known as the author of *Bambi*, as co-author in 1913, but their collaboration soon ran into difficulties. In March 1914 it was only Kremenezky's entreaties that persuaded him not to abandon the work, which was at that point almost complete.[149] Even so, he was anxious about the task, telling Kremenezky 'I fear it will be too much for me'.[150]

The pressure of so many concurrent commitments was taking a toll, not for the first time. In March 1912 he had indicated to the central Zionist office in Berlin that he wished to step down as leader of Bukovina Zionism.[151] He remained in post, however, until the war, although the Bukovina Zionists granted him a three-month leave of absence from his duties to enable his extended research stay in London.[152] Writing from London in March 1914 he admitted despairingly to Wolffsohn: 'I have had a great deal to do with public life in recent years and I have become unhealthy, emotionally unhealthy, as a consequence. The blame lies not with public life but with my temperament. I am retreating to my scholarly mouse hole. Any responsibility in public life is a torment for me.'[153] 'I am very, very tired', he wrote to Kremenezky from Berlin in June 1914, where, having returned to Vienna from London in April, he was once more attending to Zionist business.[154] Torment and exhaustion notwithstanding, the habit of many years was difficult to break, and it was as true now as it had been thirty years before that he wanted to be 'a helper to his people'. A prominent figure by this time in Czernowitz and Vienna, he was a parliamentarian, the leader of Bukovina Zionism, creator and leader of the Jewish People's Council and the Jewish Toynbee Hall in Czernowitz, a celebrated essayist whose work appeared regularly in the press at home and abroad, and a respected university professor with an international reputation.[155] Kellner was now one of

[149] Kremenezky to Kellner, 4 Nov. 1913; 6 Mar. 1914; 28 Mar. 1914; Kellner to Kremenezky, 30 Mar. 1914, all in CZA, A72/9; Wolffsohn to Kellner, 26 Apr. 1914, CZA, W1/789.

[150] Kellner to Kremenezky, 30 Mar. 1914, CZA, A72/9.

[151] Zionistisches Zentralbureau Berlin to Kellner, 28 Mar. 1912, CZA, Z3/786.

[152] *Die Welt*, 11 July 1913, 898; *CAZ*, 16 Nov. 1913, 4. Far from withdrawing, he was elected to West Austrian Zionism's Palestine Commission and attended the meeting of the World Organization's Greater Actions Committee in Berlin in the summer of 1914; *Die Welt*, 10 Sept. 1913, 122; 12 June 1914, 573. [153] Kellner to Wolffsohn, 13 Mar. 1914, CZA, A72/9.

[154] Kellner to Kremenezky, 17 June 1914, CZA, A72/9.

[155] The press took note, for example, of the marriage of his daughters or his presence at

THE CZERNOWITZ YEARS

the great and good of late imperial Austria, at one and the same time a public intellectual, politician, and scholar.

events; see e.g. *NFP*, 20 Oct. 1905, 5; 4 July 1909, 33–5; 11 Apr. 1910, 8; 3 July 1912, 8; 23 Nov. 1913, 34–5; 24 Aug. 1914, 3. His other civic commitments included a leading role in associations promoting Hebrew education (see *CAZ*, 23 Sept. 1913, 4), girls' employment (see *CAZ*, 8 Feb. 1912, 4; 27 Mar. 1913, 3), educational reform (see *NFP*, 9 June 1914, 11), and a Bukovina association in Vienna (see *CAZ*, 3 Feb. 1913, 3; 15 Mar. 1914, 4; 19 May 1914, 4).

SIX

POST-HABSBURG TWILIGHT

THE OUTBREAK OF WAR at the end of July 1914 found Kellner in Vienna. He was to return to Czernowitz just once more, when the university opened briefly in the early summer of 1916. Russian troops marched into Czernowitz in early September 1914, the first of three Russian occupations before the Austrians finally secured the city in August 1917. The first two periods of Russian rule, up to February 1915, were nasty, brutish, and short—a matter of months; the third, beginning in June 1916, lasted just over a year. The Russians deported local leaders, crippled the city's infrastructure, and terrorized its residents, tens of thousands of whom fled westward within the empire, part of a mass Austrian exodus from Galicia and Bukovina. By the summer of 1917 more than half the city's population had left.[1] The story was similar across Galicia and Bukovina, as the Russians, in control of large parts of both provinces, installed a regime of terror that singled out Jews for particularly savage treatment. Confronted by arbitrary executions, violent pogroms, rape, wholesale expulsions, and destruction and looting of homes and property, some 400,000 Jews headed west.[2] Almost 150,000 reached Vienna before the end of 1914. Many returned home as territory changed hands between Russia and Austria in the course of the war, but at least 20,000 remained in Vienna at the war's end.[3] Living conditions in the city during the war years were miserable, although infinitely superior to the devastated towns and cities of Galicia and Bukovina. Food was scarce and of poor quality, prices spiralled, wages stagnated, crime increased, disease was rife, and municipal services—gas, electricity, public transport—were severely curtailed.[4]

---

[1] Masan, 'Czernowitz in Vergangenheit und Gegenwart', 30–2. For contemporary accounts, see Menczel, *Als Geisel nach Sibirien verschleppt*, 15–31; Weber, *Die Russentage in Czernowitz*.

[2] Hagen, *Anti-Jewish Violence*, chs. 1 and 2; Mentzel, 'Die Flüchtlingspolitik', 127–46. A firsthand Jewish account is An-ski, *The Destruction of Galicia* (Yid.), vols. iv to vi.

[3] Hoffmann-Holter, 'Abreisendmachung'; Rechter, *The Jews of Vienna*, ch. 2.

[4] Healy, *Vienna and the Fall of the Habsburg Empire*, ch. 1; Boyer, *Culture and Political Crisis*, 419–28.

For Kellner, the beginning of the war marked the end of his political career, both as regional parliamentarian and Zionist leader. He took the opportunity afforded by the abrupt halt to nearly all formal political activity in the first period of the war to withdraw to his 'scholarly mouse hole'. After decades of working at high intensity on multiple fronts, at considerable cost to his physical and emotional health, not only was the spirit less willing but the flesh was now weak. He had in any case been almost an accidental politician; it had only been the uniquely troubled circumstances of Bukovina Jewry, along with his near-obsessive sense of duty, that had prompted him to assume a political role that placed him squarely in the public eye. He had long protested that politics was not his true métier, and Anna's mother's warning that it would bring him 'immense agitation' had proved prescient. As he had told Herzl in 1901, there was too much 'noise' in political activism, and the malevolence of Bukovina Jewish politics only magnified his aversion.[5] Cut off from Czernowitz and with politics in a temporary deep freeze, the time had come for him to make a change. The pendant to being a 'helper to his people' was his aspiration to be 'a servant to knowledge'.[6] Circumstances now permitted a shift from the former to the latter.

Kellner's withdrawal from politics soon became apparent. Nominally at the helm of Bukovina Zionism, he was absent in early 1915 when Austrian Zionist leaders gathered in Vienna, where many had taken refuge, to form a united front to steer the movement for the war's duration.[7] By the end of that year, he had ceded the leadership of Bukovina Zionism to his former deputy, Theodor Weisselberger.[8] In the summer of 1917 members of the Bukovina parliament's Jewish Club announced in Vienna that they had resolved their differences and had established a united party, to be led by Straucher. Kellner, the leader of the People's Council, took no part in these discussions. With Bukovina a theatre of war, the People's Council subsided into irrelevance and Kellner played no role in the new Bukovina party.[9] He retreated not just from politics but from almost all public engagement, giving very few lectures (opportunities were in any case much reduced as a

---

[5] For Anna's mother, see A. Kellner, *Leon Kellner*, 79. For 'noise', see Bein, *Theodor Herzl: Briefe und Tagebücher*, ii. 584.   [6] A. Kellner, *Leon Kellner*, 80.

[7] *JZ*, 19 Feb. 1915, 1. See also *JZ*, 5 May 1916, 1.   [8] *JZ*, 12 Nov. 1915, 3.

[9] *JZ*, 28 Sept. 1917, 1–2; *CAZ*, 25 Sept. 1917, 3–4. See also *OW*, 3 May 1918, 262–3; 5 July 1918, 417.

consequence of the strictures imposed on civic life during the war) and writing almost nothing for the press.[10] His need for a respite was such that he remained aloof even from the refugee support effort, notwithstanding his lifelong devotion to the cause of social welfare and the considerable experience he had accumulated in the course of his work in the Baron Hirsch Foundation, the Israelitische Allianz, and the Jewish Toynbee Halls. Both the state and Jewish organizations poured resources into a huge network of institutions catering to the needs of the refugees in the city, many of whom were without means of support. Kellner, however, no longer had the required energy and drive for any of this; he wanted instead to immerse himself in his Shakespeare research.

The university in Czernowitz managed a partial reopening in late 1915, the Russians having left the city in February, but most teaching resumed only in May 1916.[11] The resumption was hailed as confirmation of Austrian civilization:

In a city at whose gates the massed armies of two great empires confront one another, in a city whose walls tremble from the thunder of cannons, above whose roofs ferocious air battles take place and in whose streets bombs rain down ... in a city at the front—a university is reopened! ... Our enemies have called us "barbarians" and have accused us of savagery and lack of culture ... But now we answer them by opening a university, just a few kilometres from the front and almost in range of the cannons. This answer is so compelling, so eloquent, that even the enemy, deeply ashamed, must finally fall silent.[12]

The enemy, however, was unimpressed.

Kellner arrived in Czernowitz at the beginning of April 1916. As university buildings had been converted into military hospitals, classes in makeshift premises began in mid-May to the incessant accompaniment of the sounds of nearby war. Day and night, 'the thunder of cannons, the

---

[10] On the strictures, see Deak and Gumz, 'How to Break a State'. On lectures, see *NFP*, 26 Mar. 1915, 9; 16 Feb. 1918 (Abendblatt), 1.

[11] The theology faculty was the first to resume; see *CT*, 15 Oct. 1915, 4; 13 May 1916, 3.

[12] *CT*, 14 May 1916, 2. See also *CT*, 7 June 1916, 3.

shooting, the noise of planes' disturbed lectures and sleep. Cannon fire, said Kellner in an interview with the *Neue Freie Presse*, provided the punctuation to his lectures.[13] On 4 June, just as the teachers and their students —over 100 but far fewer than usual—had accustomed themselves to the ever-present sound of artillery, planes, and vehicles, the Russian army launched an offensive, the consequences of which were felt within days in Czernowitz. In the course of the following week, Russian shrapnel fell and the streets filled with ambulances carrying wounded soldiers and with refugees from towns in northern Bukovina. 'Fear pervaded the city . . . At night we saw mighty bursts of gunfire' and Czernowitz was 'illuminated by the glare of rocket flares and burning villages. The entire horizon was a sea of flames.' Unable to offer anything useful to those who were 'fighting, suffering, starving, thirsty, and bleeding', Kellner felt keenly 'the excruciatingly humiliating awareness of one's own superfluousness' in such a situation. Scholarship 'might be justified in a time of lofty refinement and peaceful coexistence but today, in the midst of the horror of the most terrible of all wars, it has the appearance of . . . the corpse of a long-defunct cultural mission'. Teaching in these circumstances was equally difficult. 'The semester brought little benefit to the students and little pleasure to us.' There was no escape from the 'monstrous experience' of the war. 'We may not have taught very much', concluded Kellner, 'but we have learned a great deal.'[14]

Fear did not preclude curiosity. Kellner was permitted to visit a battlefield adjacent to the city, from where he could see the Russian positions. He reported reassuringly on the 'obvious confidence' of the Austrian defenders among the dugouts and barbed wire, and took home a six-and-a-half-pound detonator fragment retrieved from a bomb crater as a souvenir. A week after the offensive began, the professors were ordered to evacuate, with only a few hours' notice. With no transport available, Kellner carried his suitcases crammed with books and papers and, along with his colleagues, boarded a cattle wagon heading south. A week later, as the Austrians surrendered Czernowitz to the Russians, the exhausted professors arrived in Vienna, having endured a stop-and-start rail journey of over 600 miles. At one point, Kellner had walked for six hours with his luggage through a mountain pass in the Southern Carpathians near the Hungarian

[13] *NFP*, 19 June 1916, 2.   [14] *NFP*, 20 June 1916, 2–3.

border.[15] No sooner had he arrived in Vienna than he learned that his son, Viktor, had been taken prisoner by the Russians at the Battle of Lutsk in Russian Ukraine in early June, part of the offensive that had driven Kellner from Czernowitz. Viktor had volunteered in 1915, interrupting his agronomy studies at the Deutsche Kolonialschule für Landwirtschaft, Handel und Gewerbe (German Colonial School for Agriculture, Trade, and Industry) in Witzenhausen in north-eastern Hesse. After a year in a prison camp near Lake Baikal in eastern Siberia, he escaped and made his way across Russia to Vienna, arriving in May 1918.[16]

None of this shook Kellner's faith in the Austrian cause. He had already articulated a spirited defence of Austria in an open letter to his American publisher, the writer and editor Christopher Morley of Doubleday in New York. Morley had suggested that Kellner, 'a scholar at a German university in the easternmost recess of the Austro-Hungarian monarchy', might wish to explain in the American press the attitude of the 'German republic of letters' towards the war. Kellner responded that he was incensed by the Anglo-American characterization of Austria and Germany as 'outlaws', no longer fit to be considered as civilized nations. His experience at the university in Czernowitz proved otherwise (at least for Austria):

Until the outbreak of the war, the professors—Germans, Romanians, Ruthenians, Slovenes—lived together in harmonious collaboration, devoted solely to their research and attentive to the welfare of the students entrusted to them. Do the Americans consider a state under whose umbrella four nations sheltered peacefully for forty years so reprehensible that it must be struck off the list of civilized nations? Was it with coercion and violence that the Austrian double eagle bound together the nations commended to its protection, or are they good Austrians because they are secure under our emperor, because they see him as the patron of the freedom and rights of the small and weak?

Could the same be said, he asked, of the English treatment of different nationalities in Welsh and Irish universities? As for the war, he dutifully trotted out the standard Austrian justification: 'We were encircled by enemies.'[17]

[15] His accounts are in *NFP*, 19 June 1916, 2–3; 20 June 1916, 1–3; *NWT*, 20 June 1916, 2–3. See also A. Kellner, *Leon Kellner*, 36, 163.

[16] Arnold, *Memoirs* (Heb.), 49–50, 88; A. Kellner, *Leon Kellner*, 85; id., 'Unsere Mutter' (1925), 222; *NFP*, 6 Apr. 1918, 19.   [17] *NWT*, 11 Jan. 1916, 8.

Now, in the wake of the debacle in Czernowitz, he reiterated his view that the war had demonstrated the merits of Austrian culture and statecraft. 'Without exaggeration it can be said that we have battled for two years against the entire world and that we have managed to keep the entire world at bay.' Just as the Greeks vanquished the Persians at Marathon and the Maccabees resisted the Hellenizing Seleucid empire, the Austrians remained confident that they would eventually prevail against overwhelming Russian firepower due to their 'spiritual superiority'. '[T]he genius of our leaders and the spirit of our army has time and again defeated the all-powerful enemy and driven it from our territory . . . Is it so inconceivable that our leaders are better acquainted with the science of war than the generals of our enemies?'[18] On a trip to Berlin in late September 1916, he observed that the German soldiers he encountered displayed what he thought of as 'English' qualities: 'the much-vaunted sangfroid . . . the calm awareness of strength, the self-imposed austerity, the depth, the taciturnity, the boundless self-sacrifice—all that made England what it is the Germans today possess in abundance. Perhaps these are not the virtues of a given race, but the traits of a rising nation.' He detected defiance and patriotic fervour even among those of his friends who had previously 'indignantly rejected patriotism and similarly outmoded sentiments'. One such friend, 'a perpetually carping enemy of the state, a sober intellectual', reported that the actions of 'our friends, the English gentlemen' were enough to 'turn even Tolstoy into a warmonger'. Like Kellner, this 'cosmopolitan' was an Anglophile, furiously building his case against the English enemy by quoting Shakespeare's *Troilus and Cressida* and urging Germans to emulate the moral fortitude of Charles Booth's Salvation Army.[19]

These were uncontentious morale-boosting contributions to public discourse at a time when the censors restricted critical voices.[20] Even so, Kellner was not dissembling. Always a patriot, though not an uncritical one, he believed fervently in the righteousness of Austria's cause and the bad faith of its enemies. With the state's very existence under threat, this was not the appropriate time for criticism. 'Will we withstand the world's onslaught?' he asked.[21] It was not difficult for him to conceive of Russia as an enemy, not just of Austria but also of the Jews. But as one of Austria's

---

[18] *NWT*, 20 June 1916, 2–3.

[19] *NWT*, 1 Oct. 1916, 4–6.

[20] Healy, *Vienna and the Fall of the Habsburg Empire*, 126–41.

[21] *NWT*, 1 Oct. 1916, 6.

most prominent Anglicists, for decades a one-man cultural exchange programme between Britain and German-speaking Europe, Kellner was caught in a terrible bind. He could no more disown his lifelong passion for all things English than he could disengage from his homeland Austria.[22] The war brought these two central, intertwined threads of his life into painful and insoluble conflict.

In August 1917 the Austrians recaptured Czernowitz from the Russians for the third and final time. The university's theology faculty restarted classes in January 1918, followed by the law faculty in mid-May, although neither was at full strength.[23] Kellner was elected dean of the third faculty, philosophy, in July 1918, although there was no immediate prospect of this faculty resuming work.[24] The city's chronic wartime insecurity had given rise to periodic discussion about relocation of the university to Salzburg (with the exception of the Greek Orthodox theology faculty, which was of particular local importance) as a means of better securing the future of this 'bastion of German culture and learning'.[25] The idea received serious consideration but foundered in the face of vocal resistance in Czernowitz and from Graz and Innsbruck, where the universities feared potential competition.[26] In March 1918 government and university authorities instead signalled their intention to open the entire university as normal at the end of the year.[27] As imperial authority crumbled in October, however, the university's plans came to look ever more unrealistic, and Kellner, along with many of his Czernowitz colleagues, opted to remain in Vienna.

By mid-November, Czernowitz was in Romanian hands, the Habsburg state had collapsed, and Vienna was the capital of the new 'Republic of German-Austria'. The end of Habsburg rule precipitated a lengthy period of turmoil on many fronts, abruptly confronting millions of people with political uncertainty and economic distress. This was change of un-

[22] He was not alone in this, of course; see Klein, 'Austrian (and some German) Scholars of English'.   [23] NFP, 15 Feb. 1918 (Abendblatt), 3; 8 June 1918 (Abendblatt), 3.
[24] ATUW, Personalakt Leon Kellner; NWT, 18 July 1918, 5.   [25] CAZ, 1 May 1918, 1.
[26] Staudigl-Ciechowicz, 'Zwischen Wien und Czernowitz', 230–2; Scharr, '"Eine überaus peinliche Lage"', 173–5.
[27] NFP, 16 Mar. 1918, 10; 8 June 1918 (Abendblatt), 3; CAZ, 17 Apr. 1918, 3; 24 Apr. 1918, 3.

imagined magnitude. For Jews, the loss of the Habsburg state was a seismic shock, and they were prominent among those who expressed regret at the passing of the old order. In October 1918 a liberal Jewish notable in Vienna declared that Jews 'were without exception and regardless of affiliation true and authentic Austrians', and he worried that this was a 'new Tishah Be'av', the latest link in the long chain of Jewish tragedies. He voiced a widespread Jewish lament: 'We bid farewell to the united fatherland . . . and we stand shaken at the grave.'[28] This kind of imperial patriotism had long been a commonplace of Jewish discourse and had been a binding force in an otherwise fractious Habsburg Jewish society.

Not only had many Jews been dynastic patriots par excellence but their post-Habsburg affiliation was far from straightforward. Unlike other ethnic and national groups in the successor states, they were a non-territorial minority who could claim no land as their own. Consequently, the process of adaptation to, and identification with, the new states in which they now found themselves was particularly fraught. Bukovina's Jews were incorporated into what for them was a culturally alien Romania. Slovakian Jews, long accustomed to Hungarian sovereignty—one Slovak politician in 1920 believed them to be 'one hundred percent Magyarized'—were now required to become loyal Czechoslovaks, as were Bohemian and Moravian Jews.[29] Bosnia's Jews also needed to adapt to an entirely new state, Yugoslavia. For some, the transition was less problematic: many of Galicia's Jews, now in 'reborn' Poland, were familiar with Polish politics and culture (and antisemitism), and the Jews of Trieste, now Italian citizens, had long been Italian in many other respects.[30] For the most part, the new political and cultural loyalties demanded of Jews by the successor states developed only gradually, grafted on to long-standing Habsburg foundations.[31]

These dilemmas were acute for the university in Czernowitz in the immediate post-war months. Its *raison d'être* as a German university was

[28] *OW*, 25 Oct. 1918, 673. For similar, see *OW*, 22 June 1917, 390; 20 July 1917, 454–5; *JZ*, 7 June 1918, 1; 9 Aug. 1918, 1.

[29] For the comment in 1920, see Klein-Pejšová, *Mapping Jewish Loyalties*, 2. See also Lichtenstein, *Zionists in Interwar Czechoslovakia*.

[30] Freidenreich, *The Jews of Yugoslavia*, esp. chs. 1, 4, and 8; Livezeanu, *Cultural Politics in Greater Romania*, ch. 2; Catalan, *La Comunità ebraica di Trieste*, esp. chs. 2, 8, and 12.

[31] These loyalties remained alive in the realm of affect and sentiment, and not just for Jews. See Moos, *Habsburg Post Mortem*; Kożuchowski, *The Afterlife of Austria-Hungary*.

at risk in an unstable Bukovina claimed both by Romania and the short-lived West Ukrainian People's Republic.[32] In mid-December, Kellner and the other professors who had remained in Vienna—around a third of the total—asked the Ministry of Education in the new German-Austrian government for advice and reassurance about 'the fate of the university', which was now open: were they obliged to return to Czernowitz (if transport became available) to resume work, or should they wait in Vienna until further notice? And what of their salaries?[33] It became clear before long that a return to Czernowitz was neither feasible nor advisable. Their German-speaking colleagues in the city were anxious and despondent, alarmed by the Romanian government's declaration in February 1919 that the university was to be an entirely Romanian-language institution by the end of the year. Those unwilling or unable to adapt faced dismissal.[34] Professor Hans von Frisch, the dean of the law faculty, welcomed students in February with the distressing news that they were 'boarding a sinking ship'. Kellner's replacement as dean of the philosophy faculty, Professor Eugen Herzog, was equally pessimistic, telling students that the 'fate of the German university of Czernowitz appears to be sealed'.[35]

The following month, the professors, Kellner among them, addressed a lengthy plea to Vienna. It was clear, they wrote, that the 'German university in Czernowitz is at an end'. Their future was 'utterly hopeless' and it was the Vienna government's 'moral and cultural duty' to rescue them from 'an unworthy, abject, and undeserved position'. They suggested two options, both of which had been under discussion since late 1918: the government should either establish a new university or redeploy them at existing universities.[36] Soon after, Frisch reported to the government in Vienna that 'from week to week, from month to month, our position becomes increasingly dismal and precarious, and prospects for the immediate future are extremely inauspicious . . . We are occupied by a chauvinistic enemy who reminds us daily that he is the victor; we Germans have become a toler-

[32] Livezeanu, *Cultural Politics in Greater Romania*, 56–60.

[33] Verhandlungsschrift, Staatsamt für Unterricht, 17 Dec. 1918, OS, AV/5C/Cz, Zl. 12230.

[34] Scharr, '"Eine überaus peinliche Lage"', 176; Staudigl-Ciechowicz, 'Zwischen Wien und Czernowitz', 232–3.

[35] For Frisch, see *CAZ/CT*, 2 Feb. 1919, 3. For Herzog, see *CAZ/CT*, 5 Feb. 1919, 1.

[36] Denkschrift über die Lage der deutschen Professoren der Universität Czernowitz, Mar. 1919, OS, AV/5C/Cz, Zl. 12230.

ated national minority who must acquiesce.' In Romanian hands, thought Frisch, Bukovina had become 'a land of profiteering and corruption', and he reminded the government of the promise made to the German professors in December 1918 by Franz Dinghofer, one of the new state's troika of presidents: German-Austria, Dinghofer had declared, 'would never abandon them'.[37]

Dinghofer's declaration was in keeping with the government's undertaking in late 1918 that it would assume responsibility for the university personnel 'of German nationality', although what this meant in practice would take many months to become clear.[38] Save for a handful who accepted the Romanians' conditions, the professors, including those still in Vienna such as Kellner, were dismissed from their posts in September 1919, by which time the Treaty of Saint-Germain-en-Laye had ratified Bukovina's incorporation into Romania.[39] Even before this the government had begun efforts to redeploy them, as neither the resources nor the will existed to create a new university in a new state struggling to establish itself. In June the Ministry of Education asked universities to consider the 'interim employment' of the Czernowitz professors. Mindful of university autonomy, this was phrased as a request rather than an instruction, and the ministry promised to absorb all costs.[40] Responses ranged from lukewarm to dismissive. Frisch had predicted as much, writing to the ministry in early May: 'we are sure that the German-Austrian faculties will not welcome us with open arms'.[41] The University of Vienna's faculty of philosophy, for example, expressed concern that their Czernowitz colleagues were not at the appropriate 'scholarly level'.[42] In Innsbruck, the dean of the philosophy faculty,

---

[37] Bericht über die gegenwärtige Lage der deutschen Professoren, wissenschaftlichen Hilfskräfte und Beamten an der Universität Czernowitz, 1 June 1919, OS, AV/5C/Cz, Zl. 12231.

[38] Staudigl-Ciechowicz, 'Zwischen Wien und Czernowitz', 232–3; Bericht über die gegenwärtige Lage der deutschen Professoren, 1 June 1919, OS, AV/5C/Cz, Zl. 12231. On the new state's policies towards the empire's civil servants, see Deak, 'Fashioning the Rest'.

[39] Scharr, '"Eine überaus peinliche Lage"', 178; CAZ/CT, 27 July 1919, 4; 3 Sept. 1919, 1. The treaty also stipulated that the German-Austrian republic change its name to the 'Republic of Austria'.

[40] Ministry of Education to Prof. Geitler, 18 June 1919, OS, AV/5C/Cz, Zl. 12230; Ministry of Education to Prof. Frisch, 10 July 1919, OS, AV/5C/Cz, Zl. 12196; Scharr, '"Eine überaus peinliche Lage"', 180 n. 48. [41] Frisch to Hofrat Maurus, 2 May 1919, OS, AV/5C/Cz, Zl. 6154.

[42] Report for the Staatsamt für Inneres und Unterricht, 29 Aug. 1919, OS, AV/5C/Cz, Zl. 13359.

138 POST-HABSBURG TWILIGHT

citing the 'mood of the local students', was even more blunt: 'Jewish professors cannot be taken on here.' They 'would face difficulties in the singular Tirolean circumstances', and their presence would disturb the faculty's 'calm and peaceful work'.[43]

During the course of the next year, most of the professors found academic positions of one sort or another, although some were shunted into early retirement.[44] Kellner, along with the handful of other Jews, fared poorly; not a single university was willing to find a place for him.[45] Since Vienna had been Kellner's home for almost forty years, relocation at the age of 60 was in any event unlikely. Even as a professor, Zionist leader, and parliamentarian in Bukovina, he had generally spent more time in Vienna than in Czernowitz. The University of Vienna, in response to Kellner's request in November 1919 that he at least be permitted to teach, made it plain that it had no interest in him even as a cost-free teacher. Worse, he would not be considered as a candidate for a chair in English literature which was vacant following the retirement of his teacher Jakob Schipper in 1913.[46] Kellner had told Herzl twenty years previously that a chair in Vienna would be a 'miracle', and this prize remained frustratingly out of reach. The case against Kellner was made by Karl Luick, with whom Kellner was well acquainted. Both men had studied with Schipper in the 1880s and had received simultaneous appointments as Privatdozenten in Vienna in 1890, after which their career paths had diverged.[47] Luick, professor of English literature in Vienna (alongside Schipper) since 1908, now wrote a lengthy and unequivocally damning assessment of Kellner's work.

Kellner's early work on syntax was original, Luick acknowledged, but lacked depth and was prone to error. His edition of Morris's *Historical Out-*

[43] Dekan der philosophischen Fakultät an das Staatsamt für Inneres und Unterricht, 11 July 1919, OS, AV/5C/Cz, Zl. 13359 and 26 Mar. 1920, OS, AV/5C/Cz, Zl. 146800. See also Scharr, '"Eine überaus peinliche Lage"', 180–2.

[44] Staudigl-Ciechowicz, 'Die österreichische Universitätslandschaft um 1918', 651–4; Scharr, '"Eine überaus peinliche Lage"', 182.

[45] Report for the Staatsamt für Inneres und Unterricht, 29 Aug. 1919, OS, AV/5C/Cz, Zl. 13359.

[46] Staatsamt für Inneres und Unterricht to Dekanat der philosophischen Fakultät der Universität in Wien, 20 Nov. 1919, AUW, PUW/2172, Zl. 2438/8; Protokol, Dekanskanzlei meeting, 18 Dec. 1919; Dekan der philosophischen Fakultät to Staatsamt für Inneres und Unterricht, 27 Jan. 1920, both in AUW, PUW/2172, Zl. 395.

[47] On Luick, see Fill, 'Anglistik und Amerikanistik', 232–45.

lines was insufficiently scholarly, and his reworking of Thieme's dictionary was marred by the 'fundamental problem' that he 'confused meaning with translation'. Luick saw the core of Kellner's work as literary history but dismissed much of his writing in this area as merely for public consumption. In *Die englische Literatur im Zeitalter der Königin Viktoria*, however, Kellner had ample opportunity to demonstrate his 'skill as a literary historian', and it was here that Luick concentrated his fire (ignoring the more recent book on North American literature). The best that Luick was prepared to say was that the book showed 'diligence and wide reading' and was 'useful as a reference work'. Kellner's judgements, though, were superficial: his portraits of writers were 'journalistic . . . and strongly subjective', and he worked with 'an amateurish conception of originality that scholarship abandoned long ago'. Kellner's fatal flaw was his failure to undertake an 'organic' reading of an author's life and work, what Luick called a 'historical-genetic account' that embedded the genesis and development of a literary work in the life of its author. Kellner had anticipated this objection in the foreword to his book, explaining there his choice to treat an author's life and work as conceptually distinct, although certainly not as entirely separate. Luick brushed aside Kellner's explanation as a ruse to disguise 'incompetence' as a 'principle of research', an attempt 'to make a virtue out of necessity'. He was, Luick said, out of step with contemporary scholarship and methodologically ill equipped 'to achieve an objective assessment of literature'. As such, Kellner's work was prone to the same kind of superficiality found in English or American handbooks, which 'German scholarship had already outgrown'. This explained Kellner's popularity in England, 'in whose schools and universities the rigorous scholarly standards of modern philologists play a far smaller role than here'. His reputation in the German lands was less good. It was telling, said Luick, that no German-speaking university besides Czernowitz had wanted to recruit him and that the University of Vienna had not considered him upon Schipper's retirement in 1913. Luick warned against granting Kellner even a purely teaching role, fearing that Kellner's students would not receive adequate scholarly training and would therefore write 'dilettantish dissertations'. Not only did he demand too little from his students but his 'grave methodological deficiencies' would 'damage tuition in the most alarming way'. Luick was also concerned for the university's reputation: if Kellner were allowed to teach, he would to all intents and purposes enjoy the 'status' of a regular professor, contrary to the university's express wish. In addition, Luick was anxious that if Kellner were part of the faculty, the hard-pressed government would not permit the university to fill the vacant chair in English literature and he would lose a valuable opportunity to build the field as he wished. 'If we review Kellner's scholarly work', wrote Luick in summary, 'we must observe, alas, that all his great industriousness and diligent endeavour have not yielded accomplishments that would signify genuine scholarly success.'[48]

Luick's devastating critique was in part a disagreement about academic method and style, expressed in the most unforgiving of terms. University politics and competition for resources were also at play. All this was standard fare. But there was an extra element that helps explain the animus towards Kellner that runs through Luick's report. A clue is provided at the outset, where, recounting Kellner's career, Luick saw fit to refer to his student days at the Jewish Theological Seminary in Breslau and to his fleeting work as a teacher of Judaism at schools in Vienna. Luick was a member of Vienna's German Club, a centre of German nationalist agitation, and of the Deutsch-akademischer Anglistenverein (German Anglicists Association), open only to 'Aryans'. Antipathy to Jews was a *sine qua non* for membership of both organizations.[49] The same was true of the 'bear's den', a secretive clique of antisemitic professors—many of whom also belonged to the German Club—who worked assiduously to reduce the Jewish presence at the university in the interwar years. Luick was sympathetic to the aims of the bear's den. The palaeontologist Karl Diener, dean of the philosophy faculty, was a leading member of the bear's den and was openly hostile to the presence of east European Jews (such as Kellner) at the university. Kellner was, at least in part, a casualty of the faculty's 'latent antisemitic hegemony' after 1918, 'a great scholar', as a University of Vienna Anglicist recounted in 1991, 'who already during and after World War 1 had become a victim of those sentiments that were to cost Germany and Austria their scholarly elite in the 1930s'.[50] For Luick, the insufficiently German nature of Kellner's

[48] Kommissionsbericht betreffs Erteilung eines Lehrauftrages an Prof. Kellner, 14 Jan. 1920, AUW, PUW/2172, Zl. 395. See also Pils, 'Disziplinierung eines Faches', 543–7.

[49] Pils, '"Ein Gelehrter ist kein Politiker"', 472–4.

[50] The first quotation is Taschwer, 'Geheimsache Bärenhöhle', 238, and see also ibid. 224–6 on Diener; the second quotation is Kastovsky (ed.), *Historical English Syntax*, 1. At least two others of those who worked with Luick on his report—Rudolf Much and Hans Molisch—

POST-HABSBURG TWILIGHT 141

work—and, by extension, of Kellner himself—was an irremediable defect. In February 1920 the Ministry of Education asked the university to reconsider its position regarding Kellner and three of his Czernowitz colleagues. Diener's report on this occasion, citing Luick's assessment, summarily rejected any consideration of Kellner, and suggested that the others, none of whom was Jewish, might find positions elsewhere in Vienna. He made no such suggestion for Kellner.[51]

Employed by the university in Czernowitz until the summer of 1919 but paid in Romanian lei rather than in Austrian currency, Kellner had requested financial support from the new government in Vienna at the end of 1918.[52] Together with those of his colleagues who had also not found a post in Austria, he turned again to the government for 'emergency relief' in March 1920. At the beginning of that month, they had finally been granted the nominal status of state employees, providing them with at least a secure, if inadequate, income.[53] The ministry, which a few months earlier had been unsure whether Kellner had been paid at all in the first half of 1919, offered only limited help and noted that the professors had already enjoyed 'significant preferential treatment of a kind not afforded to any other refugees'.[54]

From the government's perspective, the professors were far from the most needy of the many clamouring for assistance. Beset on all sides, the fragile new state's resources were stretched to the limit. Austria was 'the beggar of Europe', wrote Arthur Salter, a British civil servant (later a politician and academic) working for the League of Nations in 1919.[55] Salter

---

were of a similar persuasion, as were most of Luick's own research students, a number of whom became Nazi sympathizers. See Pils, 'Disziplinierung eines Faches', 547.

[51] Dekan der philosophischen Fakultät [Karl Diener] to Staatsamt für Unterricht, 22 Mar. 1920, OS, AV/5C/Cz, Zl. 5645.

[52] Ordentlicher Professor der Universität in Czernowitz, Dr. Leon Kellner, 18 Aug. 1919, OS, AV/5C/Cz, Zl. 17969.

[53] Adler, Zelinka, Kellner et al., An das Unterrichtsamt Wien, 20 Mar. 1920, OS, AV/5C/Cz, Zl. 5656; Staatsamt für Inneres und Unterricht, Professoren der Czernowitzer Universität, 24 Mar. 1920, OS, AV/5C/Cz, Zl. 5656.

[54] Staatsamt für Inneres und Unterricht, Professoren der Czernowitzer Universität, 24 Mar. 1920, OS, AV/5C/Cz, Zl. 5656; Staatsamt für Inneres und Unterricht, 27 Sept. 1919, OS, AV/5C/Cz, Zl. 17969. Kellner received no salary between October 1919 and March 1920; Bundesministerium für Inneres und Unterricht to Präsidentschaftskanzlei, 2 Dec. 1920, OS, AdR/01/PK/Kellner, Zl. 5923.   [55] Salter, 'The Reconstruction of Austria', 630.

feared that the republic, destabilized by political unrest and conflict with neighbouring states and regarded by many as a mere remnant of the monarchy, was 'at the very brink of chaos and destitution'.[56] William Goode, in charge of British relief and described in the *New York Times* as 'the real ruler of Austria in 1920–21', wrote that he found:

a whole nation, or what was left of it, in utter, hopeless despair. Inability to obtain a ration, in itself insufficient to support human life, and the misery of hundreds and thousands who, in an early winter's snow, shivered without heat or the hope of getting it, were bad enough, but it was nothing compared with the apathy, the helplessness and the loss of all hope that pervaded every class from the highest to the lowest.[57]

With *Anschluss* (annexation) to the new democratic Germany or the formation of a Danubian Federation being popular options, Austria's viability could not be taken for granted.[58] Vienna's distress was particularly severe. Tens of thousands of demobilized soldiers, along with former Habsburg state employees and summarily expelled Jews, had arrived in the city from the successor states, compounding the problems of a population already struggling with widespread hunger, mass unemployment, poverty, rapidly rising prices, and the Spanish flu epidemic.[59]

Kellner was more fortunate than some. He had been in receipt of a salary, even if woefully inadequate, until the summer of 1919, a measure of government assistance thereafter and a salary again from March 1920. But it was nowhere near enough. As Salter noted, the middle class was 'almost destroyed', and Kellner was no exception; his savings disappeared as inflation soared and the new Austrian currency depreciated catastrophically.[60] In February 1920, prompted by Anna, he turned to his friend Gotthard Deutsch, with whom he had studied at the Breslau seminary in the late 1870s. With a considerable degree of embarrassment, he asked Deutsch, now professor of Jewish history and philosophy at Hebrew Union College in Cincinnati, Ohio, to pay for a ten-dollar food package, offering to re-

---

[56] Ibid. See also Deak, 'Dismantling Empire', 132–3.
[57] Goode, 'Austria', 1; *New York Times*, 17 Dec. 1944, 38.
[58] Pelinka, *Die gescheiterte Republik*, chs. 3 and 5; Sandgruber, *Ökonomie und Politik*, 343–5.
[59] Haider, *Wien 1918*, 285–376.
[60] Salter, 'The Reconstruction of Austria', 631. See also Sandgruber, *Ökonomie und Politik*, 354–61.

imburse him later in Austrian currency.[61] Disturbed by Kellner's predicament, Deutsch dismissed the idea of reimbursement—an 'embarrassment' due to the absurd exchange rate—and wrote: 'I cannot enjoy my own food if I know that a man such as you must starve.' Deutsch immediately wrote to United States Supreme Court justice Louis Brandeis, honorary president of the Zionist Organization of America, and to Judge Julian Mack, the organization's president, to apprise them of Kellner's plight.[62] In mid-April, the Kellners were 'moved and delighted' to receive 'food drafts'—a coupon to be exchanged for food—not only from Deutsch and Mack but also from the Zionist Organization of America.[63] Kellner wrote to Deutsch:

Do you remember how you used to tease me because I found so much in the world curious? I was the polar opposite, you said, of Horace's *nil admirari* [to wonder at nothing]. Your shrewd observation was, and still is, true. *I take nothing for granted* [in English]. As an old fellow, the world for me is just as it was then, full of curiosities and wonders. You will have learned from our press what we must pay here for the basic necessities. You also know, as I see from your flattering letter to Judge Mack, that the noble descendants of the Romans [i.e. Romanians], the current masters of Czernowitz, have thrown us out. Is it not astonishing that one survives such misfortune and manages to stay afloat in a civilized fashion? . . . Your ten-dollar draft, then, was one of those curiosities that have so enriched my life. And imagine our astonishment when we received the mysterious news from the Joint [Distribution Committee] that American Jewry is sending us two ten-dollar drafts! Even accustomed as I am to curiosities and wonders, I have a rather sober estimation of humanity in general and of the Jews in particular, and I harbour no illusions about myself, so I know full well that American Jewry has greater worries than my humble self and I guessed immediately that in this instance American Jewry had been prodded by you. And we had barely recovered from our astonishment at this new miracle when, fresh from singing 'Dayenu' at our second [Passover] Seder, the monster draft [worth fifty dollars] from Mack arrived. Is that not the pinnacle of all wonders? A thousand thanks, dear friend.

All this, Kellner insisted, was a loan; when the currency improved, he

---

[61] Kellner to Deutsch, 22 Feb. 1920, AJA/GDP. On Deutsch, see also Kellner, 'Gotthard Deutsch'.   [62] Deutsch to Kellner, 16 Mar. 1920, AJA/GDP.
[63] Kellner to Deutsch, 18 Apr. 1920; Deutsch to Kellner, 24 May 1920, AJA/GDP. On food drafts, see Granick, *International Jewish Humanitarianism*, 90–1.

would pay the equivalent sums to the Jewish National Fund.[64] Kellner was acutely discomfited to be in such a position. As Deutsch sent more money in the following months, Kellner admitted to him: 'I am pleased and grateful but in the depths of my heart I am humiliated.'[65]

It had been his choice to withdraw from active political engagement during the war years, but the demise of the empire was wholly unwelcome and unexpected, and left Kellner in limbo. He had been a product of, and believer in, Habsburg Austria; now, like so many others, he was cast adrift. The state and society that had enabled and sustained his career disappeared almost overnight. He was no longer a parliamentarian, since the parliament of which he had been a member did not exist any more; he was no longer leader of Bukovina Zionism or the Jewish People's Council in Bukovina, as these political organizations were defunct and the region itself had become Romanian; and, perhaps most cruelly, he was no longer a university professor, except in name. Even as an essayist he foresaw irrelevance. As he wrote to Deutsch in 1920, younger Austrians could not grasp 'the significance for an entire generation of the feuilleton in the *Neue Freie Presse*'.[66]

Rescue of a sort came from an unlikely source. In November 1919 President Karl Seitz recruited Kellner to a temporary and loosely defined role as a part-time adviser on 'English affairs and personalities'. In this capacity he was expected to keep the president—whose role was more ceremonial than executive but nonetheless significant—informed about developments in British and American politics, act as his translator in meetings with British and American officials, deal with his English-language correspondence, and practise English conversation with him.[67] The presidential office, which had opened at the end of March 1919, could afford to pay only a modest honorarium, but even that constituted a useful supplement to his income, and the opportunity to contribute to the building of the new republic appealed to his abiding belief in public service.[68] Since there

---

[64] Kellner to Deutsch, 18 Apr. 1920, AJA/GDP. The reference to Horace is his *Epistles*, bk. 1, no. 6, to Numicius. *Dayenu* means 'it would be enough for us'.

[65] Kellner to Deutsch, 12 July 1920, AJA/GDP.

[66] Kellner to Deutsch, 18 Apr. 1920, AJA/GDP.

[67] Deutschösterreichische Präsidentschaftskanzlei to Kellner, 3 and 27 Nov. 1919, OS, AdR/01/PK/Kellner, Zl. 3707.   [68] Loibl, 'Die österreichische Präsidentschaftskanzlei', 159.

was little prospect of a return to a regular teaching and research post, and he had not yet resumed writing frequently for the press, it was an offer he could not refuse. He was, in fact, ideally suited to such a role—intimately familiar with English history, culture, and politics, fascinated by and knowledgeable about American society (despite not having visited), and with years of Zionist diplomacy, political leadership, and parliamentary experience which had accustomed him to the corridors of power. A gifted teacher and communicator, he had the temperament and experience to enable him to settle quickly into his new position.

His work in smoothing the lines of communication between British and American officials and the new Austrian authorities was of considerable significance, as in the republic's early years Anglo-American power and money were crucial in ensuring its survival. The British and Americans provided vital financial and political support, along with essential food supplies, without which the state would likely have been stillborn.[69] The presidential office handled a large volume of 'sensitive' English-language correspondence, and for 'all this kind of work', wrote a senior official, 'in particular the many long English letters to American relief committees, Kellner's help has proved indispensable and has fully proved its worth. Similarly, Kellner has often been called upon to act as translator when prominent Americans visit the president.'[70] His help with Hoover's American Relief Administration, the single largest enterprise of this kind and a lifeline for Austria, was 'especially extensive': 'In large part we can credit the smooth implementation of all our business with it to Professor Kellner's readiness to lend his support and to his exceptional linguistic ability.'[71] Kellner developed a good rapport with the veteran Social Democrat Seitz, a former teacher and parliamentarian who remained president until December 1920 and later became 'the presiding genius of Red Vienna' as the city's mayor from 1923 to 1934.[72] Upon leaving office as president, Seitz

[69] Sandgruber, Ökonomie und Politik, 345–7; Höbelt, Die erste Republik Österreich, 15–57.

[70] Vorstand der Präsidentschaftskanzlei to Viktor Prüger, Unterrichtsamt, 28 Sept. 1920, OS, AdR/01/PK/Kellner, Zl. 4639.

[71] Tabelle, Aug. 1923, OS, AdR/01/PK/Kellner, Zl. 5473. See also President Hainisch to Minister für Unterricht [Emil Schneider], 31 July 1923, OS, AdR/01/PK/Kellner, Zl. 5036. On the American Relief Administration, see Granick, International Jewish Humanitarianism, 72–4; Adlgasser, American Individualism Abroad.

[72] Timms, 'School for Socialism', 40. See also Spitzer, Karl Seitz, 59–70. Formally, Seitz was

was generous in his praise for Kellner, telling his successor Michael Hainisch that Austria should be 'proud' that 'our dear Professor Kellner has carried out his fruitful services for us with the English and Americans; he has always brought us great honour'.[73]

Under Hainisch, Kellner's temporary position became permanent. The paths of the two men had crossed briefly in the 1890s in Vienna's social-liberal movement, an Austrian form of Fabianism.[74] The substance of Kellner's role in the presidential office continued as before, but Hainisch also looked to him for support for his own literary endeavours. He recorded his gratitude, for example, for Kellner's 'great tact' in helping with a book of poetry Hainisch had written; he also noted that Kellner had been 'extraordinarily helpful' in a more academic study he published on land reform.[75] In the course of their work together, including years of weekly English conversations, an unlikely friendship developed. Hainisch recalled in his memoirs that they 'grew ever closer and eventually became warm friends'; Kellner called Hainisch 'the soul of kindness'.[76] Hainisch, though, was not generally well disposed towards Jews. Francis Lindley, the British High Commissioner in Vienna from 1919 to 1920, reported to London that Hainisch was 'not free from the mild form of reasoned anti-Semitism' that was 'almost universal' in Austria.[77] His memoirs bear this out.

Hainisch disparaged Jewish colleagues from the social-liberal movement, citing with approval the remark of Social Democrat (and converted Jew) Friedrich Austerlitz that 'they are neither Austrians nor Germans; they are Jewish nomads'. He approved of a *numerus clausus* at the University

president of the Konstituierende Nationalversammlung (the Constituent National Assembly) and head of state. Following the promulgation of the constitution in October 1920, the first to assume the title of Federal President was Michael Hainisch.

[73] A. Kellner, *Leon Kellner*, 84.

[74] Hainisch, *75 Jahre aus bewegter Zeit*, 124–39, 228; A. Kellner, *Leon Kellner*, 84. On the *Sozialpolitischer Verein* (Social Political Association) and the *Sozialpolitische Partei* (Social Political Party), and on Fabianism in Vienna, see also Boyer, 'Freud, Marriage, and Late Viennese Liberalism', 77–82; Holleis, *Die Sozialpolitische Partei*, 9–14.

[75] Hainisch, *75 Jahre aus bewegter Zeit*, 229; Präsidentschaftskanzlei to Unterrichtsamt [Dr Krüger], 28 Sept. 1920, OS, AdR/01/PK/Kellner, Zl. 4635. The books were published as *Die Landflucht, ihr Wesen und ihre Bekämpfung im Rahmen einer Agrarreform* (1924) and *Aus mein' Leb'n* (1930).

[76] Hainisch, *75 Jahre aus bewegter Zeit*, 228; Kellner to Präsidentschaftskanzlei Sektionschef, 12 Apr. 1923, OS, AdR/01/PK/Kellner, Zl. 2378.   [77] Carsten, *The First Austrian Republic*, 57.

of Vienna, since otherwise it would become a 'Jewish school'. He felt that the historian and journalist Heinrich Friedjung had 'outgrown the narrow confines' of his Jewishness, becoming 'one of the best sons of the German-Austrian people'; he disliked the Jewish elite of 'distinguished scholars and doctors, grand bankers and businessmen, prominent lawyers and industrialists', but expressed a patronizing sympathy for the 'true piety' of Orthodox Jews and even claimed to have read the Talmud.[78] Jews should take a less prominent part in public and political life, he wrote, as their 'mentality differed from that of the Aryans'. They were not 'an inferior people', he clarified:

On the contrary, they are a race selectively bred by intelligence and mental agility, and in this sense they are without doubt superior to the Aryan population. A moderate inflow of Jewish blood, therefore, is... advantageous. The flaw of the Jews, however, is that they entirely lack feeling for the irrational in the life of the nation (fatherland, Heimat, mother tongue, Christianity).[79]

Consequently, Jews did not possess the kind of qualities that could build a state, and he was not only sceptical about Kellner's Zionism but chose to believe that Kellner was disillusioned by Zionism and disappointed by his visits to Palestine.[80] Hainisch, like so many others of his time and place, saw the Jews, collectively, as alien and unassimilable, views that an Englishman like Lindley recognized as a familiar form of 'mild and reasoned' antisemitism. Yet such attitudes did not of necessity lead to animosity towards individual Jews. Hainisch displayed enormous generosity towards Kellner and went to considerable lengths over a number of years to offer him assistance. Presidential patronage of this sort was no small matter and proved to be a saving grace of Kellner's post-Habsburg decade.

In March 1921 Hainisch's office complained to the Ministry of Education that Kellner, who could 'render outstanding service' to higher education, was a wasted asset.[81] Conscious of Kellner's financial difficulties, and with the ministry unable or unwilling to help, the president persuaded the notoriously antisemitic Technical University of Vienna to hire Kellner as a

---

[78] For Austerlitz, see Hainisch, *75 Jahre aus bewegter Zeit*, 139. For the *numerus clausus*, see ibid. 306. For Friedjung, see ibid. 132–3. For the elite and the Orthodox, see ibid. 303.

[79] Ibid. 306.   [80] Ibid. 229.

[81] Präsidentschaftskanzlei to Bundesministerium für Inneres und Unterricht, 17 Mar. 1921, OS, AdR/01/PK/Kellner, Zl. 5923.

148 POST-HABSBURG TWILIGHT

part-time teacher of English language.[82] Kellner told Hainisch he feared he would face either demonstrations or a boycott, and wrote to Gotthard Deutsch that the Technical University 'has forgiven my Jewishness and assigned English [teaching] to me ... It remains an open question whether the students will allow me to teach.'[83] His fears were not borne out. Teaching at the Technical University, he reported (in English) to the president's office, was 'a source of pleasure'. But he admitted that:

materially and morally my position is humiliating. My Czernowitz colleague who teaches Zoology there [Carl Zelinka] was appointed as a 'professor' and gets a salary as such; I am a 'Lehrer' [teacher] and am paid ten percent less. Why? I don't know. I was never introduced to the fellow-professors, I have no room to go to when there is an occasion for waiting—I am, again, out in the cold.[84]

The humiliation was unpleasant but tolerable; he taught from the end of 1921 until his death, sometimes to more than 100 students, and on occasion delivered lectures on Shakespeare and literature in addition to regular language instruction.[85] His love of teaching was undiminished and practical considerations weighed heavily upon him: his position at the university was linked to his work with the president, and he could not afford to dispense even with this exceedingly modest supplementary income.

Hainisch's concern for Kellner's welfare went well beyond the bounds of regular collegiality. Looking for ways to bolster Kellner's meagre income, he successfully pushed the Ministry of Education to allow Kellner to continue at the Technical University following his formal retirement from teaching in December 1924, and he equally successfully lobbied the ministry to ensure a more generous pension for a man whom he had come to 'greatly esteem'.[86] But he went even further. The state's parlous finances, he

[82] Hainisch, 75 Jahre aus bewegter Zeit, 229; Kellner to Technische Universität Rektor, 27 June 1921, ATUW, Personalakt Leon Kellner; Bundesministerium für Inneres und Unterricht to Präsidentschaftskanzlei, 17 Dec. 1921, OS, AdR/01/PK/Kellner, Zl. 5923.

[83] Kellner to Deutsch, 15 May 1921, AJA/GDP. In 1923, the Technical University instituted a numerus clausus for foreign Jewish students. See Miller, 'From White Terror to Red Vienna', 312.

[84] Kellner to Präsidentschaftskanzlei, 12 Apr. 1923, OS, AdR/01/PK/Kellner, Zl. 2378.

[85] Vorlesungsverzeichnis . . . 1921/22, 43, 95; Vorlesungsverzeichnis . . . 1923/24, 29; Vorlesungsverzeichnis . . . 1927/28, 133; Hainisch to Minister for Education [Emil Schneider], 21 Nov. 1923, OS, AdR/01/PK/Kellner, Zl. 7411.

[86] On income, see Präsidentschaftskanzlei, Kellner vertragsmässige Bezüge, 23 Oct. 1922, OS,

wrote to the minister of education, Emil Schneider, in the summer of 1923, 'preclude rewarding Kellner appropriately, so we should instead acknowledge his truly selfless and distinguished work by conferring upon him a title. I feel it is of the greatest importance to express my gratitude, and that of my office, to Professor Kellner by awarding him the title of Hofrat [Privy or Court Councillor].' In a society inordinately fond of honorifics, this was an eloquent gesture. Hainisch pressed his case insistently, emphasizing to Schneider that he wanted 'special attention' paid to his proposal and telling the Federal Chancellor's office (the seat of executive power) that he expected a response 'as soon as possible'.[87] Schneider agreed without hesitation, although, in anticipation of 'recriminations' from Kellner's professorial colleagues, he asked that the award be made to Kellner in recognition of his service to the president rather than to education.[88] At the end of August, the chancellor, Christian Social prelate Ignaz Seipel, gave his assent.[89] Kellner wrote to Hainisch (in English) from the spa town of Bad Gastein, south of Salzburg, where he was helping to care for Anna's sister, who was ill: 'Believe me, I am deeply conscious of your goodwill and proud to give your offices what little services I can.'[90]

While Hainisch had a poor opinion of 'the Jews', Kellner was perhaps in his eyes the exception that proved the rule. He considered him a trusted friend and adviser, whose misfortunes—no job, precipitate loss of status, precarious finances—were shared by millions in post-war Austria. The president's empathy and respect for him were evident, and he used his position to provide moral and practical support that lightened Kellner's burden. It was a consolation for which Kellner was deeply grateful. Accus-

---

AdR/01/PK/Kellner, Zl. 6032; Präsidentschaftskanzlei, Honorar Kellner, 17 July 1923, OS, AdR/01/PK/Kellner, Zl. 4663. On the Technical University, see Hainisch to Schneider, 21 Nov. 1923, OS, AdR/01/PK/Kellner, Zl. 7411; Hainisch to Schneider, 7 Dec. 1923, OS, AdR/01/ PK/Kellner, Zl. 8097; Schneider to Hainisch, 4 Feb. 1924, OS, AdR/01/PK/Kellner, Zl. 875. On the pension, see Präsidentschaftskanzlei, Anerkennung Kellner, 16 July 1923, OS, AdR/01/PK/ Kellner, Zl. 4664; Hainisch to Schneider, 24 Dec. 1924, OS, AdR/01/PK/Kellner, Zl. 8334; Schneider to Hainisch, 29 Jan. 1925, OS, AdR/01/PK/Kellner, Zl. 782. For 'esteem', see Präsidentschaftskanzlei to Bundeskanzleramt, 24 Aug. 1923, OS, AdR/01/PK/Kellner, Zl. 5473.

[87] Hainisch to Schneider, 31 July 1923, OS, AdR/01/PK/Kellner, Zl. 5036; Präsidentschaftskanzlei to Bundeskanzleramt, 24 Aug. 1923, OS, AdR/01/PK/Kellner, Zl. 5473.

[88] Schneider to Hainisch, 8 Aug. 1923, OS, AdR/01/PK/Kellner, Zl. 5473.

[89] Präsidentschaftskanzlei, Resolution, 31 Aug. 1923, OS, AdR/01/PK/Kellner, Zl. 5340.

[90] Kellner to Hainisch, 14 Sept. 1923, OS, AdR/01/PK/Kellner, Zl. 5340.

tomed over a lifetime to the 'mild and reasoned' antisemitism that Lindley described, Kellner was able and usually willing to separate the personal from the political. Why, Anna had once asked, was he on occasion accompanied home from the university (or the coffee-house) by colleagues whom they knew to be antisemitic? 'I never impose myself upon anyone', he had replied, 'least of all an Aryan, but if a colleague volunteers to walk a little with me I cannot refuse by saying "You are an antisemite". He is first and foremost a colleague and it is my duty to be as gracious to him as he is to me.'[91]

He practised what he preached. He was on good terms, for example, with H. L. Mencken, whose writing he greatly admired. He was an occasional contributor to Mencken's journal *The American Mercury* and he agreed in 1927 to translate Mencken's *Notes on Democracy* into German.[92] That same year Mencken offered him the post of Vienna correspondent for the *Baltimore Evening Sun*, for which Mencken himself wrote. In poor health at the time, Kellner suggested that his daughter Paula might be suitable instead. Paula was by now a freelance writer and an English teacher at the Zwi Perez Chajes School in Vienna—named in honour of the nationalist-minded chief rabbi of Vienna, with whom Leon and Anna were well acquainted; she took up the role for the *Sun* in early 1928 and continued to write for it regularly, first from Vienna and after 1933 from Palestine, until her death in 1968 (she also wrote occasionally for the *Manchester Guardian*). She resolutely defended Mencken, whom she had hosted in Vienna in 1931, against accusations of antisemitism, although she believed his use of language was often flippant (as noted above, Mencken had once described Kellner as a man of 'half-European, half-Oriental culture'). Mencken went to great lengths to secure United States visas for Paula and her family in 1942 when Rommel's Afrika Korps posed a threat to Palestine (in the event, the visas were not needed) and he was also well acquainted with Kellner's youngest daughter, Dora, who translated *Notes on Democracy* into German in 1930 in place of her father.[93] Separating the

[91] A. Kellner, *Leon Kellner*, 75.

[92] On *The American Mercury*, see e.g. Kellner, 'A Note on Shakespeare'. For his view of Mencken, see *NFP*, 25 July 1925, 10. On *Notes on Democracy*, see *New York Times*, 10 July 1927, 10.

[93] Arnold, *Memoirs* (Heb.), 110–14; *Menorah*, 9 (1931), 307–10. See also Weissweiler, *Das Echo deiner Frage*, 289–92; Richman, 'Mr. Mencken and the Jews'. Dora's translation of *Notes on Democracy* was published as *Demokratenspiegel*.

personal from the political when dealing with men such as Hainisch, Mencken, or university colleagues was challenge enough. Ezra Pound, however, a man with a visceral dislike of Jews, presented a problem of an entirely different order. During Pound's extended stay in Vienna in May 1928, he visited Kellner at home a number of times and ventured with him to the outskirts of the city to one of Vienna's popular wine taverns. Kellner left no record of his impressions, but Paula, who accompanied them on their excursion, registered her surprise at the very fact of the encounter, which nevertheless passed without incident.[94]

Kellner's duties for the president and his teaching at the Technical University, although not without their pleasures, were pale shadows of his pre-war political and academic life. Making a virtue of necessity, he resolved 'to fall back for my old age on my position in the republic of letters'. There, he felt, he would at least be 'secure and not attended by humiliations'.[95] This meant, above all, Shakespeare. He wanted in particular to complete his project of 'restoration and correction' of the manuscripts of Shakespeare's plays. It will be recalled that he had spent several months in London in the winter of 1913 and the spring of 1914 examining manuscripts and 'putting together for my own use a regular "Elizabethan Palaeography"'.[96] In July 1920 he was finally able to return to London to resume this work, with the help of funds from Deutsch.[97] 'From 1914 to this day', he wrote in February 1925, 'I have been busy to the exclusion of all other work applying the key of Elizabethan handwriting to the unexplained passages in Shakespeare's works.'[98] His first post-war London trip of six weeks was a much-needed tonic and a taste of his former life. Staying at the home of William and Frances Archer—Anna did not accompany him on this occasion—he sought out other old literary friends and made new contacts. The war cast a long shadow at times: both the Archers and his friends James and Helen Fullarton Muirhead had lost sons in battle. He visited Lucy Clifford on numerous occasions, met with H. G. Wells, spent a weekend with John Mackinnon Robertson and his

---

[94] Arnold, *Memoirs* (Heb.), 116; Moody, *Ezra Pound, Poet*, ii. 118–19. Arnold wrote about their excursion, without mentioning Pound, in the *Baltimore Evening Sun*, 9 July 1928, 9.
[95] Kellner to Präsidentschaftskanzlei Sektionschef, 12 Apr. 1923, OS, AdR/01/PK/Kellner, Zl. 2378.
[96] Kellner, *Restoring Shakespeare*, p. vii.
[97] Kellner to Deutsch, 12 July 1920, AJA/GDP.
[98] Kellner, *Restoring Shakespeare*, p. vii.

wife Maude, befriended the Irish author and journalist T. W. (Thomas William) Rolleston, and was invited to meet the new Austrian ambassador, Georg Franckenstein. Henry Bradley, with whom he had published a revision of *Historical Outlines of English Accidence* in the 1890s and who was now senior editor of the *Oxford English Dictionary*, invited him to Oxford and promised to help him find a publisher. He made other trips out of London, to the Archers' country residence in Kings Langley in Hertfordshire and to see Leonard Merrick in Eastbourne. His busy social schedule was 'an unalloyed joy' but he worried, too, that 'due to so many invitations' he could barely manage to work.[99]

Protestations notwithstanding, his work rate slowed only marginally. In 1920 he finally published the biography of Herzl on which he had been working intermittently for more than a decade. In 1909, thinking it would soon be ready, he had offered to send a copy to Deutsch.[100] In 1911 he presented a draft to David Wolffsohn, who thought it rather 'sober'; Kellner's response was to quote an immodest aphorism he attributed to Herzl: 'The Bible did not embellish Moses.'[101] In early 1914 he had considered it almost finished, but it was not until 1920 that it was deemed ready for publication. Even then, however, what he published was in effect the first part of a larger work. 'Herzl's life', wrote Kellner, 'divides into two parts: Herzl the man of the world and Herzl the bearer of a historical mission.'[102] Content for the moment to leave the larger history to others, he painted a compact, sympathetic portrait of the pre-Zionist man on the basis of Herzl's own papers —a vast collection that Herzl had entrusted to Kellner as his literary executor—supplemented by correspondence and conversations with Herzl's relations and school friends in Budapest and his many collaborators in Vienna.[103] It was, commented the *Neue Freie Presse*, 'a splendid and worthy memorial to the unforgettable' Herzl, although, true to form, the paper ignored Zionism and mourned Herzl as a loss to German literature.[104]

[99] A. Kellner, *Leon Kellner*, 164–5 (p. 165).

[100] Kellner to Deutsch, 30 June 1909, AJA/GDP.   [101] Kellner, *Theodor Herzls Lehrjahre*, 6.

[102] Ibid. See also Wolffsohn to Kremenezky, 7 Jan. 1914, CZA, A74/7.

[103] Kellner and Erwin Rosenberger had gathered the papers from Herzl's apartment soon after his death, monitored with 'unusual suspicion' by Herzl's widow Julie. Rosenberger to Kellner, 7 Oct. 1904, CZA, H1/3444.

[104] *NFP*, 16 May 1920, 7. See also *Jüdische Volksstimme*, 27 July 1920, 7; *JC*, 15 Oct. 1920, 16–17; *Menorah*, 3 (1925), 162–3.

The following year, Kellner published a revised edition of *Die englische Literatur im Zeitalter der Königin Viktoria* under a new title, *Die englische Literatur der neuesten Zeit von Dickens bis Shaw* (Contemporary English Literature from Dickens to Shaw). Even this second edition did not exhaust what he wanted to say about the subject, but he conceded that anything further 'must await better days'.[105] He struck a similar note about a sequel to the Herzl book: 'Will it be granted to me beneath brighter skies, in more favourable circumstances, to complete this work? Perhaps. But meanwhile the sand is trickling through the hourglass and one is well advised not to reckon with the longer term.'[106] One year later, in 1922, he published a Shakespeare lexicon, 'a meticulous inventory' of the playwright's vocabulary for a German-speaking audience.[107] This was also part of his restoration work. Kellner had always been of the view that, assuming reliable transmission, Shakespeare's all too numerous 'opaque passages' were explicable and that every word had a sense and a meaning that could be unearthed.[108] Unshakeable in his belief that 'there invariably exists behind Shakespeare's words a clear conception, just as behind his phrases there is always a clear idea', Kellner's goal was no less than to provide 'a more definite and critical analysis of the meanings and uses of words than those hitherto available'.[109]

He pursued his goal of clarifying Shakespeare's texts with a near-obsessive single-mindedness. 'Hundreds of passages in the text of Shakespeare present a mixture of the sublime and the ludicrous such as is unparalleled in world literature. Is it not as if some lines had been written by an inspired genius, and the next by a drivelling idiot?' Far too much

---

[105] Kellner, *Die englische Literatur der neuesten Zeit*, 8. The *Times Literary Supplement* thought the book 'a typical production of German scholarship, with all its advantages and drawbacks', with the latter outweighing the former (27 Oct. 1921, 699). See also *English Studies*, 4 (1922), 122–4. A Czech translation was published in 1928, *Anglická literatura: doby nejnovější od Dickense až k Shawovi*.

[106] Kellner, *Theodor Herzls Lehrjahre*, 6.

[107] *Englische Studien*, 57 (1923), 266. See also *NFP*, 24 Sept. 1922, 23–4: 'No praise is too warm for the astonishing quantity and crystal-clear accuracy of Kellner's interpretations.'

[108] Kellner, *Shakespeare-Wörterbuch*, p. v.

[109] *Modern Language Review*, 18 (1923), 213. The first quotation is from Kellner, *Shakespeare-Wörterbuch*, p. v. For reviews, see also *Englische Studien*, 57 (1923), 263–6; *Jahrbuch der deutschen Shakespeare-Gesellschaft*, 58 (1922), 137; *Times Literary Supplement*, 10 Aug. 1922, 521. The *Wörterbuch* was called 'still valuable' in 2015; Cheesman, 'Reading Originals', 90 n. 18.

was 'found wanting, unintelligible, imperfect at the very least'.[110] The results of his long labours to remedy this situation were published in 1925—in English rather than German—as *Restoring Shakespeare*, a work he described as 'conjectural criticism'. He anticipated disapproval: 'I am perfectly aware that the Shakespearean republic of letters is not just now in favour of new emendations.' The perils of textual conjecture were obvious; it was, he acknowledged, too often born of 'ignorance and conceit'.[111] To avoid this he was scrupulous in ensuring that his palaeographical conclusions were informed by historical and cultural research. The *Sitz im Leben*—text and context—methodology of biblical criticism served as a model, in much the same way that he had applied it in his literary-historical work. The reception, as he had expected, was mixed, with praise and admiration for his scholarship, diligence, and imagination outweighed by grave reservations about most of his proposed emendations.

Restoring Shakespeare was recognized as a pioneering work that could 'possibly stand as a landmark in Shakespearean studies'. On the other hand, Kellner's fundamental thesis 'that the great source of corruption [of Shakespeare's texts] is the misreading of manuscript "copy"' was contested, as was the palaeographical analysis that was his 'master-key to emendation'.[112] Praise for his 'zeal, devotion, and learning' was undercut by dismay at his 'faulty method, serious inaccuracy, and . . . defective sense of language'.[113] Kellner himself had asked whether a German speaker should have dared to embark on such an enterprise: 'Has a foreigner any chance of elucidating passages that remained dark to English eyes?'[114] His optimism on this score was not generally shared. One reviewer, noting acidly that non-native English speakers ought to realize that 'they start with a certain handicap', believed the 'absence of the almost incommunicable sense of linguistic form' sometimes led Kellner to propose emendations that 'could be accepted by no one with any feeling for language'.[115] Kellner's 'radicalism of attitude', remarked another, 'is doubtless traceable in part to the author's very natural enthusiasm for his new method, and in part to his being a

[110] Kellner, *Restoring Shakespeare*, 2.

[111] Ibid., p. viii. On the long history of emendation of Shakespeare's texts, see Erne, 'Emendation and the Editorial Reconfiguration of Shakespeare'; Jowett, 'Full Pricks and Great P's'.

[112] *Review of English Studies*, 1 (1925), 464. [113] Ibid. 478.

[114] Kellner, *Restoring Shakespeare*, p. vii. [115] *Review of English Studies*, 1 (1925), 476–7.

foreigner'. Here, too, appreciation softened the harsh critique: 'the volume is one that future editors of Shakespeare can afford neither to overlook nor accept without verifying every detail . . . To such a work, in spite of its multitude of detailed inaccuracies, scholarship must give serious consideration.'[116]

The *Restoring Shakespeare* volume was not an end in itself. Kellner's goal was to incorporate his findings into a complete annotated edition of Shakespeare's plays for German readers. Having laid out his principles and methods, and demonstrated their application, he set out immediately on this impossibly ambitious undertaking. Here, too, President Hainisch offered vital support, subsidizing a research trip to London in the summer of 1926 that was beyond Kellner's means.[117] Kellner was not, however, able to give Shakespeare his undivided attention. In addition to his duties at the Technical University and the presidential office, he was still writing for the public, although less frequently than before the war and almost exclusively for the *Neue Freie Presse* (now without its empire-wide reach). As he had started in the 1880s, so would he finish in the 1920s; English-language literature was his greatest passion but not his sole concern. He wrote, inevitably, about Shakespeare, explaining new directions in Shakespeare research, including his own, for example, and dismissing the idea that Francis Bacon was the author of Shakespeare's plays.[118] For the rest he focused, as before, on introducing and explaining contemporary British and American writing to a German readership. He explored new works by John Galsworthy, George Bernard Shaw, William Archer, and John Mackinnon Robertson, all of whom he knew personally and had written about extensively.[119] He noted with interest D. H. Lawrence's portrayal of women ('creatures of flesh and blood') and assessed the achievements

---

[116] *The Journal of English and German Philology*, 25 (1926), 583–4. For further reviews, see *Times Literary Supplement*, 23 July 1925, 493; *English Studies*, 7 (1925), 150–4; *NFP*, 13 Dec. 1925, 31–3; *WZ*, 7 Feb. 1926, 5; *The American Mercury*, Oct. 1925, 268.

[117] Präsidentschaftskanzlei, Hofrat Kellner a.o. Remunierung, 10 and 16 Jun 1926, OS, AdR/01/PK/Kellner, Zl. 5001.

[118] *NFP*, 19 May 1919, 1–5; 17 June 1922, 1–4; 27 June 1922, 1–4. In 1919, Kellner published an edited version of Bacon's *Essays, or Counsels Civil and Moral*.

[119] On Shaw and Robertson, see *NFP*, 16 May 1926, 31. On Shaw, see *NFP*, 25 July 1926, 19; 5 Aug. 1928, 25–6. On Archer, see *NFP*, 3 July 1923, 12; 11 Jan. 1925, 25–6. On Galsworthy, see *NFP*, 30 Oct. 1921, 31.

of H. G. Wells on the author's sixtieth birthday (Wells's 'epigrammatic gift', he thought, was not well served by writing novels).[120] He remained attentive to women authors, writing appreciatively about the novelists Elizabeth von Arnim, Lucy Clifford, and Berta Ruck, the poet Elizabeth Barrett Browning, and the anonymously published satire of 'an American woman humorist'.[121] He was sceptical about the merits of James Joyce's *Ulysses*, aware that he might as a result be 'decried as a fossil of the prehistoric era of literary criticism'. Many had hailed Joyce as the new Homer, he wrote. His conclusion: 'Every age gets the Homer it deserves.'[122]

Such was his undiminished enthusiasm for America and its literature that he fleetingly considered a lecture tour of the United States.[123] Unable to arrange this, he continued to observe from afar. He wrote admiringly of Mencken as 'the wittiest despiser' of America's 'holiest qualities' and marvelled at his *American Mercury*, launched in 1924, which 'featured more compelling reading material than any other English-language journal in the world'.[124] Reconsidering Sinclair Lewis's 1922 novel *Babbitt* in the light of its runaway success—he admitted to being underwhelmed at first reading—he suggested it represented a new departure for American literature, freed from English and European antecedents; the book's 'good fortune' was that it captured the 'temper of the times'.[125] He returned to the poetry of Walt Whitman, a long-time favourite, to examine a new German translation of 'Song of Myself', and his portrait of the writer Joseph Hergesheimer, later a good friend to Kellner's daughter Dora, received favourable mention in the *New York Times*.[126]

Occasional essays on culture and politics complemented those on literature. He offered commentary on the fluctuating fortunes of English Liberalism, the career of Lloyd George, and the swings and roundabouts of parliamentary elections.[127] He pointed out the benefits to Austria of

[120] On Lawrence, see *NFP*, 31 Jan. 1926, 31. On Wells, see *NFP*, 12 Dec. 1926, 33–4.

[121] On Ruck, Arnim, and Clifford, see *NFP*, 11 Oct. 1925, 32–3. On Browning, see *NFP*, 22 May 1921, 31–2. On the anonymous humorist, see *NFP*, 21 Oct. 1922, 1–3.

[122] *NFP*, 4 Dec. 1927, 38–9.

[123] Deutsch to Kellner, 7 Aug. 1920 and 26 Jan. 1921; Kellner to Deutsch, 9 Jan. 1921, AJA/GDP.   [124] *NFP*, 25 July 1925, 10.   [125] *NFP*, 17 Mar. 1923, 10.

[126] *NFP*, 10 July 1923, 1–3; *New York Times*, 12 Aug. 1923, Book Review and Magazine section, 22; Weissweiler, *Das Echo deiner Frage*, 287–8.

[127] On liberalism and elections, see *NFP*, 25 May 1922, 2–4; 19 Nov. 1922, 4. On Lloyd George, see *NFP*, 22 Oct. 1922, 4.

joining the League of Nations, a decision that the government took in late 1920 after much public debate, and warmly recommended Wilhelm Dibelius's *England*, an attempt by a sympathetic German to understand the wartime enemy. He reviewed a biography of St Francis of Assisi and a social history of the medieval village, and examined the ideals of civic improvement promoted by the sociologist Charles Zueblin, one of the founders of a Toynbee Hall-style settlement house in Chicago.[128] Prompted by a new translation of Maimonides' *Guide of the Perplexed*, he composed an informed summary of the medieval philosopher's thought; in the same vein, he used a posthumously published book of essays by the contemporary Austrian philosopher Wilhelm Jerusalem to give a concise account of his ideas. In both cases, in keeping with his past practice in the press, he skated without comment over the important Jewish dimension of both thinkers.[129]

Although he had protested to Anna in the 1880s that he did not wish to be a 'journalist', the essay form, which he used as a carefully curated means of indirect self-expression, was close to his heart. In his choice of what and how to write, he obliquely revealed much of his own self in his essays, more than in his scholarship or politics. This was the case, for example, in a tribute to his friend Felix Salten, the writer and critic, in which he reflected on the art of writing and the role of the critic. Salten, he felt, had 'mastered the formidably difficult craft: he can write. First and foremost, thought and expression correspond like two congruent geometric pieces—a rare thing.' For Kellner, writing was an 'intricate, unlearnable art . . . The real writer never works with used currency or—to use a common modern phrase—with clichés.' He described Salten in terms that recalled his letter to Deutsch about his own enduring sense of wonder:

There is an inherent youthful vitality to Salten, which daily renders the world anew for him as the wonder that it is. Every new acquaintance is for him an

---

[128] On the League of Nations, see *NFP*, 12 Dec. 1920, 3. On Dibelius, see *NFP*, 28 Oct. 1923, 31. On Georg Terramare on St Francis, see *NFP*, 29 Mar. 1925, 29–30. On G.G. Coulton's *The Medieval Village*, see *NFP*, 13 Feb. 1927, 34–5. On Zueblin, see *NFP*, 15 May 1923, 1–2.

[129] On Maimonides, see *NFP*, 8 May 1924, 14. On Jerusalem, see *NFP*, 12 Oct. 1924, 27. This was despite the fact that Kellner had succeeded Jerusalem as a German teacher at the Israelitische-Theologische Lehranstalt (Israelite Theological Academy) in Vienna in 1902 and that he discussed Maimonides as a Jewish philosopher in reviewing the Maimonides book in *Menorah*, 2/6 (1924), 15. See also Landesmann, *Rabbiner aus Wien*, 184.

intellectual event, every worthwhile book a blessing of fate, every stage play an experience, every artistic image a pleasure, every significant musical composition a fountain of youth . . . Salten thinks with his senses, and occasionally also with his heart.

Kellner recognized in Salten something of what he himself aspired to be as a writer and critic, a worker in 'the service of the word'.[130]

From the middle of the 1920s declining health interfered with his service. In September 1925 he was forced to take a long break from teaching after a diagnosis of 'severe neurasthenia due to exhaustion'. This was followed by a mild heart attack in April 1927, leading his doctor to prescribe a prolonged period of rest.[131] Anna was now anxious that Leon was on borrowed time, and they left Vienna immediately for an extended recuperative stay in the resort town of Bad Goisern, in the mountains of upper Austria.[132] By October, Leon was well enough to risk a third trip to Palestine. He and Anna had travelled there in late 1923—sailing from Trieste on the *Helouan*, the ship that had so impressed him on their first trip in 1913—to visit their son Viktor, one of the founders of the new colony of Binyamina.[133] That Viktor was working his own plot of land as a farmer was naturally a source of great pride for Leon, for whom land had always been the key to national renewal. As he wrote to the sceptical Deutsch, a self-described 'liberal integrationist': 'You are city, I am land. Every Jewish farmer is for me a guarantee of a new future for the Jewish people.'[134] Anna's

---

[130] *NFP*, 9 Oct. 1921, 31–2. Salten had written a tribute to mark Kellner's sixtieth birthday in *NFP*, 17 Apr. 1919, 8.

[131] Kellner to Rektorat der Technischen Hochschule, 24 Sept. 1925; Bundesministerium für Unterricht to Rektorat der Technischen Hochschule, 13 Oct. 1925, ATUW, Personalakt Leon Kellner; A. Kellner, *Leon Kellner*, 90–1; Spann, 'Dr. Leon Kellner' (Yid.), 281. The doctor was the eminent neurologist Emil Redlich.

[132] A. Kellner, *Leon Kellner*, 91–2. They also spent a few weeks at the sanatorium founded in 1905 by Anna's sister Henriette in Breitenstein in the Vienna Alps. On Henriette, see Malleier, 'Das "Kaiserin Elisabeth-Institut für israelitische Krankenpflegerinnen"', 251–4.

[133] In 1923 they made trips to Tel Aviv, Caesarea, and Hadera, and visited the Berlin artist Hermann Struck in Haifa. In Jerusalem they stayed at the home of Henrietta Szold, founder of Hadassah (the Women's Zionist Organization of America), and visited Nathan Straus, the owner of Macy's. See Anna Kellner, 'Reiseskizzen aus Palästina'; Leon Kellner, 'Ein Waisendorf'. Viktor had returned to Witzenhausen in Germany to complete his agronomy studies at the end of the war and had emigrated to Palestine in 1920; [Viktor Kellner], 'Briefe eines jungen Farmers aus Palästina'; Arnold, *Memoirs* (Heb.), 88–91; Kellner to Deutsch, 16 June 1920, AJA/GDP.

[134] Deutsch to Kellner, 16 Mar. 1920; Kellner to Deutsch, 18 Apr. 1920, AJA/GDP. Viktor's

concern about Leon's health was justified. On this visit, unlike their previous demanding trip, they rarely ventured far from Binyamina, and Anna kept a watchful and anxious eye on Leon, who was content for the most part to spend time with his grandson and to potter about on the farm. He worked on Shakespeare for 'only' three hours daily: 'Never in his life', wrote Anna, 'had he taken such a long holiday.'[135] Enforced rest for several weeks came with a bout of dysentery contracted on a rare excursion, further aggravating his heart condition. At the end of December, after two months in Palestine, they returned to Vienna.[136]

Kellner resumed work, at a marginally reduced pace. He continued to teach at the Technical University as well as for adult education courses, and he remained a valuable member of the presidential office, where a 'tribute' was planned to mark his seventieth birthday and ten years of service.[137] He also continued with an unlikely project that he had pursued periodically in the post-war years, speculatively joining Shakespeare with Jewish culture, as only he could, to search for the origins of select Shakespearean phrases in the compilation of Jewish ethical maxims *Pirkei avot*.[138] In his last years, he found renewed pleasure in traditional Jewish sources, returning to his childhood study of Bible and Talmud, the very first complex

---

sister Paula joined him in Binyamina in 1933; Arnold, *Memoirs* (Heb.), 95–110. Anna and Leon's youngest child, Dora, showed no comparable interest in Zionism. A talented writer and translator like her mother and sister, Dora married Walter Benjamin in Berlin in 1917. As Walter noted to friends more than once, Leon and Anna—despite their straitened circumstances and in contrast to Walter's parents—went to considerable lengths to provide material and moral support in the early years of the young couple's terminally troubled marriage (they divorced in 1930 but remained in close contact until Walter's suicide in 1940). See Benjamin, *Gesammelte Briefe*, ii. 89, 278, 281; Eiland and Jennings, *Walter Benjamin: A Critical Life*, 91–147, 314–17. Dora moved to San Remo in Italy in 1934 and to London in 1939. Walter also stayed regularly at Anna's sister's sanatorium in Breitenstein.

[135] A. Kellner, *Leon Kellner*, 92.

[136] Ibid. 92–3. Once home, they began to plan for another visit to Palestine almost immediately.

[137] Hofrat Prof. Leon Kellner, 9 July 1928 (Kellner/Ableben), OS, AdR/01/PK, Zl. 4804; *Vorlesungsverzeichnis . . . 1927/28*, 13, 71. On adult education and other lectures, see e.g. *NFP*, 20 July 1928, 4; 22 July 1928, 17. See also *NFP*, 22 Mar. 1922, 9; 9 Sept. 1924, 7; *NWT*, 9 Dec. 1922, 8; *Arbeiter Zeitung*, 16 Sept. 1921, 5; 18 Mar. 1925, 11; *Tagblatt: Organ für die Interessen des werktätigen Volkes*, 17 Mar. 1925, 6.

[138] 'Shakespeare and Pirqe Aboth' (Dec. 1922), NLI, Schwadron Archive 01 19 916; *JC*, 22 May 1925, 34.

texts he had encountered.[139] His most precious project remained unfinished. By the end of 1928 he had completed the annotated editions of fourteen Shakespeare plays but, as a reviewer of the posthumously published book remarked, 'Death interfered'.[140] In early December 1928 he died at home of heart failure.

[139] York-Steiner, 'Leon Kellner', 4.

[140] *English Studies*, 14 (1932), 27. Kellner's *Erläuterungen und Textverbesserungen* was published in 1931. See *Shakespeare-Jahrbuch*, 70 (1934), 138–9; *Review of English Studies*, 9 (1933), 474–6; *English Studies*, 14 (1932), 27–32.

CONCLUSION

KELLNER'S DEATH was noted at home and abroad with dismay. The *Neue Freie Presse* regretted that Vienna had 'lost one of its strongest critical spirits [who] . . . united the most profound philosophical, historical-philological, and literary-historical knowledge with the most astute critical judgement'. More than just a scholar, he had been a writer with an 'exceptional gift for vivid description', a 'master stylist . . . in the most noble German tradition'.[1] The paper's London correspondent commented on the 'tremendous esteem' that Kellner had enjoyed in Britain, one of the few Austrians and Germans whose circle of British friends and colleagues had not been diminished by the war.[2] For *The Times* in London he had earned a place 'in the front rank of Shakespearean scholars'; his friend James Fullarton Muirhead added that 'there never lived a more genial or generous man, or one more fully endowed with the indefinable quality of personal magnetism'.[3]

The Austrian president, who was leaving office that very week, wrote to Anna to express his sorrow. 'I came to know him as an honest and principled man imbued with moral qualities. There developed a close and friendly relationship between us, and it is all the more painful for me that just as I am retiring from office I must also take leave from such a dear friend.'[4] Hainisch wrote later in his memoirs: 'in my long life I have met few men as outstanding as Leon Kellner.'[5] Hainisch's most senior official, Josef Löwenthal, who had planned to ask Kellner to work with the incoming president, wrote to Anna to convey his gratitude for the 'innumerable

---

[1] *NFP*, 6 Dec. 1928, 7. See also ibid. 8.

[2] *NFP*, 11 Dec. 1928 (Abendblatt), 1. See also *Prager Tagblatt*, 6 Dec. 1928, 5; *Illustrierte Kronen Zeitung*, 7 Dec. 1928, 8; *Die Stimme*, 13 Dec. 1928, 3; *JC*, 14 Dec. 1928, 8; *New York Times*, 7 Dec. 1928, 29; *Chwila*, 9 Dec. 1928, 7–8; 22 July 1939, 9–10; *Nowy Dziennik*, 12 Dec. 1928, 6.

[3] He was, said Muirhead, 'full of brilliant scholarship, wit, and geniality'; *The Times*, 10 Dec. 1928, 19. For the earlier obituary, see ibid., 7 Dec. 1928, 15. He was also praised as a devoted and creative teacher at school, university, and in adult education. See *Neues Wiener Journal*, 6 Dec. 1928, 7; *Arbeiter Zeitung*, 7 Dec. 1928, 7; *NFP*, 3 May 1930, 1–3; 3 Aug. 1930, 1–3; *WZ*, 9 Aug. 1930, 3.

[4] Hainisch to Anna Kellner, 6 Dec. 1928, OS, AdR/01/PK, Zl. 9279/28.

[5] Hainisch, *75 Jahre aus bewegter Zeit*, 229.

excellent services that Court Councillor Kellner has performed for us with his perfect command of English and with his altogether masterly style ... I can hardly describe how greatly I valued this outstanding man.'[6] For Löwenthal's deputy, Kellner had been an 'esteemed friend and patron'. He wrote to Anna that:

For ten years I had the opportunity to be in steady, often very close, contact with your late husband. Our association occasioned so much joy ... that I am truly deeply shaken to find myself at the graveside of this distinguished and eminent man ... His noble heart, clear mind, and crystalline character are an example to all of us.[7]

In the summer of 1932 the Vienna municipality renamed a street in Kellner's honour. Former president Karl Seitz, now the city's mayor, told Anna: 'I will never forget him but I would like others to remember him too.'[8] In December 1938, following the *Anschluss* with Nazi Germany in March, the city decided that Jewish street names were 'utterly intolerable' and Leon-Kellner-Weg was Aryanized accordingly. In 1947 Kellner's name was restored.[9]

'I was the happiest woman on earth', Anna wrote to Martin Buber, 'and I plunged from the highest peak of human happiness into the deepest depths of despair ... Now I vegetate, alternating between my older daughter and my son in Palestine and my youngest daughter in San Remo.'[10] Anna's biography of Leon, 'written with my heart and soul' as she told Buber, was published in Vienna in 1936; it read, commented one reviewer, like 'a beautiful, heartfelt novel' about 'a Jewish figure who brought credit to all of humanity'.[11]

---

[6] Kabinettsdirektor Löwenthal to Anna Kellner, 6 Dec. 1928, OS, AdR/01/PK, Zl. 9280/28.

[7] Kabinettsvizedirektor to Anna Kellner, 6 Dec. 1928, OS, AdR/01/PK, Zl. 9280. Kellner stipulated that there were to be no eulogies at his funeral and cremation. See York-Steiner, 'Leon Kellner', 4; *NFP*, 7 Dec. 1928, 8.   [8] A. Kellner, *Leon Kellner*, 84. See also *WZ*, 13 July 1932, 4.

[9] *NWT*, 10 Dec. 1938, 39 for the quotation; Rathkolb, *Straßennamen Wiens*, 26, 39. Leon-Kellner-Weg (for nearly ten years Wilhelm-Riehl-Weg) is a small street in the city's thirteenth district.

[10] Anna Kellner to Martin Buber, 4 Jan. 1935, NLI, Martin Buber Archive, ARC. MS Var. 350 008 361.a (Anna Kellner 1933–1937). See also Anna Kellner to Martin Buber, 14 Nov. 1935. Anna moved to Binyamina to live near Paula and Viktor, and died in Palestine in May 1941. See *JC*, 30 May 1941, 22.

[11] *Gerechtigkeit*, 29 Apr. 1937, 4. It was described in *Die Stimme* as 'poignant' and a 'monument

That a Galician Jew, immersed for almost the first twenty years of his life in a thoroughly traditional Jewish milieu, was able to establish himself as a bona fide member of the empire's cultural elite and exercise power as an elected member of a regional parliament indicates that Habsburg Austria after 1867 was a society open to talent and willing to accommodate a degree of difference. That he remained figuratively and literally east of his personal Eden (a professorship at the University of Vienna) indicates that there were limits, especially for Jews, both to how open state and society were and to how much difference they would accommodate. By temperament a realistic optimist, Kellner mostly perceived his glass as half full. Notwithstanding his elevated status in Bukovina, he retained a measure of ambivalence about life in Czernowitz. His political career there was intense and successful but brief; his academic reputation flourished but, like most of his colleagues, he was keenly aware that the university was not generally considered to be in the top flight of Austrian institutions; culturally, the city was on the eastern periphery of the empire. In other words, it was not Vienna. And it was in Vienna that he still spent more than half his time when a professor in Czernowitz. In so doing, he lived the tension—sometimes creative, sometimes destructive—between imperial centre and periphery. He managed the difficult balancing act of maintaining a simultaneous presence in both, although not without cost, and he brought something of each to the other.

He forged a similar synthesis by acculturating to European society and its high culture with enthusiasm, without renouncing the Jewish world that had formed him. Unreservedly devoted to German and English language and culture, he also read, wrote, and spoke Yiddish and Hebrew throughout his life. To his contemporaries he was an east European Jew who had become west European. He bridged the gap between these imprecise characterizations in two ways. In a letter to Anna in 1880 he had stated his credo: he wished to serve knowledge and be a helper to his people. He achieved both. The writer Heinrich York-Steiner, a friend from the Herzl era, put it succinctly: 'His vast knowledge belonged to the world; his heart to the Jewish people.'[12] In 1896 he turned to nationalism in the form of Zionism, an ideology and movement that aspired to Jewish unity

to love' (30 Sept. 1936, 7). For Anna's comment, see Anna Kellner to Martin Buber, 4 Jan. 1935, as n. 10 above.

[12] York-Steiner, 'Leon Kellner', 4.

164   CONCLUSION

and that helped him to fuse elements of 'east' and 'west' into a viable world view; neither Kellner's important role at the launch pad of political Zionism in Vienna nor his close friendship with Herzl have to date been adequately recognized. His nationalism was another balancing act, in this instance holding Palestine and the diaspora in a relatively stable equilibrium; centre and periphery in a Jewish guise. He remained not only east of Eden but also west of Zion.

Kellner's path from Jewish tradition to European high culture was not uncommon for east European Jews of the middle to late nineteenth century, although his route was unusual.[13] For York-Steiner, Kellner was a 'symbol' of precisely this kind of Jewish transformation, and the story of his life was therefore about 'more than the fate of an individual'.[14] Kellner's particular variation on this Haskalah theme—from parochialism to Enlightenment—took the form of a passion for English philology and literature, Shakespeare and German-language culture, complemented by nationalism in a Jewish key. Kellner felt the gravitational pull of European culture to be irresistible, but it did not erase his equally strong allegiance to the Jewish world. The depth of his investment in both was evident throughout his life. His steadfast faith in the Habsburg state that enabled these intermittently converging attachments to coexist was shared by many Jews in the second half of the nineteenth century and was a distinguishing feature of Jewish life in the Habsburg lands. The Jews were a minority that by and large perceived this state as benevolent and protective, the latter necessary because of the ever-present antisemitism in Habsburg society. Many of these elements were at play in Kellner's creation of the Jewish Toynbee Hall. The model was English, the language German, the culture Jewish and European, the site Viennese, the animating spirit social-liberal and Zionist. Bitter experience, however, had taught him the limits of convergence, and he feared that a London-style Toynbee Hall established and run by Jews in Vienna would be strangled at birth by antisemitism. Instead, as a *Jewish* Toynbee Hall, it would be the same but different, neatly capturing an essential aspect of the Jewish situation in imperial Austria.

Kellner's world was destroyed twice over. Habsburg Austria came to an end in 1918, east-central European Jewry in 1945. The poet Paul Celan,

[13] For parallel examples, see Prokop-Janiec, 'Jewish Moderna in Galicia'.
[14] York-Steiner, 'Leon Kellner', 3.

a frequent visitor in his teenage years to the Jewish Toynbee Hall in Czernowitz, was an admirer of Kellner's writing and politics, and later in life more than once invoked Kellner as a metonym of this lost world.[15] To write about Kellner's life and work is to recover at least part of what was lost.

[15] Winkler, "'. . . zu erörten versuchte, was ihnen Ortslosigkeit war'", 547–8, 554–6; Chalfen, *Paul Celan*, 23–4.

BIBLIOGRAPHY

Archives

American Jewish Archives, Hebrew Union College, Cincinnati (AJA)
   Gotthard Deutsch Papers, Manuscript Collection 123, Box 2, folder 17 (Kellner, Leon 1909; 1920-1921) (GDP)

Archiv der Technischen Universität Wien (ATUW)
   Personalakt Leon Kellner

Archiv der Universität Wien (AUW)
   Personalakt Universität Wien (PUW)
      2172/Kellner (1890)

Austrian National Library, Vienna (ANL)
   Nachlass Luick, 274/113 (Leon Kellner)

Central Archives for the History of the Jewish People, Jerusalem (CAHJP)
   Berlin/DBe/4/497

Central Zionist Archives, Jerusalem (CZA)
   A12/50
   A72/9
   A74/7; A74/9; A74/29; A74/33-4   K2/19
   A120/423   W1/789
   H1/1264-2; H1/1455-2; H1/1455-5;   Z2/389; Z2/390; Z2/436
   H1/1455-17; H1/1455-22; H1/1455-24; Z3/786
   H1/1455-25; H1/1455-28; H1/1455-29; Z4/0998
   H1/1455-39; H1/2605; H1/3444

National Library of Israel (NLI)
   Martin Buber Archive, ARC. MS Var. 350 008 361.a (Anna Kellner 1933–1937)
   Schwadron Archive 01 19 916

Österreichisches Staatsarchiv (OS)
   Allgemeines Verwaltungsarchiv (AV)
      5C/Czernowitz (AV/5C/Cz)
      Professorenakt-Czernowitz, Kellner (AV/PCK)
      Professorenakt-Uni Wien, Kellner (AV/PUW)
   Archiv der Republik
      AdR/01/PK/Kellner

Wiener Stadt- und Landesarchiv (WSL)
Gelöschte Vereine

Press and Periodicals

Allgemeine Zeitung
The American Mercury
Anglia
Annalen des k. k. naturhistorischen Hofmuseums
Arbeiter Zeitung
The Author
Bausteine
Beiblatt zur Anglia
Bukowinaer Post
Chwila
Czernowitzer Allgemeine Zeitung
Czernowitzer Allgemeine Zeitung/Tagblatt
Czernowitzer Tagblatt
Deutsche Wochenschrift
Dr. Bloch's Österreichische Wochenschrift
Englische Studien
The English Journal
English Studies
Frankfurter Israelitisches Gemeindeblatt
Freies Blatt
Germanisch-romanische Monatschrift
Gerechtigkeit
Illustrierte Kronen Zeitung
Das interessante Blatt
Israelitische Rundschau
Jahrbuch der deutschen Shakespeare-Gesellschaft
Jewish Chronicle
The Journal of English and German Philology
Jüdische Rundschau
Der Jüdische Volksrat
Jüdische Volksstimme
Jüdische Zeitung
Jüdisches Gemeindeblatt für die Israelitische Gemeinde zu Frankfurt am Main
Das literarische Echo
Mährisches Tagblatt

Menorah: Illustrierte Monatsschrift für die jüdische Familie
The Mississippi Valley Historical Review
Modern Language Review
Die Nation: Wochenschrift für Politik, Volkswirtschaft und Literatur
Neue Freie Presse
Neues Wiener Journal
Neues Wiener Tagblatt
Die Neuzeit
Neue Zeitung
New York Times
Nowy Dziennik
Prager Tagblatt
Die Presse
The Review of English Studies
Shakespeare-Jahrbuch
Die Stimme
Tagblatt: Organ für die Interessen des werktätigen Volkes
The Times
Times Literary Supplement
Die Volkswehr
Die Wahrheit
Die Welt
Wiener Hausfrauen-Zeitung
Wiener Zeitung

Works by Leon Kellner

'Abwechslung und Tautologie: Zwei Eigenthümlichkeiten des alt- und mittelenglischen Stils', *Englische Studien*, 20 (1895), 1–24.

American Literature, trans. Julia Franklin (New York, 1915).

Anglická literatura: doby nejnovější od Dickense až k Shawovi (Prague, 1928).

Caxton's Blanchardyn and Eglantine (London, 1890).

Englische Epigonenpoesie (Munich, 1889).

Die englische Literatur im Zeitalter der Königin Viktoria (Leipzig, 1909); published in a revised edn. as *Die englische Literatur der neuesten Zeit von Dickens bis Shaw* (Leipzig, 1921).

'Englische Wortforschung', *Germanisch-romanische Monatsschrift*, 2 (1910), 27–35.

English Fairy Tales (ed.; Leipzig, 1917).

Erläuterungen und Textverbesserungen zu vierzehn Dramen Shakespeares (Leipzig, 1931).

'Der erste Schultag', *Menorah: Illustrierte Monatsschrift für die jüdische Familie*, 7 (1929), 393–402.

BIBLIOGRAPHY

The Essays, or Counsels Civil and Moral by Francis Bacon (ed.; Leipzig, 1917).

Geschichte der nordamerikanischen Literatur (Berlin, 1913).

'Gotthard Deutsch', *Menorah: Illustrierte Monatsschrift für die jüdische Familie*, 1 (1923), 12–13.

'Herzl und Zangwill', in T. Nussenblatt (ed.), *Zeitgenossen über Herzl* (Brünn, 1929), 112–14.

Historical Outlines of English Syntax (London, 1892).

Ein Jahr in England 1898–1899 (Stuttgart, 1900).

'Jakob Schipper', *Beiblatt zur Anglia*, 26 (1915), 193–202.

Eine jüdische Toynbee-Halle (Vienna, 1901).

Jüdische Weihestunden (Czernowitz, 1914).

Lehrbuch der englischen Sprache for Mädchen-Lyzeen und andere höhere Mädchenschulen (Vienna, 1902).

Meine Schüler (Berlin, 1930).

'Mrs. Humphrey Ward und der englische Roman der Gegenwart', *Verhandlungen der zweiundvierzigsten Versammlung deutscher Philologen und Schulmänner in Wien vom 24. bis 27. Mai 1893* (Leipzig, 1894), 420–6.

Neues und vollständiges Handwörterbuch der englischen und deutschen Sprache von Dr. F. W. Thieme. 18. Auflage vollständig neu bearbeitet von Dr. Leon Kellner: 1. Theil English–Deutsch (Braunschweig, 1902).

'A Note on Shakespeare', *The American Mercury* (Feb. 1924), 237–40.

Nursery Rhymes (Leipzig, 1917).

'Oliver Wendell Holmes', *Biográphische Blätter: Jahrbuch für lebensgeschichtliche Kunst und Forschung*, 1 (1895), 413–22.

'Die Quelle von Marlowes Jew of Malta', *Englische Studien*, 10 (1887), 80–111.

Restoring Shakespeare: A Critical Analysis of the Misreadings in Shakespeare's Works (London, 1925).

Review of Thomas Malory's 'Le Morte Darthur', *Englische Studien*, 15 (1891), 424–5.

Shakespeare (Leipzig, 1900).

Shakespeare-Wörterbuch (Leipzig, 1922).

'Shelley's "Queen Mab" und Volney's "Les Ruines"', *Englische Studien*, 22 (1896), 9–40.

'Sir Clyomon and Sir Clamydes: Ein romantisches Schauspiel des 16. Jahrhunderts', *Englische Studien*, 13 (1889), 187–229.

'Suggest, Suggestion, Suggestive', *Bausteine: Zeitschrift für neuenglische Wortforschung*, 1 (1906), 1–28.

'Syntaktische Bemerkungen zu Ipomadon', *Englische Studien*, 18 (1893), 282–92.

Theodor Herzls Lehrjahre (1860–1895) (Vienna, 1920).

Theodor Herzl's Zionistische Schriften (ed.; Berlin, 1905).

'To Suggest: Ein Beitrag zur neuenglischen Lexikographie', *Beiträge zur neueren Philologie: Jakob Schipper zum 19. Juli 1902 dargebracht* (Vienna, 1902), 301–23.

BIBLIOGRAPHY

'Ein Waisendorf', *Menorah: Illustrierte Monatsschrift für die jüdische Familie*, 4 (1926), 93–6.

'Zur Sprache Christopher Marlowe's', *Sechsunddreizigster Jahresbericht über die k. k. Staats-Oberrealschule und die Gewerbliche Fortbildungsschule im III. Bezirke (Landstraße) in Wien für das Schuljahr 1886/87* (Vienna, 1887), 3–26.

'Zur Textkritik von Chaucer's Boethius', *Englische Studien*, 14 (1890), 1–53.

with PAULA ARNOLD and ARTHUR L. DELISLE, *Austria of the Austrians and Hungary of the Hungarians* (London, 1914).

with JULIUS BAUDISCH, *Sonnenburgs Grammatik der englischen Sprache* (Vienna, 1895).

with ANNA KELLNER, *Englische Märchen: Für die deutsche Jugend bearbeitet* (Vienna, 1899).

Other Published Sources

ABEL, EMILY K., 'Canon Barnett and the First Thirty Years of Toynbee Hall' (Ph.D. diss., University of London, 1969).

ADAMCZYK, MIECZYSŁAW JERZY, *Edukacja a przeobrażenia społeczności żydowskich w monarchii habsburskiej 1774–1914* (Wrocław, 1998).

ADLGASSER, FRANZ, *American Individualism Abroad: Herbert Hoover, die American Relief Administration und Österreich, 1919–1923* (Vienna, 1993).

ALEKSIUN, NATALIA, 'The Galician Paradigm? Postwar Experiences of German-Speaking Polish Jewish Survivors', *Leo Baeck Institute Year Book*, 64 (2019), 159–78.

ALMOG, SHMUEL, *Zionism and History: The Rise of a New Jewish Consciousness*, trans. Ina Friedman (New York, 1987).

——JEHUDA REINHARZ, and ANITA SHAPIRA (eds.), *Zionism and Religion* (Hanover, NH, 1998).

ALTENHUBER, HANS, *Universitäre Volksbildung in Österreich 1895–1937* (Vienna, 1995).

AN-SKI, S. [Solomon Zainwil Rapaport], *The Destruction of Galicia: The Jewish Catastrophe in Poland, Galicia and Bukovina* [Der yidisher khurbn fun poyln, galitsye, un bukovine], in id., *Collected Writings* [Gezamlte shriftn], 15 vols. (New York, 1921), vols. iv–vi.

ARNOLD, PAULA, 'Herzl and Kellner' (Heb.), *Shivat Tsion*, 4 (1955–6), 114–60.

——'Leon Kellner (1859–1928)', *Herzl Year Book*, 2 (1959), 171–83.

——*Memoirs with Love* [Zikhronot be'ahavah] (Jerusalem, 1968).

ARONSOHN, MAURYCY, 'Zur Geschichte der schlesischen Juden', *Monatsschrift der Oesterreichisch-Israelitischen Union*, 17 (June–July 1905), 12–21.

ASCHHEIM, STEVEN E., *Brothers and Strangers: The East European Jew in German and German Jewish Consciousness, 1800–1923* (Madison, Wis., 1982).

AVINERI, SHLOMO, *Herzl: Theodor Herzl and the Foundation of the Jewish State*, trans. Haim Watzman (London, 2014).

BAŁABAN, MAJER, *Historia Lwowskiej synagogi postępowej* (Lwów, 1937).

BARNETT, SAMUEL, and HENRIETTA BARNETT, *Towards Social Reform* (London, 1909).

BATO, LUDWIG, *Die Juden im alten Wien* (Vienna, 1928).

BEALES, DEREK, *Joseph II: Against the World, 1780–1790* (Cambridge, 2009).

——*Joseph II: In the Shadow of Maria Theresa, 1741–1780* (Cambridge, 1987).

BECK, ERICH, *Bukowina: Land zwischen Orient und Okzident* (Freilassing, 1963).

BEIN, ALEX et al., *Theodor Herzl: Briefe und Tagebücher*, 7 vols. (Frankfurt am Main, 1983–96).

BELLER, STEVEN, *The Jews of Vienna: A Cultural History* (Cambridge, 1989).

BENJAMIN, WALTER, *Gesammelte Briefe*, ed. Christoph Gödde and Henri Lonitz, 6 vols. (Frankfurt am Main, 1995–2000).

Bericht des Curatoriums der Baron Hirsch-Stiftung zur Beförderung des Volksschulunterrichts im Königreiche Galizien und Lodomerien 1900–1901 (Vienna, 1902).

Bericht über das erste Betriebsjahr der Jüdischen Toynbeehalle der Berliner Bnei-Briss-Logen (12. Oktober 1904–30. März 1905).

Bericht über das fünfte Betriebsjahr der Jüdischen Toynbeehalle der Berliner Bnei-Briss-Logen (19. Oktober 1908 bis Ende März 1909).

BIALE, DAVID et al., *Hasidism: A New History* (Princeton, NJ, 2018).

BIHL, WOLFDIETER, 'Die Juden', in Adam Wandruszka and Peter Urbanitsch (eds.), *Die Habsburgermonarchie 1848–1918*, iii: *Die Völker des Reiches*, pt. 2 (Vienna, 1981), 880–948.

BILLROTH, THEODOR, *Über das Lehren und Lernen der medicinischen Wissenschaften an den Universitäten der deutschen Nation* (Vienna, 1876).

BINDER, HARALD, *Galizien in Wien: Parteien, Wahlen, Fraktionen und Abgeordnete im Übergang zur Massenpolitik* (Vienna, 2005).

BLACK, EUGENE, *The Social Politics of Anglo-Jewry 1880–1920* (Oxford, 1980).

BLAZER, YITZHAK, 'A Survey of Religious Jewry in Tarnów' (Yid.), in Avraham Chomet (ed.), *The Life and Destruction of a Jewish City* [Torne: kiem un khurbn fun a yidisher shtot; Tarnov: kiyumah vehurbanah shel ir yehudit] (Tel Aviv, 1954), 217–24.

BLOCH, JOSEPH SAMUEL, *Der nationale Zwist und die Juden in Oesterreich* (Vienna, 1886).

BONAR, ANDREW A., and ROBERT MURRAY M'CHEYNE, *Narrative of a Mission Enquiry to the Jews from the Church of Scotland in 1839* (Philadelphia, 1845).

BOOTH, WILLIAM, *In Darkest England and the Way Out* (London, 1890).

BOYER, JOHN W., *Culture and Political Crisis in Vienna: Christian Socialism in Power, 1897–1918* (Chicago, 1995).

—— 'Freud, Marriage, and Late Viennese Liberalism: A Commentary from 1905', *Journal of Modern History*, 50 (1978), 72–102.

BRÄMER, ANDREAS, 'Die Anfangsjahre des jüdisch-theologischen Seminars: Zum Wandel des Rabbinerberufs im 19. Jahrhundert', in Manfred Hettling, Andreas Reinke, and Norbert Conrads (eds.), *Breslau zu Hause? Juden in einer mitteleuropäischen Metropole der Neuzeit* (Hamburg, 2003), 99–112.

BRANN, MARCUS, *Geschichte des jüdisch-theologischen Seminars (Fraenckel'sche Stiftung) in Breslau: Festschrift zum fünfzigjährigen Jubiläum der Anstalt* (Breslau, 1904).

BRENNER, MICHAEL, *The Renaissance of Jewish Culture in Weimar Germany* (New Haven, Conn., 1996).

BRIGGS, ASA, and ANNE MACARTNEY, *Toynbee Hall: The First Hundred Years* (London, 1984).

Die Bukowina: Eine allgemeine Heimatkunde verfasst anlässlich des 50jährigen glorreichen Regierungsjubiläums seiner kaiserlichen und königlichen Apostolischen Majestät unseres Allergnädigsten Kaisers und Obersten Kriegsherrn durch die k. k. Landes-Gendarmerie-Commandos N. 13 (Czernowitz, 1899).

BUSSGANG, JULIAN J., 'The Progressive Synagogue in Lwów', *Polin*, 11 (1998), 127–53.

BUSZKO, JOSEF, *Zum Wandel der Gesellschaftsstruktur in Galizien und in der Bukowina* (Vienna, 1978).

CAINE, BARBARA, *Biography and History*, 2nd edn. (London, 2019).

CAMERON, KENNETH NEILL, *The Young Shelley: Genesis of a Radical* (London, 1951).

ČAPKOVÁ, KATEŘINA, *Czechs, Germans, Jews? National Identity and the Jews of Bohemia*, trans. Derek and Marzia Paton (New York, 2012).

—— 'Jewish Elites in the 19th and 20th Centuries: The B'nai B'rith Order in Central Europe', *Judaica Bohemiae*, 36 (2000), 119–42.

CARR, GILBERT, 'Time and Space in the Café Griensteidl and the Café Central', in Charlotte Ashby, Tag Gronberg, and Simon Shaw-Miller (eds.), *The Viennese Café and Fin-de-Siècle Culture* (New York, 2013), 32–49.

CARSTEN, FRANCES L., *The First Austrian Republic: A Study Based on British and Austrian Documents* (Aldershot, 1986).

CATALAN, TULLIA, *La Comunità ebraica di Trieste (1781–1914): Politica, società e cultura* (Trieste, 2000).

CEAUŞU, MIHAIL-ŞTEFAN, 'Der Landtag der Bukowina', in Helmut Rumpler and Peter Urbanitsch (eds.), *Die Habsburgermonarchie 1848–1918*, vii: *Verfassung und Parlamentarismus*, pt. 2 (Vienna, 2000), 2171–98.

CESARANI, DAVID, *The Jewish Chronicle and Anglo-Jewry, 1841–1991* (Cambridge, 1994).

CHALFEN, ISRAEL, *Paul Celan: Eine Biographie seiner Jugend* (Frankfurt am Main, 1979).

CHEESMAN, TOM, 'Reading Originals by the Light of Translations', in Peter Holland (ed.), *Shakespeare: Origins and Originality* (Cambridge, 2015), 87–98.

CHOMET, AVRAHAM, 'On the History of the Jews in Tarnów' (Yid.), in Avraham Chomet (ed.), *The Life and Destruction of a Jewish City* [Torne: kiem un khurbn fun a yidisher shtot; Tarnov: kiyumah veḥurbanah shel ir yehudit] (Tel Aviv, 1954), 3–186.

——(ed.), *The Life and Destruction of a Jewish City* [Torne: kiem un khurbn fun a yidisher shtot; Tarnov: kiyumah veḥurbanah shel ir yehudit] (Tel Aviv, 1954).

COHEN, GARY B., *Education and Middle-Class Society in Imperial Austria 1848–1918* (West Lafayette, Ind., 1996).

——'Education and the Politics of Jewish Integration', in Mitchell B. Hart and Tony Michels (eds.), *The Cambridge History of Judaism*, viii: *The Modern World, 1815–2000* (Cambridge, 2017), 477–504.

—— *The Politics of Access to Advanced Education in Late Imperial Austria*, Working Paper 93-6 (2002), Center for Austrian Studies, University of Minnesota.

—— *The Politics of Ethnic Survival: Germans in Prague, 1861-1914*, 2nd edn. (West Lafayette, Ind., 2006).

——'Die Studenten der Wiener Universität von 1860 bis 1900: Ein soziales und geographisches Profil', in Richard Georg Plaschka and Karlheinz Mack (eds.), *Wegenetz europäischen Geistes*, 2 vols. (Munich 1983, 1987), ii: *Universitäten und Studenten*, 290–316.

COHEN, ISRAEL, *Theodor Herzl: Founder of Political Zionism* (New York, 1959).

CORBEA-HOISIE, ANDREI, *Czernowitzer Geschichten: Über eine städtische Kultur in Mittelosteuropa* (Vienna, 2003).

——(ed.), *Jüdisches Städtebild Czernowitz* (Frankfurt am Main, 1998).

——'Urbane Kohabitation in Czernowitz als Modell einer gespannten Multikulturalität', *Neohelicon*, 23 (1996), 77–93.

——'Wie die Juden Gewalt schreien: Aurel Onciul und der antisemitische Kurs in der Bukowiner Öffentlichkeit nach 1907', *East Central Europe*, 39 (2012), 13–60.

DEAK, JOHN, 'Dismantling Empire: Ignaz Seipel and Austria's Financial Crisis, 1922–1925', in Günter Bischof, Fritz Plasser, and Peter Berger (eds.), *From Empire to Republic: Post-World War I Austria* (New Orleans, 2010), 123–41.

——'Fashioning the Rest: National Ascription in Austria after the First World War', in Marcus M. Payk and Roberta Pergher (eds.), *Beyond Versailles: Sovereignty, Legitimacy, and the Formation of New Polities after the Great War* (Bloomington, Ind., 2019), 124–42.

—— *Forging a Multinational State: State Making in Imperial Austria from the Enlightenment to the First World War* (Stanford, Calif., 2015).

BIBLIOGRAPHY

——and JONATHAN E. GUMZ, 'How to Break a State: The Habsburg Monarchy's Internal War, 1914–1918', *American Historical Review*, 122 (2017), 1105–36.

DEUTSCH, GOTTHARD, *Scrolls: Essays on Jewish History and Literature, and Kindred Subjects*, 2 vols. (Cincinnati, 1917).

DICKSON, MORA, *Teacher Extraordinary: Joseph Lancaster, 1778–1838* (Sussex, 1996).

DIKAU, JOACHIM, 'Geschichte der Volkshochschule', in Franz Pöggeler (ed.), *Geschichte der Erwachsenenbildung* (Stuttgart, 1975), 107–31.

DOBRSHANSKI, OLEXANDR, 'Der politische Kampf in der Bukowina um die Landesreformen am Anfang des 20. Jahrhunderts', *Südostdeutsches Archiv*, 38/39 (1995/96), 117–32.

DORNSEIFER, MARIA, 'Geschichte der Settlements/Nachbarschaftsheime', in Franz Pöggeler (ed.), *Geschichte der Erwachsenenbildung* (Stuttgart, 1975), 229–37.

DOSTAL, THOMAS, 'Bildung zu "Volkstum und Heimat" in der österreichischen Volksbildung der Zwischenkriegszeit' (Ph.D. diss., University of Vienna, 2017).

DUFFY, CIAN, *Shelley and the Revolutionary Sublime* (Cambridge, 2005).

DYNNER, GLENN, 'Those Who Stayed: Women and Jewish Traditionalism in East Central Europe', in Antony Polonsky, Hanna Węgrzynek, and Andrzej Żbikowski (eds.), *New Directions in the History of the Jews in the Polish Lands* (Boston, 2018), 295–312.

EILAND, HOWARD, and MICHAEL W. JENNINGS, *Walter Benjamin: A Critical Life* (Cambridge, 2014).

EMERSON, RALPH WALDO, *Self-Reliance and Other Essays* (New York, 1993).

Encyclopedia of Jewish Communities: Poland [Pinkas hakehilot: Polin], 8 vols.; vol. iii: *Western Galicia and Silesia* (Jerusalem, 1976).

Die Ergebnisse der Volkszählung und der mit derselben verbundenen Zählung der häuslichen Nutzthiere vom 31. December 1880 in den im Reichsrate vertretenen Königreichen und Länder (Vienna, 1880).

ERNE, LUKAS, 'Emendation and the Editorial Reconfiguration of Shakespeare', in Margaret Jane Kidnie and Sonia Massai (eds.), *Shakespeare and Textual Studies* (Cambridge, 2015), 300–14.

FALTER, MATTHIAS, and SASKA STACHOWITSCH, '"Denn für uns Juden erhebt sich keine Stimme!": Parlamentarische Praxis des Jüdischen Klubs im Abgeordnetenhaus 1907 bis 1911', *Chilufim: Zeitschrift für jüdische Kulturgeschichte*, 7 (2009), 43–66.

FELDMAN, DAVID, *Englishmen and Jews: Social Relations and Political Culture 1840–1914* (New Haven, Conn., 1994).

——'Mr Lewinstein goes to Parliament: Rethinking the History and Historiography of Jewish Immigration', *East European Jewish Affairs*, 47 (2017), 134–49.

FEWSTER, KEVIN, 'Ellis Ashmead Bartlett and the Making of the Anzac Legend', *Journal of Australian Studies*, 6 (1982), 17–30.

FILL, ALWIN, 'Anglistik und Amerikanistik', in Karl Acham (ed.), *Geschichte der österreichischen Humanwissenschaften*, v: *Sprache, Literatur und Kunst* (Vienna, 2003), 231–55.

FISCHER, R., 'Zur Frage nach der Autorschaft von Sir Clyomon and Sir Clamides', *Englische Studien*, 14 (1890), 344–65.

FLUSSER, GUSTAV, 'Die jüdische Toynbeehalle in Prag', *B'nai B'rith: Monatsblätter der Großloge für den Čechoslovakischen Staat*, 2 (1923), 141–3.

——'Die Prager Toynbeehalle', *B'nai B'rith: Monatsblätter der Großloge für den Čechoslovakischen Staat*, 5 (1926), 173–5.

FOLTINEK, HERBERT, 'Dickens in Austria and German-Speaking Switzerland', in Michael Hollington (ed.), *The Reception of Charles Dickens in Europe* (London, 2013), 247–56.

FRÄNKEL, JOSEF, *Dr. Sigmund Werner: Ein Mitarbeiter Herzls* (Prague, 1939).

FRANZOS, KARL EMIL, *Aus Halb-Asien: Culturbilder aus Galizien, Südrussland, der Bukowina und Rumänien*, 2 vols. (Leipzig, 1876).

FREIDENREICH, HARRIET PASS, *Female, Jewish, and Educated: The Lives of Central European University Women* (Bloomington, Ind., 2002).

——*The Jews of Yugoslavia: A Quest for Community* (Philadelphia, 1979).

FRIEDJUNG, HEINRICH, *Österreich von 1848 bis 1860*, 2 vols. (Stuttgart, 1912).

FRIEDLER, MENASCHE JOSEPH, 'Die galizischen Juden vom wirtschaftlichen, kulturellen und staatsbürgerlichen Standpunkte 1815–1848' (Ph.D. diss., University of Vienna, 1923).

FRIEDMAN, ISAIAH, *Germany, Turkey, and Zionism, 1897–1918* (Oxford, 1977).

FRIEDMANN, FILIP, *Die galizischen Juden im Kampfe um ihre Gleichberechtigung (1848–1868)* (Frankfurt, 1929).

——'Die Judenfrage im galizischen Landtag 1861–1868', *Monatsschrift für Geschichte und Wissenschaft des Judentums*, 72 (1928), 379–90, 457–77.

FULTON, JOE B., 'Contemporary and Early Reception and Criticism (to 1960)', in John Bird (ed.), *Mark Twain in Context* (Cambridge, 2020), 295–304.

GAISBAUER, ADOLF, *Davidstern und Doppeladler: Zionismus und jüdischer Nationalismus in Österreich* (Vienna, 1988).

GĄSOWSKI, THOMAS, 'From Austeria to the Manor: Jewish Landowners in Autonomous Galicia', *Polin*, 12 (1999), 120–36.

GELBER, NATHAN MICHAEL, *The History of the Zionist Movement in Galicia, 1875–1918* [Toledot hatenuah hatsiyonit begalitsiyah], 2 vols. (Jerusalem, 1985).

GERTNER, CHAIM, '*Batei Midrash* in Galicia in the Nineteenth Century as Institutes for the Development of Scholars' (Heb.), in Immanuel Etkes (ed.), *Yeshivot and Batei Midrash* [Yeshivot uvatei midrash] (Jerusalem, 2006), 163–86.

GILLIVER, PETER, *The Making of the* Oxford English Dictionary (Oxford, 2016).

GINN, GEOFFREY A. C., *Culture, Philanthropy and the London Poor, 1880–1900* (Abingdon, 2017).

GOLDMAN, EMMA, *Living My Life*, 2 vols. (1931; New York, 1970).

GOODE, WILLIAM, 'Austria', *Journal of the British Institute of International Affairs*, 1 (1922), 35–54.

GOODMAN, PAUL, *Zionism in England: English Zionist Federation, 1899–1929* (London, 1929).

GRANICK, JACLYN, *International Jewish Humanitarianism in the Age of the Great War* (Cambridge, 2021).

GREENE, RICHARD, *Edith Sitwell: Avant-Garde Poet, English Genius* (London, 2011).

GRILL, TOBIAS, *Der Westen im Osten: Deutsches Judentum und jüdische Bildungsreform in Osteuropa (1783–1939)* (Göttingen, 2013).

GRUNWALD, KURT, 'A Note on the Baron Hirsch Stiftung Vienna 1888–1914', *Leo Baeck Institute Year Book*, 17 (1972), 227–36.

GRUNWALD, MAX, *Vienna* (Philadelphia, 1936).

GUTWEIN, DANIEL, *The Divided Elite: Economics, Politics and Anglo-Jewry, 1882–1917* (Leiden, 1992).

HAAS, GUSTAV, 'Toynbeehalle', *B'nai B'rith: Monatsblätter der Großloge für den Čechoslovakischen Staat*, 1 (1922), 125–8.

HAGEN, WILLIAM W., *Anti-Jewish Violence in Poland, 1914–1920* (Cambridge, 2018).

HAIDER, EDGARD, *Wien 1918: Agonie der Kaiserstadt* (Vienna, 2018).

HAINISCH, MICHAEL, *75 Jahre aus bewegter Zeit* (Vienna, 1978).

HÄUSLER, WOLFGANG, *Das galizische Judentum in der Habsburgermonarchie: Im Lichte der zeitgenössischen Publizistik und Reiseliteratur von 1772–1848* (Munich, 1979).

HAUSTEIN, SABINE, and ANJA WALLER, 'Jüdische Settlements in Europa: Ansätze einer transnationalen sozial-, geschlechter- und ideenhistorischen Forschung', *Medaon*, 3 (2009), 1–14.

HEALY, MAUREEN, *Vienna and the Fall of the Habsburg Empire: Total War and Everyday Life in World War I* (Cambridge, 2004).

HEIN, ROBERT, *Studentischer Antisemitismus in Österreich* (Vienna, 1984).

HELLMANN, ALBRECHT [SIEGMUND KAZNELSON], 'Die Geschichte der österreichisch-jüdischen Kongressbewegung: Zur Frage der nationalen Minderheitsrechte der Juden', *Der Jude*, 5 (1920/21), 204–14, 389–95, 634–45, 685–96.

HENSELLEK, THOMAS, *Die letzten Jahre der kaiserlichen Bukowina: Studien zur Landespolitik im Herzogtum Bukowina von 1909 bis 1914* (Hamburg, 2011).

HERŞCOVICI, LUCIAN-ZEEV, 'Iacob Isac Niemirower', *YIVO Encyclopedia of Jews in Eastern Europe*, 2 vols. (New Haven, Conn., 2008), ii. 1268–9.

HERZIG, FRANCZISEK, 'Tarnów od r. 1567 do r. 1907', in Jan Leniek, Franczisek Herzig, and Franczisek Leśniak, *Dzieje miasta Tarnowa* (Tarnów, 2011), 81–266.

HESS, JONATHAN M., *Middlebrow Literature and the Making of German-Jewish Identity* (Stanford, Calif., 2010).

HIRSCH, ERIKA, *Jüdisches Vereinsleben in Hamburg bis zum Ersten Weltkrieg: Jüdisches Selbstverständnis zwischen Antisemitismus und Assimilation* (Frankfurt am Main, 1996).

HÖBELT, LOTHAR, *Die erste Republik Österreich (1918–1938): Das Provisorium* (Vienna, 2018).

HÖDL, KLAUS, *Als Bettler in die Leopoldstadt: Galizische Juden auf dem Weg nach Wien* (Vienna, 1994).

——*Zwischen Wienerlied und Der Kleine Kohn: Juden in der Wiener populären Kultur um 1900* (Göttingen, 2017).

Hof- und Staats-Handbuch der Österreichisch-Ungarischen Monarchie für 1882 (Vienna, 1882).

HOFF, MASCHA, *Johann Kremenezky und die Gründung des KKL* (Frankfurt am Main, 1986).

HOFFMANN-HOLTER, BEATRIX, *'Abreisendmachung': Jüdische Kriegsflüchtlinge in Wien 1914 bis 1925* (Vienna, 1995).

HOLLEIS, EVA, *Die Sozialpolitische Partei: Sozialliberale Bestrebungen in Wien um 1900* (Munich, 1978).

HÜCHTKER, DIETLIND, *Geschichte als Performance: Politische Bewegungen in Galizien um 1900* (Frankfurt am Main, 2014).

HYE, HANS PETER, 'Die Länder im Gefüge der Habsburgermonarchie', in Helmut Rumpler and Peter Urbanitsch (eds.), *Die Habsburgermonarchie 1848–1918*, vii: *Verfassung und Parlamentarismus*, pt. 2 (Vienna, 2000), 2427–64.

Jahresbericht der Jüdischen Toynbee-Halle (für Volksbildung und Unterhaltung) der Berliner Bnei-Briss-Logen über das achte Betriebs-Jahr (1.11.1911 bis Ende März 1912).

Jahresbericht der Jüdischen Toynbee-Halle (für Volksbildung und Unterhaltung) der Berliner Bnei-Briss-Logen über das neunte Betriebs-Jahr (1.11.1912 bis Ende März 1913).

Jahresbericht der Jüdischen Toynbee Halle in Wien 1904 (Vienna, 1904).

Jahresbericht der Jüdischen Toynbee Halle in Wien über die Vereinstätigkeit im Jahre 1907 (Vienna, 1908).

Jahresbericht des jüdisch-theologischen Seminars Fraenckel'scher Stiftung 1877 (Breslau, 1878).

Jahresbericht des k. k. Staatsgymnasiums im IX. Bezirke in Wien für das Schuljahr 1885/6 (Vienna, 1886).

Jahresbericht des k. k. Staatsgymnasiums zu Bielitz für das Schuljahr 1900/1901 (Bielitz, 1901).

Jahresbericht des Privat-Mädchen-Lyzeums Luithlen Wien 1908/09 (Vienna, 1909).

Jahresbericht des Privat-Mädchen-Lyzeums Luithlen Wien 1909/10 (Vienna, 1910).

Jahresbericht des Privat-Mädchen-Lyzeums Luithlen Wien 1910/11 (Vienna, 1911).

Jahres-Bericht der Staats-Oberrealschule in Troppau für das Schuljahr 1891/92 (Troppau, 1892).

Jahres-Bericht der Staats-Oberrealschule in Troppau für das Schuljahr 1892/93 (Troppau, 1893).

JAQUES, HEINRICH, *Denkschrift über die Stellung der Juden in Oesterreich* (Vienna, 1859).

JOWETT, JOHN, 'Full Pricks and Great P's: Spellings, Punctuation, Accidentals', in Margaret Jane Kidnie and Sonia Massai (eds.), *Shakespeare and Textual Studies* (Cambridge, 2015), 317–31.

Die jüdische Toynbee-Halle in Wien im zweiten Jahre ihres Bestehens (Vienna, 1902).

'Eine jüdische Volkshochschule in Krakau: Ein Brief', *Neue Jüdische Monatshefte*, 1 (1916/17), 264–5.

JUDSON, PIETER M., *Exclusive Revolutionaries: Liberal Politics, Social Experience, and National Identity in the Austrian Empire 1848–1914* (Ann Arbor, Mich., 1996).

KADISH, ALON, *Apostle Arnold: The Life and Death of Arnold Toynbee, 1852–1883* (Durham, NC, 1986).

KAHANE, AVRAHAM, 'Tarnów, A Center of Torah, Hasidism and Culture' (Yid.), in Avraham Chomet (ed.), *The Life and Destruction of a Jewish City* [Torne: kiem un khurbn fun a yidisher shtot; Tarnov: kiyumah veḥurbanah shel ir yehudit] (Tel Aviv, 1954), 189–200.

KAINDL, RAIMUND FRIEDRICH, *Geschichte von Czernowitz von den ältesten Zeiten zur Gegenwart* (Czernowitz, 1908).

KARGOL, ANNA, *Zakon Synów Przymierza: Krakowska Loża 'Solidarność' 1892–1938* (Warsaw, 2013).

KARNIEL, JOSEPH, *Die Toleranzpolitik Kaiser Josephs II.* (Gerlingen, 1985).

KASTOVSKY, DIETER (ed.), *Historical English Syntax*, 2 vols. (New York, 1991).

KAZIN, ALFRED, *On Native Grounds: An Interpretation of Modern American Prose Literature* (New York, 1942).

KELLNER, ANNA, *Leon Kellner: Sein Leben und sein Werk* (Vienna, 1936).

——'Reiseskizzen aus Palästina', *Menorah: Illustrierte Monatsschrift für die jüdische Familie*, 2 (Aug. 1924), 20–1; (Oct. 1924), 18–20.

——[A. K.], 'Unsere Mutter', *Menorah: Illustrierte Monatsschrift für die jüdische Familie*, 3 (Mar. 1925), 69–70; (Apr. 1925), 93–5; (May 1925), 118; (June 1925), 142–3; (July 1925), 165–7; (Aug./Sept. 1925), 195; (Oct. 1925), 222; (Nov. 1925), 245–7; (Dec. 1925), 271; 4 (Jan. 1926), 60–4; (Feb. 1926), 124–5; (May 1926), 310–13; (Aug. 1926), 479; (Sept. 1926), 543–5; (Nov. 1926), 657–9; (Dec. 1926), 719–20; 5 (Feb. 1927), 134–5; (Apr. 1927), 270–2; (Aug. 1927), 498–500; (Sept. 1927), 563.

KELLNER, VIKTOR, 'Briefe eines jungen Farmers aus Palästina', *Menorah: Illustrierte Monatsschrift für die jüdische Familie*, 1: 2/3 ([Feb./Mar.] 1923), 10–16; 4 ([Apr.] 1923), 17–18; 5 ([May] 1923), 12–14; 2 (Apr. 1924), 10–11.

KERNMAYER, HILDEGARD, *Judentum im Wiener Feuilleton (1848–1903): Exemplarische Untersuchungen zum literarästhetischen und politischen Diskurs der Moderne* (Tübingen, 1998).

KERNMAYER, HILDEGARD, 'Zur Frage: Was ist ein Feuilleton?', in Hildegard Kernmayer and Simone Jung (eds.), *Feuilleton: Schreiben an der Schnittstelle zwischen Journalismus und Literatur* (Bielefeld, 2017), 51–66.

KIEVAL, HILLEL J., 'Bohemia and Moravia', *YIVO Encyclopedia of Jews in Eastern Europe*, 2 vols. (New Haven, Conn., 2008), i. 202–11.

——*Languages of Community: The Jewish Experience in the Czech Lands* (Berkeley, 2000).

KING, MICHAEL, *Tread Softly for You Tread on My Life* (Auckland, 2001).

KLEIN, DENIS B., *Jewish Origins of the Psychoanalytic Movement* (New York, 1981).

KLEIN, HOLGER, 'Austrian (and some German) Scholars of English and the First World War', in Fred Bridgham (ed.), *The First World War as a Clash of Cultures* (Rochester, NY, 2006), 245–80.

KLEIN-PEJŠOVÁ, REBEKAH, *Mapping Jewish Loyalties in Interwar Slovakia* (Bloomington, Ind., 2015).

KOCH, HANS-GERD (ed.), *Franz Kafka: Tagebücher*, 3 vols. (Frankfurt am Main, 1994).

KOHL, JOHANN GEORG, *Austria, Vienna, Prague, Hungary, Bohemia, and the Danube; Galicia, Styria, Moravia, Bukovina, and the Military Frontier* (London, 1844).

KOKOSCHKA, OSCAR, *Mein Leben* (1971; Vienna, 2008).

KÖRTING, GUSTAV, *Grundriss der Geschichte der englischen Literatur von ihren Anfängen bis zur Gegenwart* (Münster, 1910).

KOVEN, SETH, *Slumming: Sexual and Social Politics in Victorian London* (Princeton, NJ, 2004).

KOŻUCHOWSKI, ADAM, *The Afterlife of Austria-Hungary: The Image of the Habsburg Monarchy in Interwar Europe* (Pittsburgh, 2013).

KRISTIANPOLLER, ALEXANDER, 'Die Bibliothek der Wiener Kultusgemeinde (Ihre Entstehung und Entwicklung)', *Menorah: Jüdisches Familienblatt für Wissenschaft/Kunst und Literatur*, 4 (1926), 194–9.

KWAN, JONATHAN, 'Liberalism, Antisemitism and Everyday Life in Vienna: The Tragic Case of Heinrich Jaques (1831–1894)', in Abigail Green and Simon Levis Sullam (eds.), *Jews, Liberalism, Antisemitism: A Global History* (London, 2020), 131–52.

LABINSKA, BOHDANA, *Die Entwicklung des Fremdsprachenunterrichts in der Bukowina und in Wien von der zweiten Hälfte des 19. bis zum Anfang des 20. Jahrhunderts* (Vienna, 2019).

LANDESMANN, PETER, *Rabbiner aus Wien: Ihre Ausbildung, ihre religiosen und nationalen Konflikten* (Vienna, 1997).

LAVEN, DAVID, *Venice and Venetia Under the Habsburgs 1815–1835* (Oxford, 2002).

LEE, HERMIONE, *Biography: A Very Short Introduction* (Oxford, 2009).

LEHMANN, MATTHIAS B., *The Baron: Maurice de Hirsch and the Jewish Nineteenth Century* (Stanford, 2022).

LEITNER, RUDOLF, 'Die Judenpolitik der österreichischen Regierung in den Jahren 1848–1859' (Ph.D. diss., University of Vienna, 1924).

LESLIE, JOHN, 'Der Ausgleich in der Bukowina von 1910: Zur österreichischen Nationalitätenpolitik vor dem Ersten Weltkrieg', in Emil Brix, Thomas Fröschl, and Josef Leidenfrost (eds.), *Geschichte zwischen Freiheit und Ordnung: Gerald Stourzh zum 60. Geburtstag* (Graz, 1991), 113–44.

LEWIN, MAURYCY, 'Geschichte der Juden in Galizien unter Kaiser Joseph II. Ein Beitrag zur Geschichte der Juden in Oesterreich' (Ph.D. diss., University of Vienna, 1933).

LICHTBLAU, ALBERT, and MICHAEL JOHN, 'Jewries in Galicia and Bukovina, in Lemberg and Czernowitz: Two Divergent Examples of Jewish Communities in the Far East of the Austro-Hungarian Monarchy', in Sander L. Gilman and Milton Shain (eds.), *Jewries at the Frontier: Accommodation, Identity, Conflict* (Urbana, Ill., 1999), 29–66.

LICHTENSTEIN, TATJANA, *Zionists in Interwar Czechoslovakia: Minority Nationalism and the Politics of Belonging* (Bloomington, Ind., 2016).

LIPP, ADOLF, *Verkehrs- und Handels-Verhältnisse Galiziens* (Prague, 1870).

LIVEZEANU, IRINA, *Cultural Politics in Greater Romania: Regionalism, Nation Building, and Ethnic Struggle, 1918–1930* (Ithaca, NY, 1995).

LOIBL, WOLFGANG, 'Die österreichische Präsidentschaftskanzlei', in Alois Mack and Herbert Schambeck (eds.), *Verantwortung in unserer Zeit: Festschrift für Rudolf Kirchschläger* (Vienna, 1990), 157–65.

MAHLER, RAPHAEL, *History of the Jewish People in Modern Times* [Divrei yemei yisra'el: dorot aharonim], 4 vols. (Merhavia, 1952–6).

MALLEIER, ELISABETH, 'Gegen den fremden Kontinent der Armut: Die Anfangsjahre der "Jüdischen Toynbeehalle" in der Wiener Brigittenau', *Das jüdische Echo*, 54 (2005), 112–17.

——'Die jüdische Toynbee-Halle in der Wiener Brigittenau', *Spurensuche*, 17 (2006), 104–13.

——'Das "Kaiserin Elisabeth-Institut für israelitische Krankenpflegerinnen" im Wiener Rothschild-Spital', *Wiener Geschichtsblätter*, 53 (1998), 249–69.

MANEKIN, RACHEL, 'Gaming the System: The Jewish Community Council, the Temple, and the Struggle over the Rabbinate in Mid-Nineteenth-Century Lemberg', *Jewish Quarterly Review*, 106 (2016), 352–82.

——*The Jews of Galicia and the Austrian Constitution: The Beginning of Modern Jewish Politics* [Yehudei galitsiyah vehahukah ha'ostrit: reshitah shel politikah yehudit modernit] (Jerusalem, 2015).

MANER, HANS-CHRISTIAN, *Galizien: Eine Grenzregion im Kalkül der Donaumonarchie im 18. und 19. Jahrhundert* (Munich, 2007).

MARETZKI, LOUIS, *Geschichte des Ordens B'nai B'riss in Deutschland 1882–1907* (Berlin, 1908).

MARGOSHES, JOSEPH, *A World Apart: A Memoir of Jewish Life in Nineteenth Century Galicia*, trans. Rebecca Margolis and Ira Robinson (Brighton, 2008).

MARRIOTT, STUART, *English–German Relations in Adult Education, 1875–1955: A Commentary and Select Bibliography* (Leeds, 1995).

MASAN, OLEKSANDR, 'Czernowitz in Vergangenheit und Gegenwart', in Harald Heppner (ed.), *Czernowitz: Die Geschichte einer ungewöhnlichen Stadt* (Vienna, 2000), 11–44.

MASER, PETER, and ADELHEID WEISER, *Juden in Oberschlesien* (Berlin, 1992).

MEACHAM, STANDISH, *Toynbee Hall and Social Reform, 1880–1914: The Search for Community* (New Haven, Conn., 1987).

MENCKEN, H. L., 'Puritanism as a Literary Force', in id., *A Book of Prefaces* (New York, 1917), 197–213.

MENCZEL, PHILIPP, *Als Geisel nach Siberien verschleppt* (Berlin, 1916).

——*Trügerische Lösungen: Erlebnisse und Betrachtungen eines Österreichers* (Stuttgart, 1932).

MENDELSOHN, EZRA, 'Jewish Assimilation in Lvov: The Case of Wilhelm Feldman', *Slavic Review*, 28 (1969), 577–90.

——*On Modern Jewish Politics* (New York, 1993).

MENTZEL, WALTER, 'Die Flüchtlingspolitik der Habsburgermonarchie während des Ersten Weltkrieges', in Börries Kuzmany and Rita Garstenauer (eds.), *Aufnahmeland Österreich: Über den Umgang mit Massenflucht seit dem 18. Jahrhundert* (Vienna, 2017), 126–55.

MILLER, MICHAEL, *Rabbis and Revolution: The Jews of Moravia in the Age of Emancipation* (Stanford, Calif., 2011).

——'From White Terror to Red Vienna: Hungarian Jewish Students in Interwar Austria', in Frank Stern and Barbara Eichinger (eds.), *Wien und die jüdische Erfahrung, 1900–1938* (Vienna, 2009), 307–23.

MISCHLER, MARIE, *Soziale und wirtschaftliche Skizzen aus der Bukowina* (Vienna, 1893).

MOODY, DAVID A., *Ezra Pound, Poet: A Portrait of the Man and his Work*, 2 vols. (New York, 2014).

MOOS, CARLO, *Habsburg Post Mortem: Betrachtungen zum Weiterleben der Habsburgermonarchie* (Vienna, 2016).

MORRIS, RICHARD, *Historical Outlines of English Accidence*, rev. Leon Kellner, with the assistance of Henry Bradley (London, 1895).

MOSELEY, MARCUS, *Being for Myself Alone: Origins of Jewish Autobiography* (Stanford, Calif., 2006).

MURRAY, JAMES A. H., *The Evolution of English Lexicography* (Oxford, 1900).

NELSON, JOHN HERBERT, 'Some German Surveys of American Literature', *American Literature*, 1 (1929), 149–60.

NG, AMY, *Nationalism and Political Liberty: Redlich, Namier, and the Crisis of Empire* (Oxford, 2004).

OELSCHLÄGEL, DIETER, 'Integration durch Bildung: Jüdische Toynbee-Hallen und Volksheime in Österreich und Deutschland im ersten Drittel des zwangisten Jahrhunderts', in Peter Hermann and Peter Szynka (eds.), *Durchbrüche ins Soziale: Eine Festschrift für Rudolph Bauer* (Vienna, 2014), 102–39.

OKEY, ROBIN, *Taming Balkan Nationalism: The Habsburg 'Civilizing Mission' in Bosnia, 1878–1914* (Oxford, 2007).

OLSON, JESS, *Nathan Birnbaum and Jewish Modernity: Architect of Zionism, Yiddishism, and Orthodoxy* (Stanford, Calif., 2013).

OPITZ, KURT, 'Specialized Bilingual Dictionaries of the Past: Krüger's *Schwierigkeiten des Englischen* and Rabe's *Deutsch–Englisches Satzlexikon*', in Arne Zettersten, Viggo Hjørnager Pedersen, and Jens Erik Mogensen (eds.), *Symposium on Lexicography VIII: Proceedings of the Eighth International Symposium on Lexicography May 2–4, 1996 at the University of Copenhagen* (Tübingen, 1998), 243–7.

Österreichisches Biographisches Lexikon 1815–1950, 15 vols. (Vienna, 1957–2020).

Die österreichisch-ungarische Monarchie in Wort und Bild (Vienna, 1899).

OXAAL, IVAR, and WALTER R. WEITZMANN, 'The Jews of Pre-1914 Vienna: An Exploration of Basic Sociological Dimensions', *Leo Baeck Institute Year Book*, 30 (1985), 395–432.

PAPPENHEIM, BERTHA, and SARA RABINOWITSCH, *Zur Lage der jüdischen Bevölkerung in Galizien: Reise-Eindrücke und Vorschläge zur Besserung der Verhältnisse* (Frankfurt am Main, 1904).

PARUSH, IRIS, *Reading Jewish Women: Marginality and Modernization in Nineteenth-Century Eastern European Society*, trans. Saadya Sternberg (Waltham, Mass., 2004).

PAWEL, ERNST, *The Labyrinth of Exile: A Life of Theodor Herzl* (New York, 1989).

PELINKA, ANTON, *Die gescheiterte Republik: Kultur und Politik in Österreich 1918–1938* (Vienna, 2017).

PENSLAR, DEREK, *Theodor Herzl: The Charismatic Leader* (New Haven, Conn., 2020).

PILS, RAMON, 'Disziplinierung eines Faches: Zur Englischen Philologie in Wien im frühen 20. Jahrhundert', in Karl Anton Fröschl et al. (eds.), *Reflexive Innensichten aus der Universität: Disziplinengeschichten zwischen Wissenschaft, Gesellschaft und Politik* (Vienna, 2016), 539–49.

—— '"Ein Gelehrter ist kein Politiker": Die Professoren der Wiener Anglistik im Kontext des Nationalsozialismus', in Mitchell G. Ash, Wolfram Niess, and Ramon Pils (eds.), *Geisteswissenschaften im Nationalsozialismus: Das Beispiel der Universität Wien* (Vienna, 2010), 455–86.

184 BIBLIOGRAPHY

POLEK, JOHANN, *General Spleny's Beschreibung der Bukowina* (Czernowitz, 1893).

POLONSKY, ANTONY, *The Jews in Poland and Russia*, vol. i: *1350 to 1881* (Oxford, 2010).

POTOCZNY, JERZY, *Oświata dorosłych i popularyzacja wiedzy w plebejskich środowiskach Galicji doby konstytucyjnej, 1867–1918* (Rzeszów, 1998).

PRIBRAM, ALFRED FRANCIS, *Urkunden und Akten zur Geschichte der Juden in Wien*, 2 vols. (Vienna, 1918).

PROKOP-JANIEC, EUGENIA, 'Jewish Moderna in Galicia', *Gal-Ed*, 14 (1995), 27–38.

PULZER, PETER, 'Legal Equality and Public Life', in Michael A. Meyer (ed.), *German-Jewish History in Modern Times*, iii: Steven M. Lowenstein, Paul Mendes-Flohr, Peter Pulzer, and Monika Richarz, *Integration in Dispute, 1871–1918* (New York, 1997), 153–95.

RATHKOLB, OLIVER, 'Gewalt und Antisemitismus an der Universität Wien und die Badeni Affäre 1897: Davor und danach', in Oliver Rathkolb (ed.), *Der lange Schatten des Antisemitismus: Kritische Auseinandersetzungen mit der Geschichte der Universität Wien im 19. und 20. Jahrhundert* (Vienna, 2013), 69–92.

——*Straßennamen Wiens seit 1860 als 'Politische Erinnerungsorte'* (Vienna, 2013).

RECHTER, DAVID, *Becoming Habsburg: The Jews of Austrian Bukowina 1774–1918* (Oxford, 2013).

——*The Jews of Vienna and the First World War* (Oxford, 2001).

——'Kaisertreu: The Dynastic Loyalty of Austrian Jewry', in Klaus Hödl (ed.), *Jüdische Identitäten: Einblicke in die Bewusstseinslandschaft des österreichischen Judentums* (Innsbruck, 2000), 189–208.

REIFER, MANFRED, *Menschen und Ideen* (Tel Aviv, 1952).

REIFFENSTEIN, BRIGITTE, 'Zu den Anfängen des Englischunterrichts an der Universität Wien und zur frühen wissenschaftlichen Anglistik in Wien', in Otto Rauchbauer (ed.), *A Yearbook of Studies in English Language and Literature 1985/86: Festschrift für Siegfried Korninger* (Vienna, 1986), 163–85.

REIFOWITZ, IAN, *Imagining an Austrian Nation: Joseph Samuel Bloch and the Search for a Multinational Austrian Identity, 1846–1919* (Boulder, Colo., 2003).

REINKE, ANDREAS, '"Eine Sammlung des jüdischen Bürgertums": Der Unabhängige Orden B'nai B'rith in Deutschland', in Andreas Gotzmann, Rainer Liedtke, and Till van Rahden (eds.), *Juden, Bürger, Deutsche: Zur Geschichte von Vielfalt und Differenz 1800–1933* (Tübingen, 2001), 315–42.

RENDERS, HANS, BINNE DE HAAN, and JONNE HARMSMA (eds.), *The Biographical Turn: Lives in History* (Abingdon, 2017).

RICHMAN, SHELDON L., 'Mr. Mencken and the Jews', *The American Scholar*, 59 (1990), 407–11.

ROBERTSON, RITCHIE, 'Joseph Rohrer and the Bureaucratic Enlightenment', in Ritchie Robertson and Edward Timms (eds.), *The Austrian Enlightenment and its Aftermath* (Edinburgh, 1991), 22–42.

BIBLIOGRAPHY 185

ROCHELSON, MERI-JANE, *A Jew in the Public Arena: The Career of Israel Zangwill* (Detroit, 2008).

ROHRER, JOSEPH, *Versuch über die jüdischen Bewohner der österreichischen Monarchie* (Vienna, 1804).

ROSENBERGER, ERWIN, *Herzl as I Remember Him* (New York, 1959).

ROSENFELD, MAX, *Die polnische Judenfrage: Problem und Lösung* (Vienna, 1918).

ROTH, JOSEPH, *Die Kapuzinergruft* (1938; Cologne, 2011).

ROZENBLIT, MARSHA L., 'The Assertion of Jewish Identity: Jewish Student Nationalism at the University of Vienna before the First World War', *Leo Baeck Institute Year Book*, 27 (1982), 171–86.

—— *The Jews of Vienna 1867–1914: Assimilation and Identity* (Albany, NY, 1983).

RUMPLER, HELMUT, and PETER URBANITSCH (eds.), *Die Habsburgermonarchie 1848–1918*, viii: *Politische Öffentlichkeit und Zivilgesellschaft* (Vienna, 2006).

SALTER, ARTHUR, 'The Reconstruction of Austria', *Foreign Affairs*, 2 (1924), 630–43.

SANDGRUBER, ROMAN, *Ökonomie und Politik: Österreichische Wirtschaftsgeschichte vom Mittelalter bis zur Gegenwart* (Vienna, 1995).

SCHARR, KURT, '*Die Landschaft Bukowina*': *Das Werden einer Region an der Peripherie 1774–1918* (Vienna, 2010).

—— '"Eine überaus peinliche Lage": Die deutschsprachigen Professoren der Czernowitzer Universität zwischen Exil und Neuanfang 1914–1920', in Florian Kührer-Wielach and Markus Winkler (eds.), *Mutter: Land—Vater: Staat. Loyalitätskonflikte, politische Neuorientierung und der Erste Weltkrieg im österreichisch-russländischen Grenzraum* (Regensburg, 2017).

SCHEIBE, WOLFGANG, '1919–1933: Weimarer Republik', in Franz Pöggeler (ed.), *Geschichte der Erwachsenenbildung* (Stuttgart, 1975), 69–78.

SCHEUER, JEFFREY, *Legacy of Light: University Settlement 1886–2011* (New York, 2012).

SCHIPPER, JAKOB, 'Über die Stellung und Aufgabe der englischen Philologie an den Mittelschulen Österreichs', *Verhandlungen der zweiundvierzigsten Versammlung deutscher Philologen und Schulmänner in Wien vom 24. bis 27. Mai 1893* (Leipzig, 1894), 137–48.

SCHORSKE, CARL, *Thinking with History* (Princeton, NJ, 1998).

SCOTLAND, NIGEL, *Squires in the Slums: Settlements and Missions in Late Victorian Britain* (London, 2007).

SEITTER, WOLFGANG, *Geschichte der Erwachsenenbildung: Eine Einführung* (Bielefeld, 2007).

SHANES, JOSHUA, *Diaspora Nationalism and Jewish Identity in Habsburg Galicia* (Cambridge, 2012).

SHAW, GEORGE BERNARD, 'A Devil of a Fellow: Self-Criticism', *Shaw: The Journal of Bernard Shaw Studies*, 20 (2000), 247–52.

186 BIBLIOGRAPHY

SHURR, WILLIAM H., *Rappaccini's Children: American Writers in a Calvinist World* (Lexington, Ky., 1981).

SILBER, MICHAEL K., 'Hungary before 1918', *YIVO Encyclopedia of Jews in Eastern Europe*, 2 vols. (New Haven, Conn., 2008), i. 770–82.

——'The Making of Habsburg Jewry in the Long Eighteenth Century', in Adam Sutcliffe and Jonathan Karp (eds.), *The Cambridge History of Judaism*, vii: *The Early Modern World, 1500–1815* (Cambridge, 2017), 763–97.

SINGER, LUDWIG, 'Toynbee-Halle und Kinderhort', in *Festschrift anlässlich des fünfundzwanzigjährigen Bestandes des israel. Humanitätsvereines 'Eintracht' (B'nai B'rith) Wien 1903–1928* (Vienna, 1928), 72–87.

SIRKA, ANN, *The Nationality Question in Austrian Education: The Case of Ukrainians in Galicia, 1867–1914* (Frankfurt am Main, 1980).

SKEAT, WALTER (ed.), *The Complete Works of Geoffrey Chaucer*, 2 vols. (Oxford, 1899).

SORKIN, DAVID, *The Transformation of German Jewry, 1780–1840* (Oxford, 1987).

SPANN, SAMUEL, 'Dr. Leon Kellner' (Yid.), in Avraham Chomet (ed.), *The Life and Destruction of a Jewish City* [Torne: kiem un khurbn fun a yidisher shtot; Tarnov: kiyumah veḥurbanah shel ir yehudit] (Tel Aviv, 1954), 270–81.

Special-Orts-Repertorium der im österreichischen Reichsrate vertretenen Königreiche und Länder: Neubearbeitung auf Grund der Ergebnisse der Volkszählung vom 31. December 1890, xi: *Schlesien* (Vienna, 1894).

SPITZER, RUDOLF, *Karl Seitz: Waisenknabe—Staatspräsident—Bürgermeister von Wien* (Vienna, 1994).

SPYRA, JANUSZ, *Żydowskie gminy wyznaniowe na Śląsku Austriackim* (Katowice, 2009).

SROKA, ŁUKASZ TOMASZ, 'Stowarzyszenie Humanitarne "Leopolis" we Lwowie (1899–1938): Głowne kierunki działalności', *Kwartalnik Historyczny*, 123 (2016), 45–69.

STAMPFER, SHAUL, *Families, Rabbis, and Education: Traditional Jewish Society in Nineteenth-Century Eastern Europe* (Oxford, 2018).

STANZEL, FRANZ K., 'Erinnerungen an die Anglistin Helene Richter anlässlich der Wiederkehr ihres 150. Geburtstages 2011', *Anglia*, 129 (2011), 321–32.

Statistik der Unterrichts-Anstalten in den im Reichsrathe vertretenen Königreichen und Ländern für das Jahr 1881/1882 (Vienna, 1884).

STAUDIGL-CIECHOWICZ, KAMILA, 'Die österreichische Universitätslandschaft um 1918', in Thomas Olechowski, Tamara Ehs, and Kamila Staudigl-Ciechowicz (eds.), *Die Wiener Rechts- und Staatswissenschaftliche Fakultät 1918–1935* (Vienna, 2014), 641–72.

——'Zwischen Wien und Czernowitz: Die österreichischen Universitäten um 1918', *Beiträge zur Rechtsgeschichte Österreichs*, 4 (2014), 223–40.

STEIN, ABRAHAM, *Der Mensch im Bilde Gottes: Festpredigt zur Feier des nach 100 Jahren wiederkehrenden Tages der Kundmachung des ersten der von Kaiser Josef II. gegebenen Gesetze zur Befreiung der Juden aus der mittelalterlichen Rechtlosigkeit* (Prague, 1881).

STEIN, MAXIMILIAN, 'Zur Begründung einer jüdischen Toynbee-Halle in Berlin', in *Vorträge und Ansprachen von Maximilian Stein* (Frankfurt am Main, 1929), 142–9.

——*Zur Eröffnung der neuen Toynbee-Halle der Berliner Logen U.O.B.B.* (n.p., n.d.) [Berlin, 1909].

Stenographische Protokolle des Abgeordnetenhauses des Reichsrates im Jahre 1907, XI. Legislaturperiode, XVIII. Session (Vienna, 1908).

Stenographische Protokolle des Bukowinaer Landtages der ersten Session der elften Wahlperiode, 1911 (Czernowitz, 1911).

Stenographische Protokolle des Bukowinaer Landtages der zweiten Session der elften Wahlperiode, 1912 (Czernowitz, 1912).

Stenographische Protokolle des Bukowinaer Landtages der dritten Session der elften Wahlperiode, 1912/1913 (Czernowitz, 1913).

Stenographisches Protokoll der Verhandlungen des V. Zionisten Congresses (Vienna, 1901).

SURMAN, JAN, *Universities in Imperial Austria 1848–1918: A Social History of a Multilingual Space* (West Lafayette, Ind., 2019).

SZCZEPANOWSKI, STANISŁAW, *Nędza Galicyi w cyfrach i program energicznego rozwoju gospodarstwa krajowego* (Lwów, 1888).

SZNAJDMAN, JOHANN, 'Die Zeit der Aufklärung und die Juden in Österreich unter der Regierung Josef II.' (Ph.D. diss., University of Vienna, 1934).

TASCHWER, KLAUS, 'Geheimsache Bärenhöhle: Wie eine antisemitische Professorenclique nach 1918 an der Universität Wien jüdische Forscherinnen und Forscher vertrieb', in Regina Fritz, Grzegorz Rossoliński-Liebe, and Jana Starek (eds.), *Alma Mater Antisemitica: Akademisches Milieu, Juden und Antisemitismus an den Universitäten Europas zwischen 1918 und 1939* (Vienna, 2016), 221–42.

TENENBAUM, JOSEPH, *Galicia: My Old Home* [Galitsye: mayn alte heym] (Buenos Aires, 1952).

——*Żydowskie problemy gospodarcze w Galicyi* (Vienna, 1918).

THON, JAKOB, *Die Juden in Oesterreich* (Berlin, 1908).

TIETZE, HANS, *Die Juden Wiens: Geschichte—Wirtschaft—Kultur* (1933; Vienna, 2008).

TIMMS, EDWARD, 'School for Socialism: Karl Seitz and the Cultural Politics of Vienna', in Judith Beniston and Robert Vilain (eds.), *Culture and Politics in Red Vienna* (Leeds, 2006), 37–59.

TOKARSKI, SŁAWOMIR, *Ethnic Conflict and Economic Development: Jews in Galician Agriculture 1868–1914* (Warsaw, 2003).

BIBLIOGRAPHY

Toury, Jacob, 'Herzl's Newspapers: The Creation of *Die Welt*', *Studies in Zionism*, 1 (1980), 159–72.

——*Die jüdische Presse im österreichischen Kaiserreich 1802–1918* (Tübingen, 1983).

Trentmann, Frank, 'Introduction: Paradoxes of Civil Society', in id. (ed.), *Paradoxes of Civil Society: New Perspectives on Modern German and British History* (New York, 2003), 3–46.

Van Drunen, Jeroen, *'A Sanguine Bunch': Regional Identification in Habsburg Bukovina, 1774–1919* (Amsterdam, 2015).

Veidlinger, Jeffrey, *Jewish Public Culture in the Late Russian Empire* (Bloomington, Ind., 2009).

Vierzehnter Jahresbericht über das k. k. Franz-Josephs Gymnasium in Wien 1887/88 (Vienna, 1888).

Vital, David, *The Origins of Zionism* (Oxford, 1975).

——*Zionism: The Formative Years* (1982; Oxford, 1988).

Volovici, Marc, *German as a Jewish Problem: The Language Politics of Jewish Nationalism* (Stanford, Calif., 2020).

Von Rezzori, Gregor, *The Snows of Yesteryear* (London, 1990).

Vorlesungsverzeichnis, Studienpläne und Personalstand der Technischen Hochschule in Wien für das Studienjahr 1921/22.

Vorlesungsverzeichnis, Studienpläne und Personalstand der Technischen Hochschule in Wien für das Studienjahr 1923/24.

Vorlesungsverzeichnis, Studienpläne und Personalstand der Technischen Hochschule in Wien für das Studienjahr 1927/28.

Wadl, Wilhelm, *Liberalismus und soziale Frage in Österreich: Deutschliberale Reaktionen und Einflüsse auf die frühe österreichische Arbeiterbewegung (1867–1879)* (Vienna, 1987).

Walter, Edith, *Österreichische Tageszeitungen der Jahrhundertwende: Ideologischer Anspruch und ökonomische Erfordernisse* (Vienna, 1994).

Wandycz, Piotr S., *The Lands of Partitioned Poland, 1795–1918* (Seattle, 1974).

Weber, Julius, *Die Russentage in Czernowitz: Die Ereignisse der ersten und zweiten russischen Invasion* (Czernowitz, 1915).

Weiss, Samuel A., *Bernard Shaw's Letters to Siegfried Trebitsch* (Stanford, Calif., 1986).

Weissweiler, Eva, *Das Echo deiner Frage: Dora und Walter Benjamin. Biographie einer Beziehung* (Hamburg, 2020).

Werses, Shmuel, *'Awake, My People': Hebrew Literature in the Age of Modernization* ['Hakitsah ami': sifrut hahaskalah be'idan hamodernizatsiyah] (Jerusalem, 2001).

Wertheimer, Jack, *Unwelcome Strangers: East European Jews in Imperial Germany* (New York, 1987).

BIBLIOGRAPHY 189

WERTHEIMER, JOSEF, *Die Juden in Oesterreich: Vom Standpunkte der Geschichte, des Rechts und des Staatsvortheils* (Leipzig, 1842).

WINKLER, MARKUS, "'... zu erörten versuchte, was ihnen Ortslosigkeit war". Paul Celans Begegnungen mit Leon Kellner: Eine Annäherung', in Andrei Corbea-Hoisie and Ion Lihaciu (eds.), *'Toposforschung (...) im Lichte der U-topie': Literarische Er-örterungen in/aus MittelOsteuropa* (Konstanz, 2017), 547–60.

WISTRICH, ROBERT S., *The Jews of Vienna in the Age of Franz Joseph* (Oxford, 1989).

——*Laboratory for World Destruction: Germans and Jews in Central Europe* (Lincoln, Nebr., 2007).

WODZIŃSKI, MARCIN, *Historical Atlas of Hasidism* (Princeton, NJ, 2018).

WOLF, GERSON, *Josef Wertheimer: Ein Lebens- und Zeitbild* (Vienna, 1868).

——*Die Juden* (Vienna, 1883).

WOLF, MICHAELA, *The Habsburg Monarchy's Many-Languaged Soul: Translating and Interpreting, 1848–1918* (Amsterdam, 2015).

WOLFF, LARRY, *The Idea of Galicia: History and Fantasy in Habsburg Political Culture* (Stanford, Calif., 2010).

WRÓBEL, PIOTR, 'The Jews of Galicia under Austrian-Polish Rule, 1869–1918', *Austrian History Yearbook*, 25 (1994), 97–138.

YORK-STEINER, HEINRICH, 'Leon Kellner', *Menorah: Illustrierte Monatsschrift für die jüdische Familie*, 7 (1929), 3–4.

ZALKIN, MORDECHAI, *Modernizing Jewish Education in Nineteenth Century Eastern Europe: The School as the Shrine of the Jewish Enlightenment* (Leiden, 2016).

Zehnter Jahresbericht über das k. k. Franz-Josephs Gymnasium in Wien 1883/84 (Vienna, 1884).

ZIPPERSTEIN, STEVEN J., *Elusive Prophet: Ahad Ha'am and the Origins of Zionism* (London, 1993).

INDEX

A
Abdul Hamid II, Sultan 48, 60
Ahad Ha'am 54
Allen, James Lane 122
Allgemeine Zeitung 29, 31, 37
The American Mercury 150, 156
antisemitism:
  Bukovina regional assembly 116, 117
  effects on Kellner's career 2, 52–3, 140–1, 147–8, 163
  Habsburg society 2, 164
  Jewish Toynbee Halls 81, 92–3, 164
  Kellner's attitude to 26–7, 31–2, 52–3, 57, 150–1
  Polish 11, 135
  Technical University of Vienna 147–8
  University of Vienna 26, 140
Apuleius 105
Arbeiter Zeitung 42
Archer, Frances 151, 152
Archer, William 61, 68, 151, 152, 155
Arnim, Elizabeth von 156
Arnold, Edwin 38
Arnold, Matthew 68
Ashmead-Bartlett, Sir Ellis 60
Austerlitz, Friedrich 146
Austria, Republic of 2, 90, 137 n.39, 141–2, 144–5
  see also Habsburg territories

B
Bab, Julius 122
Badeni, Kasimir Felix 62
Bahr, Hermann 29
Baltimore Evening Sun 150, 151 n.94
Barnett, Henrietta 77–8
Barnett, Samuel, Canon 77–8, 79
Baron Hirsch Foundation 72, 73–4, 109, 130
Barrès, Maurice 105
Baudelaire, Charles 105
Bausteine (journal) 101–3, 106, 108, 124
Beer-Hofmann, Richard 41

Bendiener, Ludwig 85
Benjamin, Walter 2, 159 n.134
Berlin:
  central Zionist office 114, 126
  Jewish Toynbee Hall 84, 85–6, 87–8, 90, 91
Besant, Walter 68
Bezalel (Jerusalem art and crafts school) 118
Bible, English 32
Bielitz (Bielsko), Gymnasium 21–4
Billroth, Theodor 26
Binyamina 158–9, 162 n.10
Blind, Karl 68, 69 n.119
Blind, Mathilde 69 n.119
Bloch, Joseph Samuel 27
B'nai B'rith 84–5, 86–8, 90–1
Boethius 38
Bohemia 17, 76, 110, 113, 135
Booth, William 43, 77, 78, 133
Bosnia 120, 135
Bradley, Henry 35–6, 152
Brandeis, Louis 143
Breslau (Wrocław):
  Jewish Toynbee Hall 87
  Jüdisch-Theologisches Seminar 19–21, 22, 24, 26, 28, 39, 140, 142
Brontë, Charlotte 108
Browning, Elizabeth Barrett 108, 156
Browning, Robert 37, 105, 122
Brüll, Ignaz 59
Buber, Martin 162
Buchanan, Robert 38
Bukovina:
  Anna's description 106
  economy 96
  German culture 97, 104
  Jewish community 10, 114, 129, 135
  Jewish People's Council 115, 129, 144
  Jewish politics 115–17, 129
  Jewish Toynbee Halls 76, 91
  Landtag (regional assembly) 116–18, 129
  nationalist politics 109–11, 113

192 INDEX

Bukovina (*cont.*):
population diversity 95
refugees from 90 n.73, 128, 131
Romanian rule 135–7, 144
schools 73
war aftermath 128
Zionism 109–11, 113, 114–15, 118–19, 126, 129, 144
Bunyan, John 36–7
Byk, Emil 111

C

Caxton, William 38–9
Celan, Paul 164–5
Chaucer, Geoffrey 35, 38
Cholmondeley, Mary 99
Clifford, Lucy 68, 151, 156
Corneille, Pierre 30
Creizenach, Wilhelm 122
Czech language 17, 85
Czernowitz (Chernivtsi):
description 96, 103–4
Jewish nationality issue 110–11
Jewish Toynbee Hall 84, 89, 109, 126, 165
Kellner family in 75, 94, 95–6, 99, 103, 106
Kellner's career 3, 4, 72–3, 96–7, 101
Kellner's political role 70, 109
Kellner's professorship 75, 96–9
Kultusgemeinde 110, 116
population 95, 96, 128
Romanian control 134
Russian wartime occupations 128, 131–2, 134
University 72–3, 75, 97–8, 101, 128, 130–1, 134, 135–7, 163
Zionist politics 109, 111–12
Czernowitzer Allgemeine Zeitung 97, 99
Czernowitzer Tagblatt 109, 110

D

de Haas, Jacob 59
Deutsch, Gotthard 20, 21, 142–4, 148, 151, 152, 157–8
Deutsche Wochenschrift 29
Dibelius, Wilhelm 157
Dinghofer, Franz 137
Dyboski, Roman 42 n.86, 102 n.46

E

Early English Text Society 35, 38, 39
Ehrlich, Eugen 98, 102 n.46
Eliot, George 105
Engel, Eduard 30
Englische Studien 34, 44
English language:
Anna's career as translator 33, 67–8, 94
Anna's studies 24
Bible translations 32
Jewish Toynbee Hall courses 83
Kellner's academic career 4, 33, 34, 40, 72, 75, 98, 103
Kellner's role as presidential adviser 144–6, 161–2
Kellner's scholarship 1, 36, 38–9, 44, 154–5, 160
Kellner's studies 22, 27
Kellner's teaching career 28, 41, 148
Kellner's teaching qualification 34
Kellner's trips to London 35–7, 59, 68–70, 77, 100–1, 151–2
Kellner's work on English–German dictionary 47, 59, 64, 71, 99–100, 101–2
Kellner's writings 33, 34–5, 35, 38–9, 44, 123, 154–6
philology 25–6, 72, 75, 101
English Zionist Federation 59

F

Falkowicz, Philip 85
Field, Julian Osgood (X.L.) 50
First World War 90, 118, 128–34, 144
Franckenstein, Georg 152
Frankel, Zecharias 19
Frankfurt, Jewish Toynbee Hall 87, 90–1
Franz, Emperor 7–8
Franz Joseph, Emperor 8–9
Franzos, Karl Emil 97
French language:
Anna's career as translator 33, 67
Anna's studies 24
Jewish Toynbee Hall courses 83, 85
Kellner's research work 39
Kellner's studies 20, 27
Kellner's teaching career 41
Kellner's teaching qualification 34
Zionist news service 60

INDEX

Freud, Sigmund 33
Friedjung, Heinrich 29, 147
Friedwagner, Matthias 94
Frisch, Hans von 136–7
Furnivall, Frederick James 35–6, 39, 68, 101

G

Galicia and its Jews 5–12, 25, 73, 111, 135
  Jewish Toynbee Halls 89, 91
Galsworthy, John 121, 155
Gaster, Moses 59
Gautier, Théophile 105
German language:
  Anna's career as translator 67–8
  Anna's education 24
  Dora's translation of Mencken 150
  Habsburg policy 7, 11, 17
  Jewish education 12, 20
  Jewish Toynbee Hall courses 83
  Jewish use of 17, 22, 97, 110–11
  Kellner's studies 16–17, 22
  Kellner's teaching career 41
  Kellner's work on English–German
    dictionary 47, 59, 64, 71, 99–100, 101–2
  Kellner's writings 33, 53, 107–8, 153
  Leah's studies 14
  translations of Shaw's work 70
Gladstone, William 49–50, 103
Goldman, Emma 79
Goode, William 142
Gosse, Edmund 68
Graetz, Heinrich 21
Güdemann, Moritz 16
Gutmann, David Ritter von 73–4

H

Habsburg empire:
  antisemitism 164
  Bukovina, see Bukovina
  east and west 2–4, 87–9, 163–4
  end of Habsburg rule 5, 90, 134–5, 164
  Jewish attitudes to Habsburg rule 3, 7, 121,
    135, 164
  Jewish nationalism 118
  Jewish rights 7–9, 25
  language issues 7, 11, 17
  relationship between capital and province
    3, 163

Haggard, Rider 37
Hainisch, Michael 146–9, 151, 155, 161
Hamilton, Cicely 68, 106 n.64
Hebrew language:
  Baron Hirsch Foundation schools 73
  books for Vienna Kultusgemeinde
    library 29
  Habsburg policy 7, 11
  Jewish education 15
  Jewish Toynbee Hall adult education
    courses 83, 85
  Kellner reading, speaking, and writing 163
  Kellner's writings on 31
  translation into 17
Helouan, SS 119, 158
Hergesheimer, Joseph 156
Herzl, Julie 49, 152 n.103
Herzl, Theodor:
  Altneuland (Old New Land) 62
  biography 125–6, 152, 153
  death 53, 75, 109, 111
  diplomatic sorties (1896) 48–9
  El-Arish venture 74–5
  first contact with Kellner 45–6
  health 46
  Der Judenstaat (The Jewish State) 45–6,
    48, 125 n.147
  relationship with Kellner 1, 4, 49–54,
    57–66, 73–5, 164
  support for Jewish Toynbee Hall 76
  Unser Käthchen (Our Cathy) 61
  Die Welt 62, 64–6
  Zionist leadership 51
  Zionist strategy 81, 111–12, 118
Herzog, Eugen 136
Hirsch, Maurice de 74
Hirsch Foundation, see Baron Hirsch
  Foundation
Hofmiller, Josef 122
Holmes, Oliver Wendell 47, 123, 124 n.141
Hugo, Victor 30, 31
Hungarian language 17
Huysmans, Joris-Karl 105

I

Ibsen, Henrik 43, 61
Imber, Naftali Herz 59

194 INDEX

Iorga, Nicolae 98
Ipomadon 44
Israelitische Allianz 74, 109, 130

J
James, Henry 68
Jaques, Heinrich 9
Jerusalem, Wilhelm 157
Jeune, Mary 68
Jewish Chronicle 80, 111, 112
Jewish Colonization Association 74
Jewish National Fund 51, 144
Jewish nationalism:
  Bukovina politics 110, 113, 114–15
  Herzl's influence 48
  'Jewish Club' in imperial parliament 113
  Jewish Toynbee Hall movement 85, 87–8,
    91–2, 114, 164
  Kadimah student association 27, 51, 52
  Kellner's position 3, 4, 52–7, 76, 112–13,
    114–15, 117–18, 163–4
Jewish nationality 110–11, 113, 117
Jewish People's Council 115–16, 126, 129, 144
'Jewish Question' 11, 48, 50, 52–3, 88, 118,
    120 n.125
Jewish Toynbee Hall movement:
  Association in Galicia 89
  B'nai B'rith role 84–8, 90–1
  Bukovina politics 115, 126
  creation 43, 66, 76, 81–4, 91
  finances 86–7, 89
  First World War effects 90
  Kellner's work 43, 66, 76, 81–2, 89, 115,
    126–7, 130, 164, 165
  origins 43, 77–81, 91
  role and activities 43, 76, 89, 91–2
  spread 76, 84, 89–90, 92–3, 112
  Zionist role 81, 83–5, 87–8, 91
Jewish World 59
Joseph II, Emperor 5–7
Joyce, James 156
Jüdischnationale Partei (Jewish National
    Party) 112–13
Jüdisch-Theologisches Seminar (Jewish
    Theological Seminary), Breslau 19–21,
    22

K
Kadimah student association 27, 51, 52
Kafka, Franz 85
Kazin, Alfred 124
Kaznelson, Siegmund 2
Kellner, Anna (née Weiss, wife):
  biography of Leon 162
  children 33, 41, 66
  death 162 n.10
  descriptions of Leon's studies 18
  education 24
  family background 22–4, 25, 41
  finances 33, 46, 142
  Leon's death 160, 161–2
  life in Czernowitz 94, 99, 103, 106
  London trips 35, 67–8
  marriage 29
  marriage plans 27–8
  memories of Leon 22, 26, 34, 38, 52, 69,
    96, 125, 150, 157, 163
  move to Czernowitz 94
  move to Troppau 41
  Palestine visits 119, 158–9
  relationship with Leon 24, 64, 125
  return to Vienna 46, 106
  sisters 41, 65, 149, 158 n.132, 159 n.134
  translating career 33, 67–8, 94, 99, 106
  view of Leon's political career 115
Kellner, Dora (daughter):
  birth 41
  education 66, 99, 106
  friendships 156
  home in San Remo 162
  marriage 159 n.134
  translation of Mencken's work 150
Kellner, Leah (Goldstein, mother) 13–14,
    16, 19, 24
Kellner, Leon:
  adult education 42–3, 109, 159
  attitude to antisemitism 26–7, 31–2, 52–3,
    57, 150–1
  Bausteine journal 101–3, 106, 108, 124
  biography 162
  birth 13
  career 3, 28–9, 40, 44, 46, 52, 63, 70, 72–3,
    75, 96–8, 103, 108, 126–7, 134, 163

INDEX

career, post-war 136–8, 140–1, 144–6, 147–9, 151
career plans 28
Caxton's Blanchardyn and Eglantine 39
Caxton's Syntax and Style 39
character 91, 163
credo 163
death 160, 161
defence of Austria 120–1, 132–4
diplomatic skills 58–60
dress 20
editing collection of Herzl's writings 125
editorship of *Die Welt* 62, 64–6
education 15–22, 25–7, 28, 39
emigration possibilities 52–3
employment plans 27–8, 33–4
Die englische Literatur der neuesten Zeit von Dickens bis Shaw 153
Die englische Literatur im Zeitalter der Königin Viktoria 106–8, 123, 139, 153
English–German dictionary 47, 59, 64, 66, 71, 99, 108, 139
English–German lexicography 99–100
faith in Habsburg state 118, 121, 144, 164
family background 13–14, 17
finances 27–8, 33–4, 41, 46, 63, 65, 97, 103, 141–5, 151, 155
friendships 49, 51–2, 64, 68–9, 151–2
funeral 162 n.7
Geschichte der nordamerikanischen Literatur 123–4
health 66, 81, 126, 129–30, 150, 158, 159
Herzl biography 125–6, 152
Historical Outlines of English Accidence (revision) 36, 152
Historical Outlines of English Syntax 36, 44
Hofrat (Privy or Court Councillor) title 149
homes 33, 46
insomnia 64, 65, 66, 106
inspecting schools 72
Israelitische Allianz 74, 109, 130
Ein Jahr in England 68–9, 71
Jewish People's Council 115, 126, 129
Jewish Toynbee Hall, *see* Jewish Toynbee Hall

languages 16–17, 25–7, 163
lectures and talks 42–3, 46–7, 72, 103, 108, 118, 129–30
library cataloguing 29
London visits 35–8, 55, 58–9, 61–2, 66–71, 77, 91, 100–1, 125, 126, 151–2, 155
marriage 29, 64
marriage plans 27–8
move from Vienna to Czernowitz 75, 86, 94, 109
nationalism 3, 4, 52–7, 76, 112–13, 114–15, 117–18, 163–4
newspaper and journal pieces (essays, feuilletons, articles, stories, reviews) 29–38, 43–4, 45, 47, 49–50, 54, 63, 70, 72, 77, 103–5, 110, 111–12, 121–2, 126, 144, 155–8
obituaries 161–2
Palestine visits 119–20, 158–9
philological and palaeographical study of Shakespearean texts 125, 130, 151, 153–4, 159–60
politics 57–8, 113–19, 126, 129, 144
presidential adviser 144–7, 155, 159
Psalm (Zionist anthem) 59
pseudonym 51, 62
reading 17, 24, 159–60
relationship with Herzl, *see* Herzl
religious issues 55–7
representative in Bukovina parliament 116–18
reputation and status 40, 109, 126–7
Restoring Shakespeare 154–5
reviews of his writings 34, 44, 107–8, 152, 154–5, 156–7
Shakespeare biography 66–7, 69 n.120
Shakespeare lexicon 153
Shakespearean scholarship 1, 130, 151, 153–4, 159–60, 161
son Viktor's wartime experiences 132
street named for 162
study of Bible and Talmud 17, 21, 159–60
teaching 27, 28, 33–4, 41–2, 46, 58, 72, 96, 148, 159
teaching qualification 34
textbook for teaching English 71–2
translation of *Der Judenstaat* 45–6

INDEX

Kellner, Leon (*cont.*):
  wartime 128–35
  work habits 38, 45–6, 66, 159
  Zionism 51–4, 57–62, 72–4, 109, 114,
    118–19, 126, 163–4
Kellner, Paula (daughter, *later* Arnold):
  birth 33
  education 66, 94
  home in Palestine 159 n.134, 162 n.10
  memories of father 18
  teaching 106, 150
  translating 159 n.134
  view of Mencken 150
  view of Pound encounter 151
  writing 102 n.46, 106, 125 n.145, 150
Kellner, Rafael (father) 13–15, 16, 18, 19,
  23, 51
Kellner, Viktor (son) 66, 99, 106, 132, 158,
  162 n.10
Kipling, Rudyard 61, 68, 69, 99, 108
Koenig, Otto 42
Kremenezky, Johann 51, 53, 86, 112–13, 119,
  126
Krüger, Gustav 101
Kuranda, Ignaz 29

L

Landespolitik 109, 110, 111
Lawrence, D. H. 155
League of Nations 141, 157
Lee, Sidney 68
Leopold II, Emperor 7
Levy, Oscar 68
Lewis, Harry 79
Lewis, Sinclair 156
Lindley, Francis 146, 147, 150
London:
  British Museum 35, 66, 67
  Goethe Society 67
  Herzl's visit 48, 50
  Kellner's visits 35–8, 55, 58–9, 61–2, 66–71,
    77, 91, 100–1, 125, 126, 151–2, 155
  Philological Society 100–1
  Toynbee Hall 43, 77–80, 81
  Whitechapel 43, 48, 50, 78, 79
  Zionist Congress 66, 77
Löwenthal, Josef 161–2
Luick, Karl 138–41

M

MacDonald, Ramsay 69
Mack, Julian, judge 143
Macmillan, Alexander 35–6
Mahler, Arthur 98
Maimonides 55, 157
Manchester Guardian 150
Mann, Rabbi Yeshayahu 16, 18
Maria Theresa, Empress 5
Marlowe, Christopher 31, 34–5
Mencken, H. L. 124, 150–1, 156
Menczel, Philipp 97
Meredith, George 38, 105
Merrick, Leonard 61, 67, 68, 99, 106 n.64, 152
Michel, Louise 69
Ministry of Education, Vienna:
  Kellner's academic career 72–3, 75 n.145,
    98, 103, 108, 137, 141, 147–8
  Kellner's work on English–German
    dictionary 59, 66
  post-war situation 136, 137
  requirements for school textbooks 71–2
  restrictions on Kellner's Zionist activities
    46, 51
Montagu, Samuel (Baron Swaythling) 50,
  80
Moore, George 105
Moravia 8, 17, 23, 76, 84, 135
Morley, Christopher 132
Morris, Richard 35–6, 38, 138–9
Morris, William 37–8
Muirhead, Helen Fullarton 151
Muirhead, James Fullarton 68, 151, 161
Müller, David Heinrich 25–6
Müller, Friedrich 30
Murray, James 99

N

Neue Freie Presse:
  Anna's writing 106
  article on academic careers of Jews 98
  editorship proposal 63–4
  Herzl's position 45, 62
  interview with Kellner 131
  Kellner's obituary 161
  Kellner's writings 43, 45, 47, 49–50, 77,
    103–4, 144, 155

reviews of Kellner's work 34, 152
Neues Wiener Tagblatt 45, 63–4, 96, 104, 119
Neuphilologische Verein (New Philological Society) 100, 101, 108
Die Neuzeit 31
New York Times 142, 156
Nordau, Max 53, 105, 125

O
Österreichische Wochenschrift 27, 58
Oxford English Dictionary 35, 99, 100–1, 152

P
Palestine:
  Anna's death 162 n.10
  Anna's move to 162 n.10
  goal of Zionism 53–4, 60, 109, 118–19
  Kellner's visits 119–20, 158–9
  Paula's life in 150, 159 n.134, 162 n.10
  Viktor's life in 158, 162
  visas 150
Pater, Walter 105
Philippson, Ludwig and Phöbus 17
Polish language 11–12, 16–17
Pollak, Gustav 123
Pollock, Frederick 68
Pound, Ezra 151
Prague, Jewish Toynbee Hall 84–5, 87–8, 90, 91
Die Presse 31
Priebsch, Robert 68

R
Rafaels, Leo (pseudonym of Kellner) 51
Rashi (Rabbi Shelomoh Yitshaki) 18
Rezzori, Gregor von 96
Rhys, Ernest 68, 70
Rhys, Grace 70
Richter, Helene 102 n.46, 105, 122
Robertson, John Mackinnon 68, 120, 122, 151, 155
Robertson, Maude 151–2
Robins, Elizabeth (C. E. Raimond) 68, 122
Rohrer, Joseph 5–6
Rolleston, T. W. (Thomas William) 152
Romania 27, 76, 87, 91, 135–7
Romanian language 136

Rosin, David 21
Roth, Joseph 3, 96
Rothschild, Edmond de 48
Rothschild family 86, 125 n.147
Ruck, Berta 156
Ruskin, John 108
Ruville, Albert von 104

S
Salten, Felix 126, 157–8
Salter, Arthur 141–2
Schatz, Boris 118
Schipper, Jakob 28, 40, 100, 102 nn.46 & 47, 138, 139
Schneider, Emil 149
Schnirer, Moritz 52, 112–13
Schnitzler, Arthur 29, 56 n.53
Schopenhauer, Arthur 29
Schwarzenberg, Felix zu 9
Seipel, Ignaz 149
Seitz, Karl 144, 145, 162
Shakespeare, Kellner's work on:
  biography 66–7, 69 n.120
  connections with Jewish culture 159
  dissertation 31, 34
  lectures 40, 103, 148
  philological and palaeographical study of 125, 130, 151, 153–4, 159–60
  reputation 1, 154–5, 161
  Restoring Shakespeare 154–5
  Shakespeare lexicon 153
  teaching 42 n.85
  writings 122, 155
Shaw, George Bernard 1, 69–70, 122, 153, 155
Shelley, Percy Bysshe 47
Shomer Yisra'el (Guardian of Israel) 12
Sims, George Robert 62
Singer, Samuel 67
Sir Clyomon and Sir Clamydes 35
Skeat, Walter 39
Slovakian Jews 135
Smolka, Franciszek 11
Society of Authors 68
Spann, Samuel 18
Spencer, Herbert 108
Stevenson, Robert Louis 37, 108
Straucher, Benno 110, 113–15, 117, 129
Swinburne, Algernon 37, 108

T

Tarnów 13–16, 19, 22
Tennyson, Alfred 37, 108
Thieme, Friedrich Wilhelm 47, 59, 99, 108, 139
Thon, Rabbi Ozjasz 88
The Times 161
Tolstoy, Leo 61, 133
Toynbee, Arnold 77–8, 82
Trebitsch, Siegfried 70
Trieste 119, 135, 158
Trietsch, Davis 119
Troppau (Opava):
  Kellner's career 41–4, 94
  Oberrealschule 41
Twain, Mark 124 n.141

V

Vienna:
  Academy of Sciences 125
  adult education 82–3
  antisemitism 26–7, 81, 140, 164
  Burgtheater 61, 62
  capital of Republic of German-Austria 134, 136
  Deutsch-akademischer Anglistenverein (German Anglicists Association) 140
  Franz-Joseph Gymnasium 28
  German Club 140
  International Congress of Orientalists (1886) 30–1, 32
  Israelitische Allianz zu Wien (Israelite Alliance of Vienna) 74
  Jewish population 10, 11, 25
  Jewish Toynbee Hall 2, 4, 43, 71, 72, 73, 76, 81–7, 90, 91, 109, 114, 164
  Kellner family's return 106
  Kellner's career 3, 4, 25, 28–9, 33–4, 40, 44, 46–7, 63, 137–41, 144–8, 150, 159
  Kellner's departure for Czernowitz 75, 86, 94, 109
  Kultusgemeinde 29, 33, 86
  Leon-Kellner-Weg 162
  Ministry of Education, *see* Ministry of Education, Vienna
  Neuphilologische Verein (New Philological Society) 100, 101, 108
  refugees 128, 141, 142

Technical University of Vienna 147–8, 151, 155, 159
University of Vienna 24, 25–6, 40, 44, 111, 137–8, 140, 146–7, 163
Volkstheater 61
Zionism 1, 51, 109, 126, 129, 164
Zwi Perez Chajes School 151
Vieweg, Friedrich 47
Volney, Comte de 47

W

Wallas, Graham 68
Ward, Mrs Humphry (Mary Augusta Ward) 68
Weiss, Henriette (sister-in-law) 158 n.132, 159 n.134
Weiss, Klara (mother-in-law) 23–4, 27–8, 94, 99, 115, 129
Weiss family 23, 28, 149
Weisselberger, Theodor 129
Wells, H. G. 121, 151, 156
Die Welt 54, 58, 61–2, 64–6, 67, 77
Wertheimer, Josef 7–8
Whitman, Walt 156
Wilde, Oscar 68, 108
Wohlbrück, Olga 121
Wolffsohn, David 53, 59, 125–6, 152
Wyndham, Charles 61
Wyndham, George 60

Y

Yeats, W. B. 4, 70, 108, 122
Yiddish language:
  east European Jews 2
  Habsburg policy 7, 22, 110
  Kellner reading, speaking, and writing 163
  language choices 16
  Toynbee Hall lectures 89
  Toynbee Hall publications 88
  translation into 17
York-Steiner, Heinrich 52, 53, 163–4

Z

Zangwill, Israel 48–9, 50–1
Zelinka, Carl 148
Ziegler, Johannes 67, 68 n.118
Zionist movement:
  Bukovina 109–11, 113, 114–15, 118–19, 126, 129, 144

Engeres Aktions-Comité (Inner Actions Committee) 58
'Hatikvah' 59
Jewish Toynbee Halls 81, 83–5, 87–8, 91
Kellner's involvement 51–4, 57–62, 72–4, 109, 114, 118–19, 126, 163–4
Kellner's writings 51, 54, 56, 62–3, 77, 111

leadership 19, 59, 119, 125, 129
newspapers 9
Psalm anthem 59
Vienna 1, 51, 109, 126, 129, 164
Zionist Organization of America 143
Zueblin, Charles 157